RILKE,
EUROPE, AND THE
ENGLISH-SPEAKING
WORLD

RILKE, EUROPE, AND THE ENGLISH-SPEAKING WORLD

BY

EUDO C. MASON
Professor of German in the University of Edinburgh

CAMBRIDGE
AT THE UNIVERSITY PRESS
1961

PUBLISHED BY
THE SYNDICS OF THE CAMBRIDGE UNIVERSITY PRESS
Bentley House, 200 Euston Road, London, N.W.1
American Branch: 32 East 57th Street, New York 22, N.Y.
West African Office: P.O. Box 33, Ibadan, Nigeria

*Printed in Great Britain by Robert MacLehose and Co. Ltd
The University Press, Glasgow*

To the memory of

HENRY CALDWELL COOK

1886–1939

CONTENTS

ILLUSTRATIONS

PREFACE

The present book originated as an inaugural lecture, delivered in Edinburgh on 11 October 1951. It has been my object to bring together in it everything relevant to Rilke's attitude towards the English-speaking world that has already variously appeared in print, together with such other material as has happened to come my way. I have not pursued any systematic research on the subject, except in so far as it was necessary to follow up particular points. What is here presented is therefore not exhaustive. There is certainly much more material unpublished. But the material available without systematic research is so copious that the results based upon it can fairly claim to have representative validity.

One of the chief sources of such unpublished material as has here been used are the Rilke Archives, in which it was my privilege to work for several weeks in the years 1937 to 1939, when they were still housed in Weimar. The subject of my research at that time was not Rilke's relationship to the English-speaking world, but some of the notes then taken proved of value in my present task. Rilke's daughter, Frau Ruth Fritzsche-Rilke, has with great patience and kindness answered many questions for me during the last ten years and supplied me with excerpts from unpublished letters, for which I am very grateful to her.

I also owe a great debt of gratitude to the late Dr Werner Reinhart of Winterthur and to his nephew, Dr Balthasar Reinhart, for allowing me on various occasions to examine Rilke's library at Muzot. It should be noted that this library, to which frequent reference is made in the present book, has not remained completely untouched since Rilke's death. There were more books than could all be accommodated at the same time on the shelves in Rilke's study, and in the process of rearrangement some have found their way from the study to other parts of the building (or perhaps to Berne) and *vice versa*. Rilke had the habit of recording the dates of his reading and sometimes also of his purchasing of books on the fly-leaf, so that it is always easy to keep track of him in these matters.

Through a strange oversight I did not come upon the only earlier publication covering the same ground as this book, B. J. Morse's 'Rilke and English Literature' (*German Life and Letters*, April 1948), until my manuscript was on the point of going to press. I was just able to make certain corrections and additions on the lines dictated to me by Morse's admirable article; in particular I was able to take Dora Herxheimer and her share in Rilke's translation of the *Sonnets from the Portuguese* into consideration—without this my book would have been seriously incomplete and inaccurate. My debt to B. J. Morse does not, however, cease here. He has kindly supplied me with much unpublished material collected by him ten years ago or longer, allowing me to make free use of it. Wherever I have taken advantage of this generous offer an acknowledgment will be found in the notes. I would, however, take this opportunity to express comprehensively my sincere gratitude to B. J. Morse for the many ways in which he has so readily helped me.

A particular problem arising in connexion with this work is that some of the most important evidence on which it has, in the nature of the case, to be based is derived not from Rilke's writings, but from records of his conversations, the authenticity of which is nearly always open to dispute. I have had to rely somewhat more than I could have wished on two declarations of Rilke's recorded by Maurice Betz (see pp. 6 and 41-42), which are not confirmed in more than a general way by other testimonies. There are certain puzzling questions which Maurice Betz would have been able to clear up at once—but his brilliant career was cut off before he had reached the age of fifty, in 1946. In general it is to be noted that a very considerable body of Rilke's conversational utterances has been recorded in diaries, letters, jottings and memoirs of people who met him. Most of these records of conversations agree so substantially in tone and purport with one another and with everything known from other sources about Rilke, especially from his letters, that they deserve to be regarded as authentic and reliable. Rilke was a remarkable conversationalist, especially in small groups of congenial people, and still more *tête-à-tête*; his words left a vivid impression, and it was natural for his hearers often to write them down immediately afterwards, and to do so quite accurately too. A striking test case of this is the long report which Hulewicz published in Polish of conversations he had had with Rilke in October 1924.[1] Passages from this report were almost immediately translated back into German and used in evidence against Rilke by outraged patriots, causing him considerable embarrassment. These were just the passages which one might most be inclined to suspect of being apocryphal, or at least distorted—but Rilke himself acknowledged them without any reservations as his own words, only remonstrating with Hulewicz for his indiscretion, but not in any way suggesting, as he easily might have done, that his utterances had been misunderstood or garbled.[2] If Hulewicz is reliable here, he can safely be trusted elsewhere. What applies to Hulewicz applies also to most of those who have recorded conversations with Rilke. I regard these circumstances as justifying the extensive—though by no means uncritical—use I have made of such recorded conversations in the present study. I would, however, add a word of warning about two more ambitious and literary presentations of conversations in which Rilke appears as one of the speakers: *Rainer Maria Rilke auf Capri* by Leopold von Schlözer (Dresden, 1931), and *Ein Vormittag beim Buchhändler* by Carl J. Burckhardt (Basel, 1943). The former is a very mediocre, the latter a brilliant literary production; but neither is to be trusted as an account of Rilke's outlook or of his manner of thinking and expressing himself. Burckhardt ascribes to Rilke throughout a historical sense and a historical-comparative approach to things which are completely alien to his nature. For this reason I regard it as inadmissible to employ in the present study the following passage from Burckhardt,[3] which would otherwise have suited my purposes admirably:

'Nobody has translated more magnificently than Shakespeare: consider

[1] Superior figures refer to notes starting on p. 196.

for instance the passages taken over almost unaltered from Plutarch in *Antony and Cleopatra*. In the case of Racine everything becomes more transparent, more limpid—*plus limpide*,' said Rilke, 'simpler, sweeter; whereas Shakespeare, by a mere nothing, by an evanescent touch, by a rhythm heightens it and sets it in that heroic light which is peculiarly his own.'

I wish I could believe Rilke ever said anything of the sort. But I am quite certain that he did not, that he was temperamentally incapable of it. A professor might have spoken like that; Carl J. Burckhardt's great and learned kinsman, Jakob Burckhardt might have spoken like that; Hofmannsthal, the professor *manqué*, might have spoken like that—but not Rilke. As for Leopold von Schlözer, he apparently calls upon us to believe that Rilke in 1907 said to him:

And yet—the Germans could learn here (i.e. in Capri) to appreciate their own fatherland, though it does lack the charms of the south. Less palaver and pageantry and more acting on the principle of a strong nation: *Wrong or right, my country*.[1] (The italicized words are English in the original.)

One can, however, never be sure, from von Schlözer's confused manner of presentation, whether it is Rilke or he himself who is supposed to be speaking.[2] These two compilations of Burckhardt's and von Schlözer's I can then, so far as the theme of Rilke and the English-speaking world is concerned, only regard as apocryphal. Elsewhere one does sometimes in both detect the authentic voice of Rilke, but the will of the authors to produce a finished literary work of their own has too heavily overlaid it.

As this study is meant to be accessible to the non-specialist, nearly all the foreign quotations in the main body of the text have been translated into English. In the case of verse quotations the German (or French) originals have been given together with an English translation: this has also been done with prose phrases which present special problems of interpretation or translation. In the notes, which are meant in the first place for the specialist, German and French quotations have as a rule been given in the original as well as in translation.

Such verse translations as are here given are my own, and I should like here to express my gratitude to Mr J. B. Leishman, the official translator of Rilke in this country, for raising no objection to my little incursions into the domain he has for many years so competently and felicitously administered. The principle followed in these verse translations has been to avoid all archaisms, inversions and Romantico-Victorian poetic diction, but at the same time to preserve as much as possible of the rhythmical character of the original. Rilke's poetry, modern though it is, still belongs, so far as any comparison is here possible, to the pre-Eliot tradition, and one only falsifies it, if one tries to impose upon it the type either of rhythm or of diction that have established themselves in this country as a result of that poetic revolution for which T. S. Eliot, more than any other individual, was responsible. In the case of two French poems (see p. 112 and p. 139) I have given a prose instead of a verse rendering—an inconsistency which hardly needs to be circumstantially justified. My metrical translations are all intended to have in some measure an *interpretative*, rather than a literal character.

In addition to the major debts of gratitude to Frau Ruth Fritzsche-Rilke, to the Rilke-Archiv, to the late Dr Werner Reinhart, to Dr Balthasar Reinhart, to Mr B. J. Morse and to Mr J. B. Leishman acknowledged above, there are many others whom I have to thank for help in particular matters which will be found specified in the notes. Especially I would name here the Libraries of Columbia University and of the University of Edinburgh; Duchess Aurelia Gallarati-Scotti; Frau Wunderly-Volkart; Fräulein Frieda Baumgartner; Frau Baladine Klossowska; M. Pierre Klossowski; Frøken Tora Holmström; the late Professor Anton Kippenberg; Fräulein Marga Wertheimer; Miss Harriet Cohen; the late Dr Rudolf Kassner; Dr Ingeborg Schnack; Dr Hans-Egon Holthusen; Mr Augustus John; Sir Philip Magnus Allcroft; the late Herr Georg Reinhart; Herr Hans Trausil; Herr Paul Obermüller; Miss Anna Gasowska; Professors L. W. Forster, Renée Lang, M. M. Macken, D. Talbot Rice, William McC. Stewart and Henry W. Wells; the late Mr E. K. Bennett;

Mr Jethro Bithell; Dr Robert Schlapp; Dr Mary E. Gilbert; Dr Gerhard Schoebe; Dr Gustav Beckers; and also the publishers and editor of *The Queen* who have kindly allowed me to reproduce photographs from old numbers which were of importance to Rilke.

EDINBURGH
25 March 1959

E. C. M.

I

INTRODUCTORY

THE reception of Rilke's work and his literary influence in Great Britain and in the United States is a theme which has been dealt with variously by Stephen Spender, W. H. Auden, B. J. Morse and others in this country and by Hans Galinsky, Werner Milch, Karl Alban and others in Germany.[1] It is not the theme of the present study, which is concerned with the other side of the picture, that is to say with the question: 'What was the attitude of Rilke towards the English-speaking world?' On this subject nobody except Mr B. J. Morse has so far found it worth while to write, because at first sight there seems to be no more to say about it than that Rilke had no relationships to the English-speaking world at all, and did not want to have any. There have been publications on Rilke and France, Rilke and Russia, Rilke and Italy, Rilke and Scandinavia, Rilke and Spain, Rilke and Switzerland—but when we set out to talk about Rilke and Great Britain or Rilke and the United States of America, we are concerned with a relationship which apparently just did not exist. We shall, indeed, largely be considering why Rilke had, in his own judgment, practically no connexions with the English-speaking world, and whether there may not after all have been some rudiments of an at least potential relationship to that world, of which he himself was not fully conscious. In examining the evidence on these questions we shall much of the time be moving in the obscurer byways and odd corners of Rilke research, far from his great poetic work and from that which is of central interest about him. As a justification for dealing with what at first seems so unpromising a theme I would, to begin with, advance that, whether it be of great importance for the interpretation of Rilke's poetry

[1] The notes are gathered on pp. 196–246.

and outlook on life or not, it is certainly of great interest to us as members of the English-speaking community. It is valuable for us to 'see oursels as others see us'.

Let us then endeavour to see ourselves as Rilke saw us—so far as he did see us at all. And here it may be noted in advance that he saw us very much as a vague, indiscriminate mass, apparently recognizing hardly any distinction, for example, between Great Britain and the United States of America. The distinction between Scotland and England[1] would also seem to have had comparatively little validity for him. He was apparently unaware that the English-speaking acquaintance with whom he came nearest to being on friendly terms was not an American, but a Scottish laird from the Pentlands. It can at most be supposed that he may have favourably distinguished the Irish from all the other English-speaking peoples, though he made no explicit statement on the subject. For the rest, he seems to have seen Scots and English alike very much in terms of America, and that was, for him, a hostile judgment. This anticipates the conclusion, the only conclusion that anybody who faces this question will ever be able to come to. But much arises out of the question besides Rilke's sweeping and somewhat trite dismissal of all who speak the English language, much that throws an unexpected light on his personality and his work in their wider aspects. Herein lies an additional justification for dealing with the theme.

II

RILKE'S CONCEPTION OF EUROPE

—lorsqu'on parle aujourd'hui de civilisation occidentale, ce n'est pas tel pays en particulier, mais l'Europe entière qu'il s'agit de considérer.

ANDRÉ GIDE: *L'avenir de l'Europe*

IN 1925, the year before his death, Rilke spent seven months in Paris, where he was the lion of nearly all the literary salons. Since his migration to Switzerland, in June 1919, he had ceased to take more than a sporadic interest in contemporary German literature, but he read nearly every new French publication of note, formed many contacts with French writers, especially with Paul Valéry, and showed a marked predilection for the French language, not only in letter-writing and conversation even with friends who were German-speaking by birth, but also in his own poetic production. The bulk of his lyrical writing, after the completion of the *Duineser Elegien* and the *Sonette an Orpheus* in February 1922, is in French, and at the time of his long triumphant visit to Paris of 1925 these French poems were beginning to appear in print under Valéry's sponsorship. His generally acknowledged rank as the greatest living German lyrical poet made too much of a public figure of him for these things to pass unnoticed in Germany. Furthermore a few of his indiscreet utterances in praise of France at Germany's expense leaked out, and it is not surprising that, from November 1924 until his death, he was again and again attacked in the German nationalistic press[1] as a renegade who had deserted Germany in the hour of her affliction and gone over to the hereditary enemy. In Rilke's own eyes, however, as in those of his large and influential French and Swiss following, he was simply behaving like a 'good European'.

One of the things that attracted him to post-war Paris was the entirely new openness to foreign, particularly German cultural influences[1] which, in his eyes, distinguished the new generation of French writers alike from their predecessors in their own land and from their contemporaries in other countries.

It was as a good European that Rilke wanted to be welcomed and in fact was welcomed in Parisian literary circles. Paul Valéry, seeking for points of contact between Rilke and himself, says: 'Finally, we were both of us good Europeans.' Again he describes Rilke as 'the most international mind conceivable', and speaks of him as having 'gradually become a citizen of intellectual Europe'.[2] Rilke talked much on these questions with his translator and friend, the Alsatian writer Maurice Betz, who gives us a valuable summary of these conversations:

> Europe, its towns, castles, cemeteries, museums and libraries seemed to Rilke a domain vast enough to occupy the lifetime of one man. The uplands of this spiritual continent were for him Russia, Denmark and France. Germany, Austria and even Italy only came after, as complementary colours, bridging over, so to speak, the transitions between his favourite environments.[3]

Many other recorded utterances of Rilke's on these subjects bear out the trustworthiness of Betz's report—only Spain and Sweden should be added to Russia, Denmark and France as 'spiritual uplands' or 'favourite environments'.

It should be noted that this 'Good-Europeanism' of Rilke's was something utterly different from that liberal-humanistic rejection of all nationalism in the name of universal human brotherhood which many would on *a priori* grounds expect of him. In December 1920 he could, indeed, write of his 'entirely cosmopolitan, un-national disposition'.[4] But Rilke was in reality very far from committing himself here to liberal humanism, with which, like Nietzsche, the inventor of the term and conception of 'Good-Europeanism', he had all his life been on strained terms, and it is only a superficial judge who could suppose that he was betraying, repudiating, contradicting or even forgetting anything he had ever earnestly stood for, when on 14 February 1926, in championing Mussolini against the liberal humanism of Duchess Aurelia Gallarati Scotti, he wrote:

It is not by cultivating a vague internationalism that the nations will come closest to one another.... Do not forget, my dear Countess, that this poor Europe of ours has all but wasted away through nourishing itself on abstract ideas. For 'internationalism' is an abstract idea, and so is 'humanism'. It is a healthy thought to revert to more solid forms of nutrition, if the country is such as to permit it.[1]

The conception of the 'United States of Europe'[2] did indeed present itself to him in these years, but as something too remote to have any practical importance for the present. Thus in the same letter to Duchess Aurelia Gallarati Scotti he goes on:

In order that some day (which I think still far off) we may arrive at an unforeseeable European concord, the different countries should (in the meantime) advance along different paths. It will even be necessary that... each nation, on its own particular route, should not think too much of the common goal, but concentrate on its own personal effort, its own task, its own national sentiment, which the others perhaps will scarcely comprehend.[3]

Just as the Europeanism in which the later Rilke believes is quite compatible with nationalistic exclusiveness, so also it is in turn itself exclusive in its relationship to what lies outside the boundaries of Europe. Theoretically it does not even provide for that sense of affinity with various aspects of oriental culture and particularly with ancient Egypt, which had characterized Rilke's middle phase. Much though he liked and admired the demi-Uruguayan Jules Supervielle, Rilke felt bound to explain to him that he could not respond to some of the more exotic images in his poetry, because 'undoubtedly his own keyboard was *too European* to contain the key which they were out to strike'.[4] In thus insisting on the 'Europeanness' of his keyboard, Rilke indicates that what lies outside Europe also lies outside the normal range of his own sensibility and interest.

Seen in this setting, the question we are examining takes on a preciser form: what place did Rilke assign to England in the 'spiritual continent' of Europe as he conceived of it? Betz gives us the answer to this. 'It cost Rilke nothing', he tells us, 'to expunge England, with which he had only difficult and disappointing relations, from his Europe.'[1] That is the final verdict of the mature Rilke upon England—that it does not belong to Europe (as Russia in his opinion does, despite the communist régime, which he views with great distrust), and that it can therefore have no real significance for him. As for America, that meant for Rilke, as Betz informs us in the same passage, 'an absolute void.'

This question, whether England belongs to Europe or not, is one on which English people have felt strongly and also differed acrimoniously amongst themselves during the last two hundred years or so. Never has it been a more urgent question than at the present moment, when history appears to be forcibly teaching us that, not only culturally, but also politically and economically, we can never really make ourselves independent of the rest of Europe. Those of us for whom the value of English culture lies not least in its being part and parcel of the greater common European cultural tradition, will spontaneously suspect that, so far as Rilke's mentality and experience were genuinely European, factors from the English-speaking world must have entered very much more extensively into them than he was ready to admit to Betz in 1925. He can, for example, hardly have overlooked how, in Jules Romains' long poem *Europe*,[2] which was one of the first books he bought himself on escaping from Germany to Switzerland in June 1919, and certainly also one of the important sources and inspirers of his Pan-European sentiment, it is warmly and unreservedly taken for granted that England belongs to Europe. This assumption, repugnant though it evidently was to him, Rilke encountered, as will be seen, at every turn throughout his life, especially amongst just those minds that most commanded his respect. What we are here investigating is then not a question that is of interest only to the Rilke specialist; it is also—and that is not the least important aspect of it—the wider question of the relationship between the English-speaking world and European cultural tradition, as exemplified in a peculiarly complex and peculiarly revealing test-case.

III

RILKE AND HIS NATIVE AUSTRIA

It is no mere chance that those out-of-the-way things 'appeal' to them and that what is near at hand and familiar means nothing to them.

RILKE: *King Bohusch*

BEFORE we ask what were the 'difficult and disappointing relations' that Rilke had had with England, we should clearly realize that his sense of the peculiar unity and value of Europe, and of himself as an exemplary good European, was a new development of his last years, no traces of which are to be found before 1914.[1] From about his twenty-fifth year to the outbreak of the first world war we find Rilke always thinking and speaking of himself not positively as a European, but negatively and also lugubriously as a homeless wanderer with no fatherland at all and ultimately with no earnest desire for a real fatherland; free to savour all countries, including those outside Europe, and to turn his back on them again, as the mood seizes him. When, in the years 1900 to 1905, and very occasionally later, he speaks of Russia, which he never seriously contemplated revisiting after his two important journeys there (1899 and 1900), as his true homeland or elective fatherland ('Heimat' or 'Wahlheimat'),[2] that is above all his way of expressing how little he feels himself as belonging to or being truly at home in any of the other countries in which he had ever lived. In particular he felt himself as not belonging to Germany, to Austria or to the narrower land of his origins, Bohemia. It was above all the shock of the 1914 war and the ordeal of being confined, against all his intentions, for five years within the frontiers of Germany and Austria, that led him to re-interpret his old negative sense of homelessness, of 'Heimatlosigkeit', in terms of a positive Pan-European consciousness, of a capacity to feel himself in a figurative sense equally a native of countries so different and distant from one another as Russia, Denmark, France and Spain, and in a lesser measure of most of the rest of Europe.

On closer examination Rilke's refusal to regard England as belonging to Europe turns out to be not the only one—or anything like the most important one—of the reservations and hesitations which attend his claims in the last years of his life to be equally a denizen of every, or almost every European country. There are, as we shall see, others, which Maurice Betz knows about very well, but which, for good reasons, he slurs over and in part suppresses. In fact, the Francophile Pan-Europeanism of the older Rilke is to a large extent an operation on paper, the substitution of a plus for a minus sign, by which the actual earlier state of his mind, his sense of being at home nowhere, with all that it implies, is not so much structurally altered as given a more reassuring and up-to-date façade. That Rilke could now on occasion approvingly speak of himself as a citizen of all Europe did not at all mean that he had really ceased to think or also at times to speak of himself in the old mournful way as a homeless wanderer. Only four months before the beginning of that stay in Paris when he confided his Pan-European sentiments to Betz, he was asked by his Polish translator, Witold Hulewicz,[1] whether he was happy in Switzerland and if he missed his own country. 'What country?' said Rilke in his reply to this; 'I never had a fatherland, never.' Hulewicz answered: 'Yes, there have been several German poets who, having once left their country, never returned.' At this Rilke gazed upon him with surprise and said: 'But I am not a German.' It was as bad as if one had inadvertently spoken of Burns as an English poet. At once we remember that Rilke was by birth an Austrian and, at the time of this conversation, technically a Czecho-Slovakian. We think of Vienna, of Salzburg, of the Tirol, of everything that makes Austria seem to us, and also to many Germans, so much more a land of grace and romance, of music, of delicate, playful urbanity and the art of living than Germany itself, at least post-1870 Germany under Prussian ascendancy, as Rilke had alone known it; and we think at once how much more appropriate Austria was to be the native land of a Rilke or a Hofmannsthal than Germany, and what a *faux pas* it was to address Rilke as a German and not as an Austrian. Some such considerations as these must have gone through the mind of the unfortunate Hulewicz, who at once hastened to retrieve his blunder and corrected himself: 'Well yes—an Austrian.' But with this he had only made matters far worse. He did not know that the mellow, seductive charm which Austrian tradition and culture have for nearly all the world simply did not exist for Rilke and never had existed for him; that loathing of Austria was one of the oldest, most deep-seated and permanent of all his loathings; that he had in his youth fled to Germany to escape from Austria and had up to 1914 intermittently felt considerable enthusiasm for the German mind and its culture. To call Rilke a German was in his eyes only a venial offence compared with the really deadly one of calling him an Austrian. With asperity he told Hulewicz that he was not Austrian. 'Not at all! When the Austrians entered Prague in 1866 my parents drew the window-curtains, so as not to see them. *Everything happened to be against my having a fatherland.*'

The ruling Teutonic minority in Bohemia, to which Rilke's family belonged, were, indeed, as easily happens in all cases of colonization, annexation, occupation or conquest, not only on hostile terms with the repressed and turbulent indigenous population which far outnumbered them, but also, in spite of the links of race and language, often at loggerheads with or estranged from the remote sovereign power. So it was, for example, with many of the Anglo-Irish before 1921. A high proportion of mankind have, however, through all history, found themselves thus uncomfortably situated between two tribes, races or nationalities as between two stools or between the upper and the nether millstones; there is nothing exceptional about it, and it is not in itself sufficient to account for that devastating sense of 'never having had a fatherland', of total 'Heimatlosigkeit', which Rilke constantly complains of. In a letter of 21 January 1920, expressing himself more temperately than in the exuberant conversations with Hulewicz, Rilke does indeed once speak of his homelessness as though it were nothing more than the common lot of all Austrians: 'Jetzt merke ich doch die Heimatlosigkeit des Oesterreichers.'[1] In reality, however, Rilke conceives all along of his homelessness as something unique and peculiarly his own, and it means for him above all that his Austrian nationality, acknowledged with the worst possible grace and sometimes denied altogether, has no genuine, intrinsic validity. 'All I need say is that I (a born Austrian) never had a fatherland,' he writes to Pol de Mont on 10 January 1902. 'Anywhere but in Austria!'[2] he says programmatically and defiantly at the age of twenty, when it is a question of where his poems should be published. 'It is almost impossible to express how loathsome everything Austrian is to me,'[3] he writes to Lou Andreas-Salomé on the eve of producing the first *Duinese Elegies* in January 1912. And in 1915 to Ilse Erdmann: 'As for Austria, which has remained through the ages a superficial compromise (dishonesty as the state)—as for Austria, the idea of finding a home there is simply unendurable to my mind and to my feelings.'[4] His most intimate friend, Lou Andreas-Salomé, apostrophizing him rhapsodically after his death, writes: 'I often ask myself how injurious it may have been to your destiny that you had so strong an antipathy to your own Austrian nationality.'[5] The ancient Austria into which he had been born had first to be annihilated by the Treaty of St Germain (1920), before Rilke could bring himself to speak about it for once with some show of pity and attachment, using (in January 1923) the startling phrase: 'en bon Autrichien que je suis;'[6] and here, too, he at once goes on:

> Also, without indulging in a vague and delusory cosmopolitanism, I must admit that Germany has contributed scarcely anything towards forming me, nor have the jumbled influences of Austria and Bohemia —but Russia, the vast and ineffable, France, Italy, Spain and all the inward and remote past that those countries, which I have inhabited and admired one after the other, have been able to awaken and, so to speak, authorize in my blood.

What is important is that Rilke loathed and disowned his native country and his native city, Prague ('this, God forgive me, miserable city of subordinate existences'[1]), regarding them as mere breeding-places of unmitigated philistinism, and that this fierce antipathy preceded and determined all his enthusiastic contacts with other lands and cities, and continued for all practical purposes undiminished till the last. The vague, non-committal cosmopolitanism of his earliest phase ('Weltgedusel'[2] he once ironically called it in 1896) and the more concrete and programmatic Good-Europeanism of his last phase are never so comprehensive as to include within them his own native land,[3] from which his whole life and all his travels are one unintermitting flight. Both Austria, as it had been left after the Treaty of St Germain, and Czecho-Slovakia were thrust so much into the background of that ideal conception of Europe which Rilke entertained during the last years of his life that they might just as well have been left out altogether, and in his own inner sentiment indeed were left out.

In the letter to Duchess Aurelia Gallarati Scotti of January 1923 already quoted above, Rilke amplifies the theme that he feels himself less a native of Austria than of Russia, France, Italy or Spain as follows:

> We are born, so to speak, provisionally, it doesn't matter where; it is only gradually that we compose, *within ourselves*, our true place of origin, so that we may be born there retrospectively, and each day more definitely. For some people their spiritual birthplace coincides with that which one finds mentioned in their passports, and it must confer an unheard of happiness to be identical to such a point with external circumstances.[4]

It is very seldom that Rilke speaks, as he does here, of his peculiar form of cosmopolitanism (or, for the matter of that, of any of his views, particularly his religious views) as something which he has himself consciously 'composed within himself' and in which therefore his own faculty of choice, his own will and his own processes of thought have played a considerable part. As a rule he much preferred to regard himself as only having received immediate intuitions from the profundities of nature, pure being or the universal spirit, intuitions in whose genesis his own will, his own likes and dislikes and the activities of his own mind or of other minds have no share whatever. He sometimes even liked hyperbolically to conceive or at least to speak of himself as an altogether exceptional being without any preferences, any will, any mental activity at all, a pure receiving apparatus for cosmic emanations and communications, for 'rätselhafte Diktate'.[1] So also in this matter of understanding and belonging to all the different European countries as though he were a native of each—with certain exceptions, amongst them the country of which he actually did happen to be a native. It was as a rule uncongenial to him to think of this faculty to which he laid claim as of something acquired by the ordinary trial-and-error process of human experience, of hard work and study, of careful observation and of instruction through others, and as liable to the limitations and uncertainties of all such human acquisitions. Actually that is just what it was, in the main, and as such it was a remarkable achievement of the mind and the will. Rilke, however, usually preferred to the glory justly due to him for such determined and effective exercise of his faculties of acquisition the other kind of glory—whether it should be esteemed higher or not is a difficult question—which attaches to the undeserving favourite of hidden powers behind the scene, to him who himself does nothing, but has all things given to him. Thus it is not to his mind, nor to his assiduity, nor to his will, nor even, except in a very small measure, to his actual experience that he normally attributes his almost all-embracing and, as he sees it, quite unparalleled European consciousness, but to his 'blood', to the 'manifold blending and widespread education of his blood' ('die vielfältige Zusammensetzung und weite Erziehung meines Bluts'), which, he claims, confers, upon him a 'peculiar detachment' ('eine eigentümliche Distanz')[2] from each single nation, especially from the Germans. A year later, in 1924, he takes up this same phrase in a slightly varied form, speaking of the 'multiplicities of his blood' ('die Vielfältigkeiten meines Bluts'.)[3] What Rilke means by this is that the blood of practically all the European nations is mingled in his veins in a way in which it apparently never has been in those of any other individual, and that he is therefore, while never completely at home in any one country, sufficiently at home in nearly all European countries to understand them as well from within as the simple native; better indeed, since he can understand them not only in their national isolation, but also in their relationship to the larger European community of nations. And this is not an understanding with the mind, but immediately and intuitively through the *blood* itself, to which Rilke in his own way attaches quite as much importance as did the National Socialists. Above all he feels able to identify himself in this way with the Latin races. So he writes in his letter to the Italian Duchess in defence of Mussolini

It would have been difficult for me to be a soldier anywhere else, but I could have been one with conviction and enthusiasm in one of those countries, if I had been born there: an Italian soldier, a French soldier, yes, I could have been one, confraternally, to the point of the supreme sacrifice: to such an extent does nationality in those two countries seem to me bound up with gesture, with action, with the visible example. Amongst you, even more than in France, blood is truly *one* and, at some moments, the idea, borne along by this blood, can also be *one*.[1]

From the circumstance that Rilke was born in Prague it is often assumed that he must at least have had a good deal of Czech blood in his veins, and that this is what he was above all referring to when he spoke of the 'manifold blending of his blood'.[2] Czech blood was, however, next to Jewish, the last kind of which he desired or claimed to have any share; and he believed, probably quite correctly, that there was not a drop of it in his veins. The hostility between the German colonizers, to whom his family belonged, and the native Czechs was so great that an uncodified but effective system of *apartheid* was spontaneously and by mutual consent adopted and maintained between them. Under these circumstances intermarriage, as Rilke himself points out, seldom occurred. 'Since my family settled in Bohemia,' he writes in 1904 'it has been emphatically German, as was entailed by the conditions there which compel clear-cut decisions.'[3] It is the situation already touched upon in connexion with Rilke's lament to Hulewicz: 'Everything happened to be against my having a fatherland.' It was a situation that affected not only the Rilke family, but also the entire German-speaking minority in pre-1914 Bohemia. They were placed between three fatherlands, none of them quite satisfactory, and not to be harmonized with one another: the Austrian-Hungarian Empire as wider, all *too* wide and heterogeneous fatherland; Bohemia as actual, all too narrow and hostile fatherland; and Germany proper as ultimate racial and spiritual fatherland. It would seem that Rilke was brought up with a strong sense of belonging in some ways quite as much to Germany as to Austria. Quite certainly he was brought up to despise and dislike the Czechs, and that was one element in his upbringing which he never really rid himself of, though he made a great effort to do so around his twentieth and twenty-first years, even professing himself for a time a partisan of the Czech movement for independence.[1] What underlies this curious episode in his early life is in the first place exasperation with his own family and their outlook, and the will to differentiate himself from them and shock them; certainly it is not any deepseated affection for the Czechs, of whose language he never acquired more than a superficial knowledge; still less is it a sense of racial kinship with them. 'The Czechs, admittedly, are not much to my taste,'[2] he writes in 1904.

Rilke hardly ever thought of himself as a Central European mongrel. He does indeed in April 1921 use the expression: 'the composite character of my Austrian nationality' ('das Komposite meines Oesterreichertums') in order to explain 'how difficult it is for him to understand what it is that the German needs'.[3] But this phrase, in which he is in any case concerned rather to dissociate himself from the Germans than really to associate himself with the Austrians, stands quite isolated amongst his numerous utterances on these questions. In speaking of the 'manifold blendings of his blood' he had something very different from the 'composite character of his Austrian nationality' in mind—the tradition, namely, that he was descended from the ancient and extinct Carinthian noble family of the Rülkes whom he liked to imagine as linked by dynastic marriages with the aristocracies of all Europe,[1] especially of Russia. An unconfirmed supposition that he might, through his great-grandfather on the maternal side, Franz Entz, be of Alsatian stock, had indeed a certain minor importance for him as 'possibly accounting for his obviously so deep-seated affinity with the French Mind',[2] but otherwise he almost entirely ignored his mother's[3] certainly not aristocratic family when he spoke of the 'multiplicities of his blood'. Actually the endeavour to establish a genealogical link between him and the Carinthian Rülkes led shortly after his death to the unexpected discovery, which would certainly have disconcerted him, that he was descended from simple Sudeten-German peasants and tradesmen, who are extremely unlikely ever to have had any connexion with the Carinthians.[4] In fact, there is no reason to suppose that Rilke's blood was any more 'manifoldly blended' than that of any other German families in Thuringia, Saxony, Silesia and the Sudeten fringe of Bohemia, most of whom in any case had a certain Slavonic component in their make-up from intermarriage in remote colonizing days with the original Wendish or Sorbish inhabitants of those regions—for conditions had been infinitely more favourable to a certain measure of German racial fusion with these Wends or Sorbs than with the Czechs or the Poles. This implies, however, no more mingling of various racial strains than is to be found, one way or another, in most Europeans of all countries, Great Britain not excluded, since the migration of the nations in the Dark Ages. At most it could be supposed that the never officially impugned rumour of a slight Jewish strain in Rilke's blood from the maternal side is true, as indeed it very well may be. But although that would help to account for Rilke's sense of being ethnically a misfit or changeling, and for much else about him, it would still not make anything like an exceptional case of him in a region where innumerable families had Jewish connexions. In other words, that unique mingling of bloods which Rilke postulated for himself and made responsible for nearly everything about himself, especially for his exemplary Pan-Europeanism, turns out to be a myth, and the real explanation for his half-dismal, half-exultant sense of being at home in no country and yet in many very different countries must be sought elsewhere.

It is, after all, quite common for modern men of genius with a strong individualistic bent to dissociate themselves as much as possible from the people and land of their origin, to regard themselves as changelings and postulate for themselves curious, undocumented, remoter origins of a more interesting kind, on which they can lay the responsibility for their waywardness. That 'Family Romance' ('Familienroman') which Freud[1] treats as an almost universal psychological phenomenon assumes here, it would seem, dimensions appropriate to the greater tensions, aspirations and powers of genius. Thus Nietzsche attached great importance to his highly improbable Polish ancestry; D. H. Lawrence liked to think of himself as descended illegitimately from an emigrant French aristocrat; and Joyce dissociated himself from Celts and Sassenachs alike by assuming that he had a decisive Scandinavian streak in his blood. Rilke's procedure—if one may apply the term 'procedure' to what is, of course, in the main a subconscious process—is on the same lines, only more ambitious, and in his case, as in these others, the one thing we can be certain of is that it all begins with a violent spirit of opposition to the world into which the individual concerned happens to have been born, and to everything that is taken for granted by that world, and with an urge to differentiate oneself as much as possible, at all costs, and in no matter what way, from that world and its sacrosanct formularies. The validity of all the specific circumstances of time, place, class and everything else attending one's birth is flatly denied: 'Nous naissons, pour ainsi dire, provisoirement, quelque part....'[2]

This spirit of revolt itself, with the accompanying sense of being different from everybody else and the will to become more different still, is something which in its turn has also to be accounted for. It manifests itself, however, so extensively in human nature, wherever the discipline of tradition relaxes, that there is no need to have recourse to esoteric doctrines of blood and race to explain it. Certainly Rilke came at an early age to be at loggerheads with his family and with his entire environment, but this can be far more convincingly accounted for by the particular combination of in themselves quite unmysterious circumstances which happened to attend his unfortunate boyhood, than by his own assumption that he belonged through the peculiarities of his blood to a race apart. That assumption appears to be rather one of the *results* of the situation of which it professes to tell us the *cause*. And just as Rilke's spectacular myth of the 'multiplicities of his blood' is of no real service to account for his youthful revolt against his immediate origins and early environment, so also it is of just as little use to account for his feeling in later life that he belongs in a semi-detached way, as a quasi-native, to nearly all the European nations. That feeling itself is at bottom nothing more than an extreme, but still incomplete sublimation of his youthful spirit of revolt.

IV

RILKE AND GERMANY

For a variety of reasons, some of them sounder than others, many are likely to feel a good deal more respect and sympathy for Rilke's virtual exclusion of Germany from the visionary Europe in which he professed his faith during his last years than for his virtual exclusion of Austria. For he did virtually exclude Germany as well, or at least relegated it to a position where it was scarcely perceptible on the horizon.

To some extent Rilke's treatment of Germany runs parallel to his treatment of Austria, and it should be remembered that he had been brought up to regard Germany, at least spiritually, as hardly less his fatherland than Austria.[1] What filled him with resentment against Austria, however, and blinded him completely[2] to all its mellow cultural charm, was in the first place the misery and humiliation which he had to endure as a boy in the Austrian military academies of St Pölten and Mährisch-Weißkirchen. That was something he never got over and could never forgive.[3] Of Germany, where things had nearly always gone comparatively well with him, he thought on the whole much more favourably up to 1914, in spite of occasional outbursts of impatience. His most virulent—or perhaps it would be more accurate to say, his most petulant—outbreaks against Germany in these earlier years are aimed at German tourists abroad, especially in Italy, at what he feels to be conventional, theatrical or otherwise not quite genuine in their cult of the beautiful and in their mode of expressing it. 'Rome began to swell and became all fat and German, enthusiastic through and through,'[4] he writes in April 1904. Similarly he says of Capri in December 1906 that 'it seems to be made up of the ineptitudes of German admiration', and that 'particularly the German "temperament" ['Gemüt'] has let itself go here deplorably'.[1] In such moods as these he can superciliously remark: 'Not to be amongst Germans is, of course, always a good thing.'[2] In reality, however, without feeling that he belonged to Germany—that could not be expected of him—Rilke got on well enough with her in these years, and his criticisms of her, unlike his criticisms of Austria, were as a rule fairly moderate and well-founded and such as were often advanced by thousands of cultured, open-minded native Germans themselves.

In particular Rilke was, whether he liked it or not, strongly linked to Germany by the German language, the only one in which he could, up to 1923 or so, effectually write his poetry. This was indeed a restriction to which he had not all along tamely submitted, but at last he was forced to accept it, after various abortive attempts in French and above all in Russian, which he had for a time contemplated adopting exclusively for all literary purposes[3]—those were the days when he wore a Russian peasant-blouse in Berlin and spoke broken German interspersed with Russian tags.[4] Rilke distinguished sharply between German as he himself used it for his poetry, and German as the language of the German people, regarding it as a 'peculiar obligation' of the poet to differentiate his words fundamentally and intrinsically from the words of mere intercourse and communication. 'Not a single word (and by this I mean every *und* or *der, die, das*) in a poem is *identical* with its homophone in practical everyday conversation,'[5] he writes to Countess Sizzo in March 1922. He goes on to relate in the same letter how he had shocked Dehmel by the practical application he gave to this in itself sound enough aesthetic principle. 'I told him,' he says,

that when I am working I cannot endure to hear German spoken around me (spoken, as it mostly is, in a revolting, bad and slovenly way!), but prefer to be encompassed then by some other language, which is familiar and congenial to me as a medium for ordinary conversation. Through such isolation (which Dehmel probably regarded as terribly 'unpatriotic'), the German tongue, I explained to him, then assumed *within me* a peculiar concentration and clarity, and I felt it to be a magnificent medium, appropriate to myself; (how magnificent! Russian is perhaps the only language which, if one could master it, would afford one a yet ampler gamut, even greater contrasts of expression!)[1]

But although Rilke thus maintained that he could write German better in foreign countries, where he had the German language, as it were, all to himself, he never quite forgot or denied that the headquarters of this, his poetic medium, were after all in Germany. 'The German language was not imposed upon me as something alien,' he admitted in 1925; 'it acts through me, it speaks out of my nature. How could I ever have worked on it and attempted to enrich it, if I had not felt it as belonging to me from the very beginning of things?'[2]

There is a remarkable contradiction between what Rilke says in his letter to Countess Sizzo of March 1922 in praise of the German language as inferior only perhaps to Russian, and certain other somewhat earlier remarks of his on the same theme, which have been given far wider currency. Here he is found complaining bitterly of the German language, and not merely of the way in which it is abused in everyday conversation and by the semi-educated, but of certain supposed defects which are intrinsic to it even at its best, and vitiate it as a poetic medium. His outbreak of this kind which has been given the greatest publicity was in a conversation of 26 January 1914 with André Gide, who records in his journal and elsewhere the exact phrase of Rilke's that so much struck him: 'This inadequacy of our language' ('cette insuffisance de notre langue').[3] The extremest and most ample formulation of Rilke's dissatisfaction with the German language would appear to have been in a letter written in French to Frau Wunderly-Volkart[4] of May 1921, which has so far been made known only in the form of a fragmentary German paraphrase. It was evidently above all concerned with the fundamental inferiority of German as a literary medium to French. These two dates, January 1914 and May 1921, indicate also for practical purposes the beginning and the end of Rilke's serious quarrel with the German language in its essential as opposed to its merely fortuitous characteristics, a quarrel which, as is pointed out by F. W. Wodtke,[5] was ultimately concerned less with the inadequacy of any one language than with the absolute inadequacy of all language—T. S. Eliot's

> Words strain,
> Crack and sometimes break, under the burden,
> Under the tension, slip, slide, perish,
> Decay with imprecision, will not stay in place,
> Will not stay still.[1]

One easily comes to false conclusions if one interprets all that Rilke says in these years 1914–21 against language in general, or against the German language in particular, quite literally, without making allowances for what may be merely figurative, hyperbolical and subjective in it, and above all without taking into consideration that at the back of all these complaints, and expressing itself through them, there lies Rilke's despair during these years over the apparent cessation of his own creative powers just when he was so anxious to complete the *Duinese Elegies*, begun in January 1912. Once this greatest longing of his life had been fulfilled, in February 1922, his quarrel with the German language as such was forgotten, and in the very following month he could, as we have seen, write of it enthusiastically as a 'magnificent medium' to Countess Sizzo. He was indeed shortly after this—a remarkable *tour de force*—to make greater use of French than of German for poetic purposes, but we no longer find him disparaging the German language, as in the days when he could not complete the *Duinese Elegies*. For the rest, it may be noted that out of all he has to say against the German language only one quite meagre concrete indictment emerges, namely that there are no exact German equivalents to the French words 'paume' (Italian 'palma') and 'verger'—to which two words, constantly adduced in this connexion, he also on one occasion adds 'offrande', and 'absence' —'in the great positive sense in which Paul Valéry has used it.'[2]

It is significant for a curious distinction which Rilke contrived to make between the German language and German culture that the very time when he begins to quarrel seriously with the German language is also the time when he is on the most cordial terms with German culture, and that the time when he becomes reconciled with the German language again is also the time when he most stubbornly turns his back on German culture. The four years before the outbreak of the first world war are years in which Rilke draws steadily nearer in interest, sympathy and admiration to the great tradition of the German mind and its best contemporary manifestations.[1] This goes so far that for the first few days of the war he is even carried away by the general wave of patriotism and writes a remarkable cycle of poems (*Fünf Gesänge —1914*), in which he comes close to identifying himself with extreme German nationalistic sentiment. Later, indeed, he disowned this work. The reaction had set in very quickly, and here at least we know that what turned his sympathy irrevocably away from Germany was her militarism, her claim to dominate the rest of Europe. His mind is here working on quite clear and intelligible lines, nor are there any discrepancies to be allowed for between the literal meaning of his words, taken at their face value, and what really underlies them. In September 1915 he writes in a letter:

> To understand what an ordeal these times are for me, you must consider that I don't feel in a 'German' way—not in any respect. Although the German spirit cannot be alien to me, since I am spread out to my very roots in its language, the way in which that spirit is now operating and its present overweening consciousness can only estrange and offend me so far as my thoughts reach. . . . How is it possible for me, whose heart has been nurtured by Russia, France, Italy, Spain, the desert[2] and the Bible,[3] how is it possible for me to chime in with the vauntings of those who surround me here?[4]

At the end of the war Rilke took cognizance with some pity but no regrets of the extinction of the old Austria he had known: 'Austria, to which, in spite of everything, I did belong a little more than to Germany, has ceased to exist,' he wrote in March 1921.[5] He even gave his theoretical approval to that factor in the new order which most affected his own technical status and which was also most resented by German nationalists, the creation of the Czecho-Slovakian state. 'I have no objections to Czecho-Slovakia,' he wrote on 25 May 1925 to Anton Kippenberg; and again, on 14 February 1926 to Duchess Aurelia Gallarati-Scotti:

'It has delighted me to see Prague become a Czech capital once more.' Three[1] months after this he accepted an invitation to tea in Montreux with President Masaryk's daughter, whom he goes out of his way to designate as 'une compatriote'.[2] One of the things Rilke was most violently attacked for in the German nationalistic press was sending a complimentary message to Masaryk, addressing him as 'the great humanist'.[3] Commenting on this incident, he writes:

How could I help feeling called upon to express my approbation, when a man of universal intellectual eminence assumed the highest position in my native land, from which I am sufficiently aloof to keep faith with it, independently, in the particular turns taken by its destiny.[4]

The condition tacitly implied by the terms 'aloof' ('abgelöst') and 'independently' ('unabhängig'), with which Rilke qualifies his approval, is that he would under no circumstances himself think of returning to Bohemia, still less of permanently living there. A few scraps of the Czech language overheard in a public park in Geneva in August 1920, when there still seemed to be some danger that he might be forced to go to Czecho-Slovakia, filled him with dismal and disgusted thoughts of what an awful fate that would be.[5]

In writing in March 1921 to a Swedish friend, from whom he he had heard nothing since 1914, Rilke sums up the effect that the war had had upon him:

I suffered with everybody—that was all I was capable of—but least of all with the Germans, because their character remains the most alien to me, not indeed perhaps in its deepest roots, but measured by the uses to which it puts itself at this present epoch of its history.[6]

Noteworthy here is the term 'the most alien to me' ('mir am fremdesten'). Rilke uses it frequently in his later years, and the Germans are not the only nation to whom he applies it. It turns up again in 1924, in the conversations with Hulewicz, when he says: 'As to the Germans, there is nobody more alien to their spirit than I am.' Rilke still concedes, indeed, that the Germany which he so resolutely disowns may not be the only or the most essential Germany:

One has to go back to the drawings of Albrecht Dürer and the ancient masters to discover the authentic German face; one of its essential features was that tough and enduring humility of the peasant and the good citizen, of which no trace remains in the present-day ambitious grimace....[1]

So Rilke writes of Germany in the letter to Duchess Gallarati Scotti of February 1926 already quoted more than once in this study. In this same letter, having justified nationalism in general and even in its excesses as something which every nation ought to experience, he goes on to make certain exceptions:

It is different in the case of unities which are too new and of recent construction. The example of the German people since their great national success of 1870 would be calculated to render suspicious all striving after deliberate nationalism.[2]

It is in this connexion that Rilke speaks of the 'authentic German face' ('la véritable figure allemande') found in the drawings of Dürer, which has ceased to exist since the whole country came under the 'rod of preponderant and arrogant Prussia'. 'I have', he says, 'always detested German nationalism, as the pretentiousness of a vaguely americanized *parvenu*.' This phrase 'parvenu vaguement américanisé' is worth noting as an indication that there may be a closer subterranean link between Rilke's feelings about Germany and the main theme of this study, his feelings about the English-speaking world, than one would at first have suspected.

In the last three or four years of his life Rilke certainly felt that, apart from certain personal friends and a few ineffectual minority groups—especially the youth-movement that went under the name of Wandervogel[3]—he had no longer any real connexions with Germany beyond the circumstance that he happened to have employed the German language in the great bulk of his writings. And of this use of the German language he had said as early as 1918: 'The German word, once it is poetically intensified, withdraws itself from the community, and has then somehow or other to be caught up by them again.'[1] The French language, on the other hand, he asserts in the same letter, 'introduces the private experience of the poet so to speak into the domain of common humanity.' One sees here how Rilke, in turning about 1923 from German to French as the chief medium of his lyrical production, was consciously writing for a community, as he hardly ever had been so long as he wrote German.

In 1925 Rilke stated his position in these matters to Walter Mehring as follows: 'Is it then, in view of all I have given in the German language, necessary to emphasize the fact that I belong to German poetry?'[2] Which is, being interpreted: 'Well, if you insist on it, I suppose I am a German poet, but only on my own terms. The Germans may refuse to accept those terms, if they like—or if they dare—but that will be their loss, not mine. I am making no concessions.' It is much the same attitude as that assumed towards English literature by James Joyce and D. H. Lawrence. Homer, Vergil, Dante, Shakespeare or Racine would have found such an attitude of the poet towards the community incomprehensible. Rousseau would have understood it very well. It follows from the ultra-individualistic assumptions of what, up to about 1930, could, without qualifications, be called the specifically modern mind, if they are consistently enforced, that this is the normal, indeed the only right and proper attitude for the 'pure' poet to adopt, and it is still often quite unhistorically postulated that it must therefore have been the attitude of a Dante or a Shakespeare—against which Mr T. S. Eliot has rightly and not ineffectually protested. In Milton the beginnings of the intransigently individualistic modern attitude can be clearly observed; only Milton could still persuade himself that at least Puritan England was behind him; whether he still felt assured of this when he wrote *Samson Agonistes* is doubtful.

On his deathbed Rilke declined to become a member of the German Dichterakademie, as he had also, a year and a half before, declined to represent Czecho-Slovakia at a banquet of the Pen Club, to the great relief of his publisher; but at the very moment when he was rejecting the invitation to become a member of the German Dichterakademie he was also negotiating to accept the highly academic office of adjudicating conjointly with Paul Valéry a French literary prize.[1] The Germany from which Rilke thus pointedly dissociated himself was, it should be noted, not National-Socialist Germany,[2] which did not come into existence till seven years after his death, but of which he seems to have had some horrified foreboding; it was the democratic Germany of the Weimar Republic.

It is therefore a euphemistic understatement when Betz says that Germany and Austria belonged to the Europe of the later Rilke 'only as complementary colours, . . . bridging over the gaps between his favourite environments'. They were, as Betz knew, less even than that: they were 'completely alien' to him, a status exactly the same as that which he assigned to England; and could it have been made geographically plausible, it would have cost him as little to expunge them from his ideal map of Europe as it did to expunge England. Austria and Germany Rilke knew, however, extremely well, with an immediate intimacy with which he knew no other country, not even France or Switzerland—in fact, he knew them far too well. Of England, on the other hand, he knew but little.

V
RILKE AND THE ENGLISH LANGUAGE

It is difficult to determine how much Rilke knew about England and the English-speaking world, except that he felt he knew enough about them not to like them—and for a man as guided by 'instincts' and 'intuitions' as he was that did not need to be very much. Everything turns here upon the question of how much he knew of the English language, and the evidence on that point is curiously contradictory. If one takes all his own declarations at their face value, one is, as will be seen, forced to the paradoxical conclusion that he knew English quite well before he had begun to learn it, and that once he had learnt it, he no longer knew it at all.

It is important in this connexion that Rilke had a remarkable natural gift for languages, acquiring with little effort a considerable command[1] of Italian, Russian, Danish and French and some smattering of Czech, Swedish, Spanish, Latin and even Arabic. This inspired polyglottism was, indeed, one of the chief factors in that spiritual economy whereby Rilke strove to transfigure his Byronic sense of being a highly exceptional kind of Displaced Person into the more comforting consciousness of exemplary Good-Europeanism. 'At bottom,' he wrote in 1918 to a fellow-sufferer, 'one ought really to write in all languages just as this sense of being without a fatherland (which you now, intelligibly enough, express as a lament) could also profess itself jubilantly in a positive form as membership of the entire family of nations.'[2] 'One ought to write in all languages,' Rilke says here—but with the mental reservation, 'in all languages except English.' In his dealings with foreign languages Rilke's entire sensibility was always in full play; he apprehended them at once sensuously as living organisms with distinctive physiognomies, more or less attractive to him, making enormous short cuts through the arid territory of mere grammar, which was not his strongest point. His chief criticism of the English-speaking peoples was that he could not stand their language, which at the same time he declared he did not know; and this same confessed ignorance of it was in his eyes a conclusive justification for his disliking it. His line of argument would seem to have been: 'It is clear that English cannot be a language of any true cultural standing, for if it were, I should know it, shouldn't I?' The decisive fact, many illustrations of which will be cited in various connexions in the present study, was that Rilke could not hear or imagine English spoken without its getting on his nerves. Frau Klossowska, one of his closest acquaintances during his later years, records how, on hearing English spoken in a shrill voice by a woman passing in the street (possibly an American) Rilke exclaimed: 'And that is supposed to be a language!' ('Das soll eine Sprache sein!')[1] Many similar instances could be cited of scraps not only of English, but also of German thus overheard in the street, in trains or in restaurants, especially abroad, getting on Rilke's nerves, but the distinction which he made in the case of German between the 'revolting, bad and slovenly way in which it is mostly spoken' (see above p. 19) and the fundamental character of the language, it apparently never occurred to him to make in the case of English.

We here have one quite objectively attested fact to go by. It is, however, nowhere alluded to by Rilke himself in his numerous recorded utterances about his relationship to the English language, and indeed it seems difficult to reconcile with some of those utterances. In one at least of the phases of his education, the one he most disliked being reminded of, when, at the age of sixteen, he attended the Commercial College ('Handelsakademie') at Linz from about September 1891 to about June 1892, he was formally taught English, receiving in his certificate the mark 'Satisfactory' ('befriedigend').[2] Whether he had learnt any English before this at his military academies, and whether he continued to be instructed in it later by one or other of the private tutors who in the years 1892 to 1895 prepared him for the

Austrian school-leaving examination, is uncertain, as there is no mention of it in any of his other certificates.

The hypothesis that best meets all the ascertained facts (as opposed to the legendary accretions) is that Rilke throughout his life, from well before 1900 onward, had a bare working knowledge of English, derived probably from the Linz Commercial College, which he never seriously cultivated, but could, if occasion arose, with the help of his curious intuitive facility for languages and of a good dictionary, temporarily furbish up for more exacting purposes, such as, for example, the translating of Elizabeth Barrett-Browning's *Sonnets from the Portuguese*. But if this is true, we must also assume that, so long as his footing in the world was not fully assured—that is to say, up to about 1910—he occasionally went out of his way to let it be supposed that he knew English much more thoroughly than he really did, and that once his footing was firmly assured and he could afford, without endangering his status, openly to avow an insufficiency in what was normally regarded as indispensable for any educated person, he went just as much out of his way to create the impression that he was far more ignorant of English than he actually was. After all, for a man of his standing there was more *cachet* in knowing no English at all than in having merely an inadequate, bungling knowledge of it.

Many of Rilke's friends and critics have been puzzled to explain how he could, in spite of his often avowed total ignorance of the English language, produce his impressive translation of Elizabeth Barrett-Browning's *Sonnets from the Portuguese*, a difficult enough specimen of English poetry. It is a very arbitrary transposition of the original into Rilke's peculiar poetic idiom and mode of feeling; many instances of misunderstandings of the text can be found in it; but it really was rendered from the English original and not, as has sometimes been suggested, through the intermediary of some already existing translation in a language Rilke knew well. Careful comparison shows that when Rilke translated these sonnets he really did, at least for the time being, know English well enough to feel and appreciate them as

English poetry, though not to understand them correctly in every detail. He himself dwelt at the time on the 'perfection and precision of the diction',[1] and insisted that it had been one of his principal objects to reproduce not merely their meaning, but also their tone—'diesen Ton zu treffen.'[2] This is borne out by what Professor William McC. Stewart of Bristol records of Rilke's statements to him in 1925 about the translation of the *Sonnets from the Portuguese*: 'This he had made with the help of a friend.... He said he had felt himself at the time completely immersed in and at home in the English language, enjoying its rhythms, and yet later forgetting it completely.'[3]

'The Sonnets of Elizabeth Browning were translated in honour of a friend who was of English descent from her mother's side and loved these poems above everything,' Rilke explained to Professor Pongs on 21 October 1924. These Sonnets were by their emotional theme peculiarly congenial to Rilke, and they remained virtually the only English poetry for which he ever expressed any enthusiasm. It is almost as though he regarded himself as dispensed by his response to them from ever again making a whole-hearted attempt to appreciate any English lyric in the original. In 1901 he must have read and may very well have been impressed by what Rudolf Kassner says in passing about the *Sonnets from the Portuguese* in an essay on Robert Browning:

Out of the soul of this tiny, half-paralysed creature the love of Browning, who is so robust and faces life so confidently, conjures up the finest poetic work to be written by any woman since Sappho—the *Sonnets from the Portuguese*. They constitute a culminating point of destiny, and he who evoked it celebrates the moment in verse. These fifty sonnets of Elizabeth Barrett-Browning are the only great event in Browning's life.[4]

It was probably above all this essay of Kassner's on the Brownings of 1900 that Rilke had in mind, when he wrote on 18 August 1903 in one of his early letters to the Swedish reformer and authoress Ellen Key:

Poorly read as I am, and unfamiliar with the English language, I knew hardly any of the works of the Brownings and was *acquainted only with one or the other felicitous stanza from the poem of their lives*; but now I am full of eagerness to learn a great deal about these two emblems of a more passionate and profound humanity.[1]

This is Rilke's earliest reference to the Brownings, and the occasion of it must have been some allusion to them in the letter of Ellen Key's which Rilke is here answering, most probably to her long study on them of 1899. This study of the Brownings by Ellen Key was not translated into German till about 1910 (in the volume *Menschen*), but it may be taken as certain that Rilke read it in the original in 1904, at the time when he was acquiring a reading knowledge of Swedish and making extensive use of it.

There are various mysteries about Rilke's translation of the *Sonnets from the Portuguese*. One of these mysteries indeed, that arising from his supposed total ignorance of the English language, is, as I have already maintained, more apparent than real. It is certain that he would never have been able to understand the sonnets at all, still less to translate them, without the help given to him by the 'friend' of whom he speaks to Pongs and to Professor Stewart, and it is possible that she provided him with literal prose renderings of the more difficult passages.[2] But it is also certain that with all this help, and with all the 'linguistic inspirations' ('Sprachinspirationen')[3] which he speaks of as sometimes enabling him to read languages he does not really know, he would never have been able to translate the sonnets as he did, if he had not had some previous grounding in English to work on. That he must have had such rudimentary previous knowledge of English, however acquired, as early as 1899 is proved by the circumstance that, when engaged on his intensive study of Russian language, literature and history in that and the following year, he was able to utilize certain standard English publications on the subject,[4] especially W. R. S. Ralston's *Songs of the Russian People* (1872), from which he made excerpts. The most explicit and also probably the most reliable statement Rilke himself makes on this point is in a letter of April 1902 to Wilhelm Schölermann: 'I read English badly and with a fair amount of trouble' ('Ich lese Englisch schlecht und mit ziemlicher Mühe').[5]

More complex and difficult of solution are the problems when and where the translation of the *Sonnets from the Portuguese* was made and also who was the 'friend' responsible for his undertaking it. It turns out that no fewer than three different friends had a share in this. One was Ellen Key, to whom Rilke wrote on 11 August 1908, in promising her a copy of his translation: 'Your visit to Capri was the real inducement to this work' ('die eigentliche Veranlassung zu dieser Arbeit'). This is, however, little more than a non-committal complimentary phrase, which it would hardly be necessary to draw attention to at all, if it had not been given undeserved prominence, at the expense of the other more important evidence, by Nora Wydenbruck on p. 138 of her *Rilke: Man and Poet* (London 1949): 'her [Ellen Key's] visit was fruitful, for she had given the poet an idea. Owing to her suggestion he undertook to translate Elizabeth Barrett Browning's *Sonnets from the Portuguese*.' Ellen Key had been of great importance to Rilke in the years 1901 to 1904, and he owed her much for the help she had given him by finding hospitality for him in Sweden, but he had been much annoyed by her well-meant essay on him of 1904, and by the time of her visit to Paris of May and June 1906 he regarded her with acute exasperation, which finds refreshingly malicious expression in his letters of those weeks. He was indeed somewhat mollified in his attitude towards her when she turned up at Capri from 12 to 16 March 1907, and it may be assumed that on this occasion she brought up Elizabeth Barrett-Browning and her Sonnets, in which we know she was deeply interested, as a topic of conversation. But all genuine sympathy between Rilke and her was by now at an end, and there were other, stronger inducements to him to undertake the translation. According to his own often repeated account the decisive figure here was Frau Alice Faehndrich, who was his hostess at Capri from December 1906 to April 1907, to whose memory the translation was dedicated and to whom he wrote on 14 February 1908 (only a few weeks before her death): 'I am now reading the proofs of *the work we did together* last year; it seems to me very beautiful and perfect.'[1] Thus also in a letter to Gudrun Baronin

Uexküll of 15 April 1907 he mentions the translation, 'the accomplishing of which I owe to my hostess here.' So also seventeen years later, in reply to Pongs' question: 'What was the first occasion of your translations?' Rilke refers, as we have already seen to 'a friend who was of English descent from her mother's side and loved these poems above everything', in whose honour the *Sonnets from the Portuguese* were translated—words which cannot apply to anybody but Alice Faehndrich. It is to be assumed that between 16 March (the date of Ellen Key's departure) and 10 April (the day when the translation was completed) Rilke and Alice Faehndrich went over the Sonnets together one by one, she reading each out loud to him in the English text and Rilke producing his versions at the rate of one or two a day. Ingeborg Schnack's[1] statement that Alice Faehndrich furnished him daily with a 'rough translation' ('Vorübersetzung') is, of course, not to be interpreted as meaning that he worked without having the English original before him or taking it constantly into consideration.

This official version of how the *Sonnets from the Portuguese* were translated was challenged in 1948, when B. J. Morse[2] made known what he had heard about 1930 from Dora Heidrich (*née* Herxheimer) regarding her share in it. Dora Heidrich, a sculptress who specialized in animal figures, was apparently of mixed German and English descent, taking considerable pride in having been born in London—to be precise in Camberwell, on 4 August 1884. Later, as a national of Czecho-Slovakia through marriage, she narrowly escaped being victimized by the Nazis on account of the Jewish strain in her blood. She came as an art student to Paris in spring 1906 and must have made the acquaintance of Rilke by May of that year. They would seem almost from the outset to have addressed one another with the familiar 'thou' ('du'). On 14 June of this year Rilke writes to his wife:

Only think: two days ago I read my Rodin lecture to six young people in a studio (rue Campagne Première—hardly three yards wide and three long). It came about as follows: there was only one of them that I knew slightly—Dora Herxheimer about whom I told you, who makes the big lions—but it was pleasant and earnest and warm.

This is the only allusion to Dora Herxheimer in Rilke's published letters. He must have introduced her to Ellen Key, who was causing him so much vexation in Paris in those weeks. He invited Dora Herxheimer to share his evening walks with him, and this she seems to have done fairly regularly, often accompanying him to a *laiterie,* where he would drink the cup of milk that constituted his evening meal when he was on his working regimen. He admired her art and wrote to her in September 1908 about an exhibition in Rome which he had gone to especially to see some of her work in the previous April. About 1909 to 1910 her student days in Paris came to an end, but Rilke appears to have continued to correspond with her till about 1916. Of capital importance is his letter to her of 14 July 1907[1] about the troupe of Parisian street acrobats later celebrated in the fifth Duinese Elegy. In so far as Dora Herxheimer was partly English, she is in any case highly important for the purposes of our investigation; but the greatest interest of all attaches to her having, as she informed Morse, collaborated with Rilke in translating the *Sonnets from the Porguguese* in Paris in summer 1906, some eight months before the Capri version of spring 1907 was produced in collaboration with Alice Faehndrich. Morse writes:

> the first approaches to the task were made with the preparation of the prose renderings, which, with the assistance of Dora Heidrich, had come into being at Paris in 1906. The technique adopted was that followed by Rilke in all his subsequent translations from languages with which he was not perfectly acquainted: each sonnet was first read aloud by Dora Heidrich, and, when points of grammar and meaning had been discussed and elucidated, then reproduced in German by Rilke. The versions that were produced at Capri were only a redaction of this prior draft.

It is a pity that no further evidence about this prose rendering of the *Sonnets from the Portuguese* of summer 1906 has so far emerged, either in Rilke's letters to Dora Herxheimer herself, so far as all the memorable passages in them were transcribed and published by B. J. Morse, or in his numerous utterances to the most various people about the *Sonnets from the Portuguese*—unless we are to assume that, in speaking to Professor Stewart of having made the translation 'with the help of a friend', he was referring no longer to Alice Faehndrich, but to Dora Herxheimer instead. In her own recollections of Rilke, written shortly after his death and published in the Orplid Rilke Memorial number of 1927, Dora Herxheimer has no word to say of her share in the translation of the *Sonnets from the Portuguese*. She does, however, record something else that is worth noting in this connection:

> A clean little hotel in the Rue Cassette, a narrow staircase, the first door on the left. I knock and enter a small room, where Rainer Maria Rilke comes to meet me from his standing-desk by the window. He looks into my eyes joyfully: 'I have done some good work to-day. Would you like to hear it?' And I sit down in my corner silently and listen. Out of deep peace sounds, words ascend, assuming form, living, gleaming, dying. . . . The reader stops, completely exhausted, overcome by the experience. *The Panther in the Jardin des Plantes* had been written that same afternoon.

The chief point to be noted here is that Rilke's 'Panther', perhaps the most famous of all his poems, had been published in the magazine *Deutsche Arbeit* in September 1903 and must have been written well over three years before Dora Herxheimer first met Rilke and before he moved into the Rue Cassette. Something has gone wrong here—at the remove of over twenty years Dora Herxheimer's memory has deceived her about the 'Panther', a poem that must have appealed particularly powerfully to her as a 'maker of big lions'; and in the absence of all confirmatory evidence the question arises whether her memory may not similarly have deceived her regarding some of the details in her still later oral account to B. J. Morse of how she had collaborated with Rilke in translating the *Sonnets from the Portuguese*. If Rilke did indeed take with him to Capri a complete prose translation of the whole sonnet sequence, which he had produced in the previous summer, there was a slight disingenuousness (of which one can, admittedly, not say that he was quite incapable) in his allowing Alice Faehndrich to give him help of a kind that he no longer really needed—for that he would ever have let her have any say in the actual final moulding of his own poetic version is out of the question. Dr Ingeborg Schnack,[1] who was in the confidence of Rilke's fellow-guests at Capri in the winter of 1906–7, Manon zu Solms-Laubach and Elisabeth Freiin Schenk zu Schweinsberg, gathered from them that Rilke found his hostess comparatively difficult to get on with, and therefore thinks that the instigation to translate the *Sonnets from the Portuguese* may well have proceeded in reality far more from him than from her, as a means towards establishing a more cordial atmosphere. His numerous published letters of this winter, in which there are many references to Alice Faehndrich, do not however suggest that he felt any undue difficulty in getting on with her—and such tensions, when they were present, as a rule betrayed themselves promptly and unmistakably in his more intimate correspondence. In any case, it was not till he had been Alice Faehndrich's guest for over three months, and the end of his stay was already in sight, that the question of these translations was broached.

Another point to be taken into consideration here is that the eleven weeks from 12 May to 29 July 1906 were amongst the most industrious in Rilke's life; in addition to writing at least forty of the *Neue Gedichte* (I), he was at this time kept busy preparing the second edition of the *Buch der Bilder* for the press and revising the text of his *Cornet*. It seems unlikely that when he was so much taken up with his own creative work he should have found the time, energy or persistency to translate all forty-four of the *Sonnets from the Portuguese* into German prose, when one reflects that for each single sonnet a session of at least one hour with Dora Herxheimer must have been necessary. In view of all the conflicting evidence I am inclined to suppose that Dora Herxheimer and he only made a start on the translation at this time, and that what most mattered to him about it at this stage was the actual linguistic exercise on the English text, rather than the translation for its own sake. If we thus assume that he had with him in Capri in March 1907 prose translations of say about half a dozen of the *Sonnets from the Portuguese* from the previous summer, we can also suppose that he really did need and receive help from Alice Faehndrich, and did not merely pretend to do so. What can be regarded as quite certain is that he did do *some* reading and translating of the *Sonnets from the Portuguese* together with Dora Herxheimer in Paris in summer 1906, and that is for us a fact of great importance. It is likely that he had this experiment in reading Elizabeth Barrett-Browning with Dora Herxheimer in mind, when he wrote on 15 January 1909 to Jessie Lemont,[1] who had presented him with an English book, that he was looking forward to reading it, 'when I shall have somebody handy who will be able to help me to penetrate a little into the English language, which to my regret I read only with great difficulty.'

When Rilke offered his manuscript of the Elizabeth Barrett-Browning translation to his publisher, Kippenberg, and when it appeared in 1908, the impression naturally arose that he was quite as much a master of the English language and an adept in English literature as the average cultured German man of letters was in those days expected to be, and some years were to elapse before he did anything to dispel this misleading impression. Thus when, in 1909, the first manuscript of translations of his own poems into English (by Jethro Bithell) was submitted to him, he sent it on to Kippenberg with the critical comment: 'These attempted translations seem to me unobjectionable, but cold and mechanical.'[2] There is nothing here as yet of those protests he was regularly to make in later years on such occasions that he knew far too little English to be a competent judge.

The translation of the *Sonnets from the Portuguese* was not the only thing likely to create the mistaken impression in the minds of Rilke's early readers that he was familiar with much of English literature in the original. When he published his monograph on Rodin in 1903, he prefixed to it as motto an English phrase from Emerson: 'The hero is he who is immovably centred.' It can be taken as certain, however, that Rilke first came upon this phrase when he read Emerson in German translation in winter 1897–8,[3] and only looked it up in the English original when he was preparing his *Rodin* for the press. It is easy to arrive at wrong conclusions about Rilke's knowledge. Thus he is found writing to the publisher Fischer in 1901 of the 'days when I still read a lot of Middle High German',[1] and confiding three years later to his most intimate friend, Lou Andreas-Salomé, that he wishes he could at last study Middle High German poetry, of which he 'knows nothing, nothing at all'.[2] Similarly one should not conclude that he knew Greek from the circumstance of his reproducing 'Platon, Symposium' in Greek characters in 1898 in his story 'Die Flucht'[3] and prefixing a Greek motto to his *Life of the Virgin Mary* in 1913 and giving a tag from Sophocles as a note to his poem 'Kore'[4] of February 1907.

If we had no other evidence to go by here than that contained in such of Rilke's letters as have so far been published, no serious problems would arise as to how much English he knew or when and how he acquired it. What he writes, for example, to his American admirer and translator, Jessie Lemont, in June 1912 of his 'connaissance malheureusement très incomplète de l'anglais',[5] which has nevertheless not prevented him from reading the English article on Rodin she had sent him, in no way conflicts with the hypothesis already advanced here that Rilke had a bare knowledge of English from before 1900 onwards; nor does his declaration less than a year before his death to Duchess Aurelia Gallarati Scotti: 'l'anglais m'échappe depuis longtemps.'[6] It was chiefly in conversation that Rilke sometimes allowed his vivacity to run away with him on this, as on a number of other themes, heightening with legendary nimbus or anecdotal piquancy facts which were in themselves quite humdrum and unmysterious. When one tries to clear up the contradictions and misunderstandings which this has given rise to, there are many possible sources of inaccuracy to be allowed for in the actual reports themselves that have come down to us of Rilke's conversational utterances about the English language: his original words may have been imperfectly heard, imperfectly apprehended or imperfectly remembered; and in some cases there are the strongest reasons for supposing that the writers in question are not only recording what they themselves remember hearing Rilke say, but also bringing in what they know other people heard him say on the same subject, together with their own unproven hypotheses about it. But when all due allowance is made for these possible sources of error, there can be no doubt that Rilke frequently, and particularly in the last six or seven years of his life, gave in conversation mythically or anecdotally heightened accounts of his relationship to the English language, which will not fit in altogether with the ascertainable facts.

It was about 1910 that Rilke first began openly and even defiantly to proclaim his ignorance of the English language (and, for the matter of that, also of *Hamlet* and of Goethe's *Faust*). His hearers, having the Elizabeth Barrett-Browning translation before them, naturally found it hard to know quite what they should make of such declarations. His publisher's wife, Katharina Kippenberg, who saw much of him in the years 1910–14, gives the following account of his attitude towards the English language and those who speak it:

With a curious bias he excluded the English from his spiritual world. In spite of his translations from the English and of his respect for the admittedly very narrow segment of Shakespeare's work that he knew, he manifested a kind of dislike ['eine Art Abneigung'] for their character and their language; at the age of thirty he still knew none of their poets.[1]

Rudolf Kassner, whose intimacy with Rilke fell in the years 1909 to 1919, sums up his impressions on the question in the following words, which were published only four months after Rilke's death and therefore have the additional interest of being almost the first statement[2] about the subject to appear in print:

He loved France because he saw there the higher race ['die höhere Art']. It would be completely wrong to see in Rilke's love for France nothing but the ordinary German love for the foreign as such. Thus *the English race and the English language had always remained alien to him, nothing could persuade him to go to London; the American appeared monstrous to him....*

One of his principal confidantes on the last seven years of his life,

Frau Wunderly-Volkart of Canton Zürich, is the chief source for the following account, given by J. R. von Salis, of how Rilke spoke about England after his migration to Switzerland in 1919:

Rilke always declared that he did not understand English, and nothing would induce him to visit England.... But one day Elizabeth Barrett-Browning inspired him with unconditional, self-surrendering enthusiasm, such as only he was capable of feeling. By guesswork and intuition he acquired on the spot that knowledge of the language which enabled him, with the help of a collaborating friend, to translate the *Sonnets from the Portuguese*. He never read any more English books after that and said he had forgotten what he had known of the language. But those who knew him well maintain that he had not entirely forgotten it, and that they sometimes looked up with surprise, when Rilke would, with a malicious smile, if the conversation happened to turn on points of the English language, suddenly come out with the correct grammatical form, or the expression that was being looked for.[1]

This account of J. R. von Salis, which has come to be accepted as having a quasi-official validity[2] and which clearly embodies together with the author's and Frau Wunderly-Volkart's own firsthand information much inferred from other, remoter sources, rests on the assumption that such formal study of the English language as Rilke would confess to having indulged in can only have taken place in 1907, immediately before he translated the *Sonnets from the Portuguese*, and that these sonnets were the only English poetry he ever attempted to read. There are, however, good reasons for suspecting that these assumptions formed no part of what either Frau Wunderly-Volkart or von Salis themselves ever heard Rilke *say* in so many words, but that they belong rather to what von Salis, in view of various circumstances, concludes that he must have *meant*. Difficulty arises when one compares von Salis' account with two records of Rilke's conversations in Paris in 1925, the one by Fréderic Lefèvre,[3] editor of *Les Nouvelles Littéraires*, the other by Maurice Betz, the translator of whom we have already variously heard. What Lefèvre gives us on 24 July 1926 is the first statement about Rilke's attitude towards things English to appear in print, and the only such statement to be published during Rilke's lifetime. Within three weeks it was reprinted in German translation in the *Neue Leipziger Zeitung*.[1] Lefèvre writes:

It is a strange thing, Rilke said, to me, that I learnt English in hardly more than a few months, only in order to be able to read Browning in the original; but the genius of that language then seemed so alien to me that, once my curiosity had been satisfied, I so completely forgot it again in less than six months that at the present day I no longer understand a single word of it.

Lefèvre's report, of which this, of course, is only a small portion, has the advantages of priority and contemporaneity; for the rest he writes as a professional journalist, carelessly and for the day only; interviewing important authors is a routine job with him; this is his only meeting[2] with Rilke, of whom he had previously known next to nothing; much of what he says is demonstrably inaccurate.[3] One would have preferred to have a more reliable witness; in particular one would like to know whether what Rilke really said was not that he had learnt English in order to be able to *read Browning* ('à seule fin de lire Browning dans l'original'), but in order to be able to *translate Elizabeth Barrett-Browning*. A certain check on Lefèvre's report is supplied, however, by Maurice Betz, who knew Rilke well personally, was thoroughly familiar with all his writings and had innumerable long conversations with him in Paris in 1925, keeping careful notes on them. It was Betz who introduced Lefèvre to Rilke—and in doing so he was undoubtedly above all concerned, as a kind of unofficial literary agent, to obtain some of the right kind of publicity for his author. It seems possible that Betz may himself have been present at Lefèvre's interview with Rilke, which took place in a restaurant in Montmartre one hot afternoon in June or July 1925. In his *Rilke vivant* of 1936 (which embodies in an appendix some passages—though not the one that interests us—from Lefèvre's interview), Betz writes:

Rilke told me one day that he had learnt English in a few months in order to be able to read Keats and Browning. But on being disappointed by these poets he had at the same time felt himself so alienated from England and the English language that he almost as quickly forgot everything he had just learnt. He had realized that England lay without the magic circle of his nature and its experiences and possibilities. From that moment his memory expelled everything it had absorbed, just as though it had never been there.[1]

These were the 'difficult and disappointing relations with England' which Betz speaks of elsewhere (see above p. 6) as having led Rilke to 'expunge England from his Europe'. Whether Betz is here supplementing notes and recollections of his own from Lefèvre's report, or correcting that report in the light of his own knowledge, or reproducing quite independently of Lefèvre an entirely different conversation, he is deserving of more trust, as one who writes on Rilke with authority and with a due sense of responsibility. In particular we can trust him in the one point where his report most strikingly deviates from that of Lefèvre, in the addition of Keats' name to that of Browning as having first induced Rilke to learn English.

It seems beyond dispute that Rilke's unsuccessful attempt to find anything to his taste in Keats and Browning must have been a quite distinct experience from his enthusiastic discovery of Elizabeth Barrett-Browning in 1906–7,[2] which curiously and puzzlingly enough, does not figure at all in the reports of Lefèvre and Betz, although Betz must have known about it. It is here, however, that chronological difficulties arise. The only thing we can be certain of is that Rilke was fond, during his last years, of telling the anecdote (heard by Frau Wunderly-Volkart, Fréderic Lefèvre, Maurice Betz and possibly also by von Salis) of how he had at some unspecified earlier period acquired (apparently from scratch) for some particular purpose a working knowledge of the English language in a remarkably short time, the great point of this anecdote being, however, that he had totally forgotten the language again just as rapidly. So far as the name 'Browning' occurs in all the recorded versions of this anecdote, we might at first, in spite of the obvious objection that 'Browning' is not at all the right name under which to refer to Elizabeth Barrett-Browning, assign the formal study of English, which Rilke here speaks of, to summer 1906 and spring 1907—and that is just what von Salis does. But we are forced by the decisive testimony of Betz, which introduces the name of Keats into the discussion, to date Rilke's formal study of the English language, such as it was, after January 1914, instead of before April 1907. On 17 January 1914 Rilke saw in the house of André Gide a reproduction of Joseph Severn's sepia drawing of Keats on his deathbed,[1] and was greatly moved by it. The following day he wrote his poem on Keats ('Zu der Zeichnung, John Keats im Tode darstellend'). The tone of this poem is utterly incompatible with any sort of disillusionment as to the value of Keats' poetry, and since such disillusionment is, according to Betz, all that Rilke felt, once he had actually attempted to read Keats in the original, we can be certain that it must have been written *before* that attempt was made. There is no objection at all to that assumption. The poem runs:

Nun reicht an's Antlitz dem gestillten Rühmer
die Ferne aus den offnen Horizonten:
so fällt der Schmerz, den wir nicht fassen konnten,
zurück an seinen dunkeln Eigentümer.

Und dies verharrt, so wie es, leidbetrachtend,
sich bildete zum freiesten Gebilde,
noch einen Augenblick,—in neuer Milde
das Werden selbst und den Verfall verachtend.

Gesicht: o wessen? Nicht mehr dieser eben
noch einverstandenen Zusammenhänge.
O Aug, das nicht das schönste mehr erzwänge
der Dinge aus dem abgelehnten Leben.
O Schwelle der Gesänge,
o Jugendmund, für immer aufgegeben.

Und nur die Stirne baut sich etwas dauernd
hinüber aus verflüchtigten Bezügen,
als strafte sie die müden Locken lügen,
die sich an ihr ergeben, zärtlich trauernd.

In translation:

On seeing the drawing of John Keats in death

His countenance, the task of praise completed,
with wide horizons' distance now is blended:
so pain, by which our minds are still defeated,
reverts to its dark owner, when all's ended.

And there remains this mask which, woe-surveying,
moulded itself to freest figuration,
—a moment yet—in new-learnt gentle fashion
scornful alike of flowering and decaying.

O face of whom? What doom has overtaken
the chords but now consentiently swinging?
O eyes that life, its dearest treasures bringing,
from dark renouncement never more could waken!
O threshold of sweet singing,
o lips of youth, for ever now forsaken!

Only the brow seems bent upon achieving
some permanence, where all is disconnected,
as to confute the locks that, tired, dejected,
give way upon its curve to tender grieving.

This poem, one of Rilke's finest, is really nothing but an ampler and more fluid variation upon his earlier 'Der Tod des Dichters' ('The death of the poet') of 1906, inspired in its turn by Rodin's group of the same name. Not only the theme, but also the structural imagery is the same in both poems. Severn's drawing had renewed older vibrations in Rilke's spiritual make-up, and all he needed to know about Keats[1] when he wrote his poem in January 1914 was that he was a great poet who had died young. Keats stands generically for any poet, for all poets, for 'Orpheus', for Rilke himself.[2] It can only have been *after* and *as a result of* his being so much moved by Severn's drawing of Keats that Rilke decided to find out for himself what the poetry of this Keats was actually like, and it was not until the war had forcibly put a stop to his travel-fever of this epoch, confining him for practical purposes to one spot, that he can have settled down to the requisite formal study of the English language of which he spoke to Betz. That he was interested in Browning as well as in Keats just about this time is shown by his appealing in October 1914 or very shortly after to 'Robert and Elizabeth Browning' as examples of the possibility of solving the, for him, insoluble problem of 'living in fellowship with the beloved.... We must find out the way too.'[1] Unless we are to dismiss the report of Betz as quite unreliable, the only satisfactory hypothesis is that the more or less systematic but ultimately abortive study of the English language which Rilke talked about after 1920 not only to Betz, but also to Lefèvre, to Frau Wunderly-Volkart and presumably to others as well, must have taken place fairly soon after August 1914.

Time was heavy on Rilke's hands during the war years, when he so seldom found himself able to produce original work, and foreign travel was impossible. We know that he sought to occupy his mind with various desultory courses of private study, for example of astronomy, astrology and mathematics. It may well be supposed that he made a similar desultory study of the English language at this time—only it is clear from all that we have already seen that he cannot have embarked on this study as an absolute beginner, with no previous knowledge, but must rather have brushed up a certain sketchy and seldom exercised knowledge which he had long since had, trying to put it on a firmer basis. The circumstances were unfavourable for such an undertaking. During the war years Rilke was incapable of tackling anything with zest or tenacity; hardly anything could give him real pleasure or rouse him to enthusiasm. It is to be presumed that he set about working on English grammar and reading Keats and Browning half-heartedly and listlessly, with many misgivings, and very soon gave it up again. Thus the curious situation arises that Rilke would seem, if all his own utterances are taken at their face value, to have known English quite well *before* he had begun (about 1914) to learn it, and to have been totally ignorant of it *after* he had made considerable progress in learning it. From all the evidence before us we may assume that Rilke from his early years to his death knew more English than he would admit after 1912, but that he never at any time came to know English well enough to be entitled to pronounce a judgment either on the cultural and aesthetic value of the language as such, or on the merits of such a poet as Keats.

Rilke's declarations to Frau Wunderly-Volkart, Betz and

others during his Swiss years that he had completely forgotten every word of English that he had ever known are certainly not to be taken literally. It has already been seen that he would at times put his friends right on points of English grammar and vocabulary (see above p. 40). In 1922 he transcribed without any errors a passage that interested him from an English society and fashion journal for ladies,[1] copies of which seem to have come his way fairly regularly. Interesting in this connexion is almost the only letter of Rilke's recorded in the Rilke Archives to one of the many who had translated him into English—he would seem as a rule to have left it to his publisher to deal with all such correspondents. To a certain Mrs Goodwin-Winslow,[2] who had sent him specimens of her English translations from his *Book of Hours*, together with a letter in English, he replied on 25 November 1923 not in German, which would have been the obvious language to use, failing English, but, very characteristically, in French, as follows:

Of the various languages which I have more or less cultivated, English has always remained the least accessible to me; I could pretty well understand your kind lines,—but you will excuse my replying to you in another language: that of the country where you are at present residing. / It goes without saying that I remain extremely grateful to you for your exertions as a translator: I regret that I am incapable of judging the results, of which you have kindly let me see some fragments.

This is quite typical of Rilke's way of writing about the English language, when occasion arises, in the letters of his Swiss years. Thus he writes on 6 January 1922 to Gräfin Sizzo:

I have before me Mr R. G. L. Barrett's English translation (of the *Life of the Virgin*), which has just appeared . . . a little volume produced with much good taste. I can't make much beyond that out of it, however, as this language has, of all those with which I have ever tried to enter into relationship—and in spite of my translation of the Browning Sonnets—remained the most insuperably alien ['die unüberwindlich fremdeste'] to me.[3]

Similarly in 1924 Rilke writes to Professor Pongs of his translation of Elizabeth Barrett-Browning's Sonnets as 'my only attempt from English, the language which is the remotest and most alien for me ('die mir entlegenste und fremdeste Sprache')'.[4] These epistolary declarations represent so to speak the penny-plain version of what we have already come across in the twopence-coloured state in the records given by Betz, Lefèvre, J. R. von Salis and others of Rilke's conversational utterances on the same theme in the same years—but in these latter it can safely be assumed that the colouring is in considerable measure Rilke's own.

The question naturally arises how far Rilke, who makes such lavish use of foreign—in the first place, of course, French—loan-words in his poetic work, his letters and his conversation, is to be found employing English tags. In this connexion it should be noted that, apart from the considerable influx of English borrowings into the German and, for the matter of that, also into the French language, due to general scientific, industrial, commercial and social developments during Rilke's lifetime, the circles he moved in were full of people who knew English well, loved it and were constantly interlarding their German and even their French with English terms and phrases. Fürstin Marie Taxis[1] in her correspondence with Rilke speaks in the middle of a German context of being 'anxious', 'out of place', 'down in the pit', 'up in the clouds', 'disgusted' or 'tranfixed'; she uses such phrases as 'a fluttering heart', 'Complimenten-Fischerei', 'last not least' (sic), 'the great majority', 'I wonder', 'long long ago', 'make me wild with delight'; 'babies', 'daffodils' and 'spirits' belong to her regular vocabulary in writing German; she can, without turning a hair, write to Rilke: 'Doch jetzt sind wir in for it'; 'ich bin etwas downhearted'; or: 'heute nur diese Zeilen um Ihnen . . . A merry Xmas and a happy New Year von ganzem Herzen zu wünschen.' Katharina Kippenberg, without letting herself go quite so much as this, introduces into her letters to Rilke such English words as: 'beefsteaks', 'cottage', 'gentleman', as well as the continental 'high-life' Anglicisms: 'five o'clock tea', 'smoking', 'boys', 'hall'. Claire Studer,[2] after a prolonged stay in the United States, produces a volume of poems with the barbaric title *Lyrische Films,* which Rilke unsuccessfully recommends to his own publishers. Even Baladine Klossowska,[3] who writes to Rilke chiefly in French and has only slight English affinities, can occasionally employ such phrases as: 'Als mir der postmann sagte...' or: 'Outre ces women anglaises...' Rudolf Kassner, like Hofmannsthal, very frequently employs English loan-words. The same is certainly true of at least half of Rilke's acquaintances. English or pseudo-English nicknames were liable to turn up amongst his friends—so he is found referring in 1897 to Sophia Goudstikker as 'der Puck'[1] and in 1915 to the much-married Marianne Mitford as 'Baby Friedländer'.[2] Rilke has quite enough linguistic sense to appreciate the preposterousness of the pseudo-English name 'Somegod' with which Barbey d'Aurevilly designates Maurice de Guérin in his Amaidée, and to cite it ironically in the note to his own translation of de Guérin's *Le Centaure*.[3]

All these circumstances considered, it is not to be expected that that there should be no English loan-words at all in Rilke's vocabulary. What is surprising is that he should use no more of them than he does[4]—his personal prejudice would appear to have been stronger here than the influence of his environment. Among the technical jargon of the literary profession which he early assimilated there was the word 'Essay',[5] used by him, though not to the exclusion of the Teutonic 'Aufsatz', intermittently from 1897 to 1918, if not later. It is to be put down to hardly escapable Anglo-Saxon economic and social influences that he is occasionally in his letters found using such words[6] as 'Lift' (1915), 'Bank-safe' (1919—but side by side with 'Eisenschrank', 1910), 'Generalstreik' (1919), 'bridge-Tisch' (1923) and 'Hall' (1923—in the context: 'ce bureau au "Hall"'). There are, however, other cases where Rilke appears to be using English loan-words not merely without reflection and automatically, in conformity with general practice, but deliberately and with conscious interest. In his quite early years, when he still indulged comparatively crudely and obviously in the naturalistic trick of hoisting prosaic modern phenomena and phraseology into poetry, he was evidently fascinated enough by the English words *tramway* and *pony* to exploit them repeatedly for such purposes. Thus in 1895, in the poem 'Künstler-Los' in *Wegwarten I*, he writes:

Flott angespannt!
Pony, du kleines, du ziehst den grünen
prächtigen Wagen . . .

And in 1896, 'Mein Geburtshaus' in *Larenopfer:*

Wo ich, einem dunklen Rufe
folgend, nach Gedichten griff,
und auf einer Fensterstufe
Tramway spielte oder Schiff.

In another poem in *Larenopfer* ('An der Ecke') the two words are somewhat monstrously combined:

So trefflich schmort auch keine die Maroni.
Dabei bemerkt sie, wer des Weges zieht,
und alle kennt sie—bis zum *Tramwaypony*;
sie treibts ja Jahre schon, die alte Toni . . .
Und leise summt ihr Herd sein Lied.

Another English word which Rilke, in later years, seems to use with a certain relish, is 'clown'; thus on 10 May 1911, in writing to Fürstin Marie Taxis: 'sie spielen ihre Rollen, sie schreiben Briefe, und dabei bleibt noch Zeit übrig, zähe Zeit, auf die sie laut loshauen, wie auf einen *Clown*, um sie nur loszuwerden.' Similarly, in writing about his grandmother to Lou Andreas-Salomé on 19 February 1912: 'Das Leben hat heftige Späße mit ihr unternommen, aber sie begriff, wie die *Clown's* (sic), immer nur den Knall. . . .' It is curious that Rilke prefers to 'Schal', the normal German transliteration of Persian S H Á L, the English transliteration 'shawl' which, used quite regularly still by Goethe and Mörike, sounds very out of the way, archaic and affected in modern German. This is all the more important because Rilke in his last years, largely under the influence of the collection of Cashmere shawls in the Historical Museum in Bern, made of the shawl one of his favourite symbols. In 1923 and 1924 he wrote three poems entitled 'Shawl',[1] using the word in this English form also elsewhere in his poems and letters of these later years.

It is very much the 'high-life' Rilke who writes in February 1907 to his wife: 'Wir waren zum Lunch wieder da—', in March

1914 to Magda von Hattingberg: 'Wollen wir um Eins lunchen?'[1] and in July 1919 to Rudolf Junghanns: 'Ich ... stieg genau zur Lunch-Zeit, um halb-eins, vor dem Palazzo Salis ab';[2] and in January 1920 to Elisabeth von Schmidt-Pauli: 'In Luzern, im National, saß ich beim Lunch nicht weit von den griechischen Höchsten Herrschaften.'[3] This is the same Rilke who also sometimes, in writing German, uses not only the word 'Lunch', but also, alternatively, 'Déjeuner'—a practice for which, however, Swiss polyglottism may in part be held responsible.

Rilke apparently managed to get on very well without what is usually regarded as the most indispensable and certainly is one of the most popular English loan-words on the continent, the word 'gentleman'. Hofmannsthal can be found using it, even Stefan George can be found using it—and in an amusing context[4] too—but I have so far never come across an instance of Rilke's using it. One might well suppose that the aristocratic ideal so dear to Rilke's heart would have appeared to him too diluted and compromised by concessions to the middle classes and to merely common-sense standards of behaviour in the conception of the gentleman. Rilke does, however, on one occasion employ the English word 'snob', when he characterizes Proust as only just having escaped the danger of being one—'wie nah am Snob vorbei.'[5] (That was, of course, Rilke's own danger, quite as much as it was Proust's; one of his closest friends, Lou Albert-Lasard,[6] confesses, evidently with some satisfaction, to having once in a moment of anger called him a 'snob' to his face.) Another 'indispensable' English loan-word which Rilke once or twice uses in his last years is 'sport'. In his unpublished jottings of February 1922 he has a long meditation in French on 'sports' as 'an active method for replacing the feeling for nature with sensation etc.'. In a letter to Baladine Klossowska of 15 February 1924 he reflects upon 'le sport moderne', and upon what would have been the probable results, if he himself had been given 'une éducation sportive'. In a French poem of February 1926 he expresses his lukewarmness about winter-sports:

> J'aime les hivers d'autrefois qui n'étaient point encore sportifs.[7]

It was one of Rilke's little idiosyncrasies, for which he was taken to task as precious by at least one of his friends, Paula Becker,[1] to spell the three months 'Mai', 'Juni' and 'Juli' archaically with a final 'y', instead of the now normal 'i'. One would like to know whether he realized that he was thereby, in the case of May and July, merely adopting the most ordinary English spelling. It would also be interesting to know whether he realized that the English language, of which he thought so poorly, has perfect equivalents for those two French words, 'paume' and 'verger', the untranslatability of which into German constitutes in his eyes so disgraceful a deficiency of the German language. (See above p. 21.) 'Palm', fully naturalized in English for centuries, expresses everything that Italian 'palma' or French 'paume' can express, while the admirable native Anglo-Saxon 'orchard' has all those nuances which Rilke praises in the French word 'verger', saying that they alone had been a sufficient inducement for him to write poetry in French instead of in German: 'A meadow planted with fruit-trees, neither garden nor field, but rather both together.'[2]

Not only from the living, but also from the dead were Rilke's sensitive ears liable to be assailed with scraps of the uncongenial English language. On 4 October 1912, at Schloss Duino, when he was keeping the minutes of a spiritualistic séance conducted particularly to please him, the *planchette* suddenly switched over from German to English with the words: 'Once more,' and Rilke found himself obliged to transcribe the following dialogue:

Princess Marie Taxis:	Who is here, please?
Answer:	No friend. . . . I hate allof you (sic)
Princess Marie Taxis:	Can you say your Name? (sic)
Answer:	No.
Princess Marie Taxis:	Why dou (sic) you hate us?
Answer:	Why st. . . .(?) not[3]

At a later séance, in April 1915, at which Rilke was not present, but the results of which were communicated to him as probably in some way concerning him, all that could be got out of the 'Unknown One' or some other spirit supplanting her was a volley of 'awful abuse in English' ('schauerliche Grobheiten auf Englisch').[1]

There is a curious epilogue, without which our survey of Rilke's relationships to the English language would not be complete. In Autumn 1932 Countess Nora Wydenbruck, who, without ever meeting Rilke personally, had corresponded quite a lot with him, largely about spiritualism, in the years 1921 to 1925, and who had made, but not as yet published, an English version of the *Duinese Elegies*, was working, as she records, with Mrs Hester Dowden, 'the famous automatic writing medium.'[2] At one of these sessions, in reply to the question: 'Who is it?' the answer received was: 'Rilke.' The Rilke who thus announced himself was a Rilke with a profound mastery of and interest in the English language and also with very precise ideas about how he wanted his *Elegies* to be translated into that language. It was for this reason that he had presented himself; 'Yes. I must speak to you, but not with others,' he declared; 'Give me an evening. Bring the poems and your translations; we shall discuss it.' He assured Countess Wydenbruck, on being asked, that he had helped her with her translation, the whole of which was eventually gone over and corrected line by line in various later séances. Of these corrections, which were 'of the most subtle nature, and absolutely in accordance with Rilke's method of working', Countess Wydenbruck gives us a few specimens. Where a line in the second *Elegy* had originally been rendered: 'Pivots of radiance, pathways, ladders, thrones....' Rilke objected to the use of 'pivots' for 'Gelenke', and of 'ladders' for 'Treppen'; eventually the improved reading arrived at was:

Links of all radiance, pathways, steps and thrones.

Most interesting of all, however, is the objection raised by the spirit-Rilke to the word 'verdant' used in the translation of the fourth Elegy, on the ground that 'it was derived from a Latin, not an Anglo-Saxon root'—and the authoress here goes on to say that this 'corresponds to his (Rilke's) method of working in German'. 'Almost invariably,' she continues, 'Rilke would object to words derived from Latin roots, and substituted *allowed* for *permitted, whole* for *entire, robbed* for *despoiled*.' This is a remarkable development to conceive of Rilke going through, even in the spirit world, Rilke, who uses foreign loan-words so lavishly on all occasions. While he was eliminating the non-Anglo-Saxon words 'verdant', 'permitted', 'entire' and 'despoiled' from the English version of his *Duinese Elegies*, he might also have left instructions for the deleting in the original German text of such words of non-Germanic extraction as: 'Kontur', 'Szenerie', 'Maske', 'Figuren', 'Chaos', 'Pollen', 'Tumulte', 'Vase', 'Urne', 'Fransen', 'Minuten', 'metallen', 'Modistin', 'Rüschen', 'Kokarden', 'Fontäne', 'Tempel', 'Pylone', 'Musik', 'Porzellan', 'Kruste', etc. It is time that the spirits found out that the English language, as a consequence of the Norman conquest, so modified itself, particularly its system of intonation, that it can absorb and has absorbed thousands of words of Latin origin, completely naturalizing them in a way for which there is no analogy at all in German.

In conclusion the spirit-Rilke said to Countess Wydenbruck:

> Allow me to say that when you put my poetry into English words I feel I have done it to a great extent myself, for you sing the same harmonies as I do, but when a note jars I long to set it into tune myself. Therefore forgive me for my suggestions, when they seem unreasonable.... I thank you very much. You seem part of myself when I speak like this, not a personality apart.... I have been warned not to come again until the call is given to me. I had worked with you and found you in a very receptive frame of mind, when it was easy to guide your mind in my direction. It was an honour to come.

The satisfaction one might have derived from the thought of Rilke in the spirit-world having so thoroughly overcome his old aversion for the English language and even having extensively adapted it for his own purposes is largely neutralized by the unfortunate circumstance that he has nothing to say in it but banalities. This applies also to his later communication of 1949, still in English and still addressed to Countess Nora Wydenbruck, but this time transmitted by a sensationally circuitous route, in which Miss Kathleen Raine and even the Third Programme of the B.B.C. played a part: 'Tell Nora that death is no longer a weariness and I have got hold of my fragment of eternity. Tell Nora.'[1] This is an allusion to the phrase in the first Duinese Elegy, 'dass man allmählich ein wenig / Ewigkeit spürt' ('so that one may gradually feel a little eternity'), as it is somewhat arbitrarily and effusively rendered by Countess Wydenbruck: 'Until we begin / to grasp a fragment of eternity.' If Rilke, clairvoyant as he was, had any presentiment during his lifetime of the curious things that were to happen with him through the medium of the English language in a later state, his irrational aversion for that language was after all fully justified.

VI

STEREOTYPED ESTIMATES OF ANGLO-SAXON CULTURE

Many of Rilke's acquaintances, as he often notes in his letters,[1] travelled for one reason or another, sometimes for longer periods or habitually, to England or even to America, and it was naturally expected of him that he should, like most people of his circle, at least make the journey to London. But, as we have already seen (above p. 39), Kassner records that 'nothing could persuade him to go to London', and J. R. von Salis that 'nothing would induce him to visit England'. Actually it appears that Rilke did in the years before the 1914 war more than once contemplate going to England—though the only records of these plans that have so far come to light all take the form of decisions not, after all, to risk such a step. On 17 August 1904, when Arthur Holitscher had suggested, presumably on the ground of some tentative, earlier, oral plans, that he and Rilke should spend some time together in London, Rilke replied from Sweden: 'I imagine London as something very torturing. You know my fear of very large cities. Furthermore I shall probably never travel any further westward, since everything always summons me to Russia.' (For the rest of what Rilke says about England in this letter see below pp. 64-5.) On 26 May 1910 Rilke writes to his wife from Paris: 'And now I also know that what I have to do at this time is not to go to England, but to pull myself together here.' Two years later, when there is a rumour circulating amongst his friends that he is going to London, he indignantly denies it: 'No, London is not in the least on my programme.'[2]

One may say both of Rilke's thoughts of travelling to England and of his dealings with the English language that, so far as he advances at all, it is only for the sake of drawing back again with an expressive and also characteristic gesture. *Il sautait pour mieux reculer.*[1] But although he took good care never actually to go to England, and although he regarded the unfavourable reaction of his subtle organism to the English language as a conclusive demonstration that England did not belong to Europe, there were many other guises under which he was, whether he liked it or not, brought face to face with manifestations of Great Britain and of the United States, and compelled to react to them—and by no means always with hostility either. Wherever he moved in the European continent, in every stratum of experience, from the most inward to the most external, from the most material to the most spiritual, he was liable to encounter us and our works. The study of his letters alone is an object lesson in the manifold ways in which we are, despite our insularity, despite the English Channel and the North Sea, despite even the Atlantic, interwoven in the fabric of continental European life. Though Rilke did not go to England, England in a certain sense came to him, especially when he was in France; and so also did Scotland, if it was only when, in 1905, he registered the pleasant feeling of really being at home in Paris at last, after a long absence, on reading in a menu: 'Marmelade dundee';[2] or when, twenty years later, he was invited to a great literary reception in the 'Prunkräume' of the 'Dotation Carnegie' in the Boulevard St. Germain.[3] One of the favourite tunes recorded as being whistled by the 'Herr Inspektor', a caricature of Rilke's own father, in his early autobiographical novel, *Ewald Tragy*, is 'My object all sublime' ('So such' ich den Humor') from Gilbert and Sullivan's *Mikado*. Rilke was not indifferent or unsympathetic when, to the glory of Theodore Roosevelt, the first teddy-bears 'conquered the world' in 1906.[4] He was called upon to commiserate with Lou Andreas-Salomé, when she had to install an ugly iron stove in her room in January 1922, because the inflation made it impossible for her to obtain English anthracite.[5] In October 1920 his nostrils were called upon to remember the peculiar aroma of Baladine Klossowska's Swiss-Virginian cigarettes: 'Je fume mes bonnes Flags, vous les sentez?'[6]

All the impressions which educated foreigners and particularly Germans receive through the most various channels of the character and culture of the English-speaking peoples tend to sort themselves into two categories. Either they bear witness to the view of us as peoples with a distinctive and impressive still living cultural tradition of our own, closely affiliated and not inferior in status to the cultural traditions of the continental European nations and linked to them in a give-and-take relationship which could not be broken off without some real loss to the continental Europeans as well as to ourselves. Or they bear witness to the view of us as materialistic, thick-skinned, unphilosophical arch-philistines with a strong streak of Pharisaism in our make-up, given over to commerce, manufacturing and empire-building, and with no still living culture, except what a few scarcely representative individuals parasitically acquire from more favoured lands, without being able to communicate it to more than an ineffectual minority; in fact, as people from whom nothing is to be learnt except the arts of money-making and (in earlier days at least) successful but unscrupulous foreign politics.

These two contrasted ways of envisaging the English-speaking peoples are, after all, not unfamiliar to us who belong to those peoples. They have both been present in our dealings with ourselves ever since the later eighteenth century, when, simultaneously with the industrial revolution, the culture of the mind[1] came more and more to be regarded as an end in itself, perhaps the supreme goal of human aspiration, a serious rival to older religious postulates about the purpose of man's existence. The threat of debasement or extinction to the finer life of the mind and imagination from an increasingly one-sided Anglo-Saxon concentration upon mere technological progress and material prosperity called forth criticism, often very bitter criticism, within the Anglo-Saxon countries themselves, quite as early as it did elsewhere, and has continued to do so uninterruptedly from the beginnings of the Romantic Movement to the present day. It is chiefly from documents of this Anglo-Saxon self-criticism that foreigners have all along derived and still derive the material for their often so very uncomplimentary estimates of Anglo-Saxon culture. That we are a 'nation of shopkeepers' was a harmless little joke of Adam Smith and others at our own expense, before it became a bitter sneer in the mouths of Barère and Napoleon. More perhaps than in any other country, the self-appointed champions of unadulterated intellectual and aesthetic culture in Great Britain and the United States of America have tended to insist to the utmost, and even with some complacency, on their status as a high-brow or third-programme minority group, at loggerheads not only with the masses, but still more with the bulk of the upper classes and with the established educational system and academic institutions of their own nation. They have tended to conceive of true culture as in principle supranational, but in practice better appreciated and more at home in almost any other country than their own. This has been, in varying degrees, the mental attitude not indeed of anything like all, but of many who during the last century or so have themselves been the leading representatives of contemporary Anglo-Saxon culture, especially of those who have attracted most attention abroad. So far-reaching a divorce between cultural aspirations and natural partisanship for one's own nation is not to be found in other countries, least of all in nineteenth century Germany or France. Some of the material evidence for the worth and vitality of contemporary Anglo-Saxon culture could therefore often be interpreted instead as evidence for its inferiority and effeteness. One could either see in such portrayals of the English-speaking peoples as Matthew Arnold's *Friendship's Garland*, Galsworthy's *Island Pharisees* or Sinclair Lewis's *Main Street* and *Babbitt* a final, authoritative verdict of condemnation on their whole mentality, or else one could see that mentality as impressively represented by those who purchased, read and admired the writings of Matthew Arnold, Mr Galsworthy and Sinclair Lewis, and also, of course, by the Matthew Arnolds, Galsworthys, Sinclair Lewises, Frank Harrises and Ezra Pounds themselves.

Both of these contrasted ways of envisaging the English-speaking world are mingled in varying proportions in the complex and fluctuating picture of it which is constantly forming and re-forming itself within the mind of each one of us who ourselves belong to that world. The foreigner, however, looking on us from without, is less inclined to suspend his judgment; not unnaturally, and like ourselves in analogous cases, he wants a final black or white verdict of acceptance or rejection. It is not to be expected of him that he should say with William Cowper, as we do, even when we are most critical of ourselves: 'England, with all thy faults I love thee still.' He forms a one-sided, stylized picture of us, that he can either like or dislike.

In reality, of course, very few people ever have an opportunity or even a genuine inclination to form an independent estimate of any foreign nation, based substantially on their own immediate observation and experience. Where, as in the case that concerns us here, the nation involved has played and still continues to play a major part in the world's history, ready-made conceptions, favourable or unfavourable, of what its character and culture are like inevitably impinge upon the individual beyond its frontiers through newspapers, books, schools and conversation during his formative years, and one or other of these stereotyped conceptions gains the upper hand in him, before he sets foot in the country in question. Even if he is highly educated, he will nearly always, in the nature of things, whether he is conscious of it or not, expect and desire, in travelling abroad, as in all his other dealings with foreign nations, to be confirmed in preconceived ideas of which he would find it impossible to declare whence he has derived them or how much true authority attaches to them. Even if his attitude towards the nation concerned changes radically, as it well may do, from admiration to contempt or *vice versa,* he is still liable just to be exchanging one current and stereotyped opinion for another, rather than forming a genuinely independent judgment of his own. It can even turn out that the opinion of a man of genius about some particular foreign nation is in substance very much less his own personal opinion than the opinion of the man in the street, which he has unconsciously and uncritically taken over. The question arises whether this could ever have happened to Rilke. He did indeed detest stereotyped opinions on any subject, and was as a rule particularly anxious to go out of the way of them in this matter of sizing up foreign nations. What he has to say about the foreign peoples in whom he is most interested, the Russians, the Scandinavians and the French, can be criticized as arbitrary, subjective and remote from facts,[1] but never as hackneyed. When he discusses the English-speaking world, on the other hand, he is hardly ever sufficiently interested in it to make any serious effort to get away from or beyond the trite, conventional generalizations about it which are current all around him. Nearly everything he has to say about us, favourable or unfavourable—and it will be seen that he very occasionally has something favourable to say—remains well within the grooves of stereotyped German ways of reducing us to a schematic type. He never wanted to form a conception of his own about us, and it irritated him that he was expected—as he constantly was—to take any interest in us at all. If he was nowhere else conventional, he was so in this one connexion.

Of the two contrasted ways of envisaging the English-speaking world which presented themselves to Rilke from his early youth to his death, the unfavourable view of us as materialistic philistines with no true sense for the finer things of the spirit was more firmly established and widely accepted, and therefore also more stereotyped, than the favourable one of us as a people with a culture deserving respect. Sympathy with and respect for Anglo-Saxon culture were on the other hand older, going back to the mid-eighteenth century, when England, with Shakespeare as the dominant figure, had afforded the most important model and inspiration for the great efflorescence of German culture which culminated in Goethe. A certain esteem, sometimes warm-hearted and active, sometimes merely perfunctory, for England, above all as the land of Shakespeare and the land which had given to the rest of Europe the idea of the gentleman, was a constituent factor in that liberal-minded, comparatively cosmopolitan German humanism which in the period of Rilke's childhood and early manhood was unsuccessfully trying to maintain the ideals of

Goethe and Weimar against the harsh, increasingly Anglophobe nationalism of the new Hohenzollern Empire. In humanistic circles one owed it to Goethe and Weimar, one owed it to oneself, to think the best of England, whatever people said, and even if one had no lively consciousness of owing it to England herself. But since Goethe's days much had changed. Klopstock's prophetic demand in his ode 'Die beiden Musen' of 1752—a poem, by the way, which Rilke seems particularly to have admired[1]—that German poetry should emulate English poetry, had been fulfilled. Germany had produced in Goethe a figure of a stature comparable to that of Shakespeare, together with many other outstanding minds in literature and philosophy, and she had not been slow to feel and proclaim herself greatly superior, at least in emotional fervour and philosophical profundity, to the nation from which she had up to so recently been glad to learn. The industrial revolution had changed England considerably, and not in all respects for the better. The United States had developed on a vast scale and were beginning to overshadow Great Britain in continental eyes. As early as 1800 the Romantic generation of German poets and thinkers had begun to speak disparagingly of contemporary England as debased with materialistic empiricism and far inferior to the England of Shakespeare's day, and in the 1820s the Napoleon-worshipping Francophile Heine infused into these criticisms his own virulent malice, repeatedly attacking the Englishman as the typical Philistine: 'It makes me feel sick to reflect that Shakespeare was English and belonged to the most repulsive nation created by God in His wrath.'[2] Similarly Nietzsche had branded the English as a nation without 'any true spiritual power, any true depth of spiritual discernment, in brief any philosophy' and also as 'lacking in music'.[3] Above all, Germany herself had become a powerful, united Empire, in whose consciousness the things that Weimar stood for could no longer assert the central place. Economic and political rivalry, growing more and more bitter from year to year, inevitably led practical-minded, up-to-date Germans to focus their attention on the less prepossessing aspects of English civilization. Those aspects were there too, right enough, not to be overlooked, even if scores of the best contemporary English minds had not been busily engaged in pointing them out and making the most of them in vehement publications which were meant, indeed, in the first place for home consumption[1] and not for the eager Anglophobe readers abroad who gave them a specially enthusiastic reception. The old friendly Weimarian way of regarding England lost more and more ground to a rancorous view of her which, about the time of the Boer War, came to prevail in German public opinion, at least amongst the ruling classes and in considerable measure also amongst the intelligentsia. Some of the chief purveyors and supporters of this hostile estimate of England as the paradise of the philistine and the pharisee, the land without a true living culture, were to be found in the ranks of the German university professors of English and of history, who could speak authoritatively on the subject.

These, then, were the two possible ready-made ways of seeing Anglo-Saxon culture between which Rilke had to choose, if he was not prepared to make the effort of going into the question at first hand—and he was not. In one of his earliest works, *Two Stories of Prague*, published in 1899 and written about 1897, there are two passing references to England which are of interest in this connexion. In the first story, 'King Bohusch', a charming little madcap princess is described, 'defying her *stiff and horrified English governess*' by running off on her own 'like a little stray swallow into the free expanses of a rustling park'.[2] The prudish, inhibited English governess, as 'Miss', it should be remembered, used to be no less a stock figure in German novels and comic papers than the equally prudish and inhibited German governess, as 'Fräulein', in English ones. In fact, this unfortunate creature served as a symbolic type of England altogether in the Anglophobe caricature of the nationalistic press of the second German Empire and of the National-Socialistic régime. In the second of his *Stories of Prague*, however, 'Brother and Sister', Rilke speaks of 'bright English colour-prints'[3] in the shop-windows of the Prague art-dealers, and in so doing touches on one of the aspects of contemporary English culture which was at that very time, as we shall see, exercising an important positive influence on him.

In a variety of ways pressure was again and again brought to bear upon Rilke to make him take a more favourable view of England, and he frequently did veer quite a long way in the direction of recognizing something valuable and congenial to him in what England had to offer, only to withdraw again and in the end expunge England from his ideal map of Europe—a favourite gesture, if he had but realized it, of the strident Pan-German ideologists whom he so much detested, and also, after his death, a favourite gesture of the National Socialists, whom he would have detested even more. In his first enthusiasm for the Swedish feminist and educational reformer, Ellen Key, in 1902, Rilke was forced to recognize that the true centre of these reforming movements in which he was interested, and the place where most was being done about them, was England.[1] But above all he had several friends who, either because they were adherents of the old Weimarian humanistic tradition, with its sense of affinities to English culture, or because they were partly English by extraction or had spent happy and profitable years in England, were disturbed by his hostile judgment and tried to make him revise it. Particularly to be noted in this connexion are Rilke's publisher, Anton Kippenberg and his wife, both of them champions of the old liberal Weimar ideals, and also Fürstin Marie Taxis, who had many personal links with England, often travelled there and filled her letters, as has already been seen (above p. 47), with English phrases and her palaces with English guests. Rilke did not, however, as a rule respond favourably to such efforts to convert him. 'When something is clearly and insistently presented to me and people push it nearer and nearer to me,' he writes, 'in the end it bumps up against my stubbornness, which is of considerable density.'[2]

What probably did more than anything else to prejudice Rilke so permanently against England is the circumstance that Lou Andreas-Salomé, whose influence on him from 1897 to his death was far greater than that of any of his other friends, was anything but a lover of the English. This imperious woman, whose judgment Rilke relied on particularly in such questions as this, was, without actually having any Russian blood in her veins, born and brought up in Russia, where her father served as a general, and felt a deep devotion to Russia. It was through her alone that Rilke came to be interested in Russia and for a time to regard it as his true fatherland. The only connexion that Lou Andreas-Salomé ever seems to have had with the English-speaking world is that she attended an English private school in St Petersburg—perhaps a sufficient explanation of her aversion. She knew Nietzsche quite intimately, owed a great deal to him and was probably influenced by his very hostile views on England. She says herself that she never felt drawn to travel further west than Germany.[1] How she felt about England comes out most clearly in a letter written by her to Rilke on 20 March 1904, shortly after the outbreak of the Russo-Japanese War, which was, of course, a matter of great concern to both these lovers of Russia. Having declared that nobody in the whole of pacifist Russia wanted this war, Lou Andreas-Salomé goes on: 'And yet, in the end, Russia *had*, in spite of everybody, to want the war, *because—England wanted it.* Ah, how can one help hating and being filled with rage over this! One could sit down and howl at the bare thought of it.' The hysterical violence with which Lou Andreas-Salomé here casts upon England the blame for something which was neither in England's power nor in England's interests, betrays a deep-seated pre-existent aversion. It is likely, however, that these irresponsible words of Lou Andreas-Salomé's made a profound and lasting impression on Rilke. On 16 August of the same year he wrote to her about how deeply he felt the sufferings of Russia through the war with Japan, adding that he wished Russia were his own fatherland—'Und ich wollte es wäre meine Heimat auch.' It was on the following day that he wrote to Holitscher, telling him that he could not consider travelling to London (see above p. 55). In this letter he uses for the first time the phrase which from about 1917 onwards recurs with automatic regularity, whenever England is mentioned to him: 'Everything English is remote and alien to me.' 'I do not know the language of that country,' he goes on; 'I know hardly any of its art, none of its poets.' When he says in conclusion that he will 'probably never travel further westward'—much the same phrase as Lou Andreas-Salomé uses—'because everything always summons him towards Russia', one may reasonably suppose that he has, under the influence of Lou's blind hatred and rage against England on the occasion of the Russo-Japanese War, come to regard England as the exact antithesis of his beloved Russia. This may have been the true beginning of his anti-British bias, which was, however, to remain comparatively in abeyance for some years to come, so that it did not, for example interfere with his translating, in 1906 and 1907, Elizabeth Barrett-Browning's *Sonnets from the Portuguese*.

Rilke's privately expressed anti-British sentiments resemble, in a somewhat milder form, those so stridently proclaimed before him by Heine, and still more by Nietzsche, who, it may be noted, in expounding his conception of Good-Europeanism, treats England as hardly belonging to Europe or to the true European tradition.[1] This resemblance, which goes too far to be dismissed as a mere coincidence, is perhaps sufficiently accounted for by the circumstance that Heine's and Nietzsche's hostile ideas about England had long before 1914 been popularized, stereotyped and made common property by German journalists. It is hardly likely that Rilke derived them direct from Heine and Nietzsche themselves, neither of whom can he be supposed to have read more than casually and superficially—and, at that, only in his early years.[2] It is possible, however, that Lou Andreas-Salomé may have served as an intermediary to indoctrinate Rilke unconsciously with Nietzsche's views on England, as also on various other subjects.

The Austrian, Rudolf Kassner,[3] (see above p. 39), of whom Rilke saw much in the years 1909 to 1919, and in whom he unhesitatingly recognized a mind fully of his own calibre, had, without any English family connexions, and without being moulded in the specifically Weimarian tradition, stayed some time in England in his youth and revisited the country more than once later.[4] He knew the language excellently and, breaking boldly through all stereotyped German ideas about English culture, favourable or unfavourable, he had formed his own truly independent conception of it. Few foreigners could be named whose pronouncements on England would not look meagre and shallow, if placed side by side with the penetrating, eccentrically phrased and by no means uncritical utterances on the same subject scattered through Kassner's innumerable publications. Nobody could have been better qualified or better situated than Kassner to convince Rilke that there was really something almost childish about his way of regarding England. But Kassner, who looked upon Rilke as at bottom in a paradoxically sublime sense childish, and found therein the secret of his genius, seems to have contented himself with bantering him on the subject and, for the rest, treating him as incorrigible.

Nevertheless it is likely that Kassner's admirable book on nineteenth century English poetry, *Mysticism, the Artists and Life* (1900)[1] had some share in inducing Rilke to try his luck so successfully with Elizabeth Barrett-Browning in 1906 and 1907, and so much less successfully with Keats and Browning probably about 1915. Kassner himself, indeed, assumes that this was the one book of his that Rilke certainly never read: 'The *English Poets* were not at all in his line,'[2] he writes. Kassner assumes this because the book in question—his earliest one—had been published seven years before he and Rilke met for the first time, in November 1907 in Vienna, and because it was in any case bound, by its theme, to fail to appeal to him. But that Rilke actually did read it within a year of its publication is proved by his trancribing a long passage from the chapter on William Morris and Burne-Jones in the manuscript of the second part of the *Book of Hours* (between 15 and 18 September 1901). In those days, about the turn of the century, Rilke was, for reasons which will appear, much interested in just those English poets and painters with whom Kassner deals. That was, however, an episode in his discarded past which Rilke had forgotten, or at least become ashamed of, by the time of his first meeting with Kassner, six years later; therefore Kassner gathered no inkling of it from him.

VII

'NEUROMANTIK' AND ITS ENGLISH PRECURSORS

To the impact made upon him by English literature, at least when it had been translated into some less obnoxious language such as German or French, Rilke quite often yielded more readily than to the tactics of personal persuasion employed upon him by his Anglophile friends. Up to the age of thirty or so he was not able to write without associating himself with some advanced contemporary literary and artistic group or other, though his associations of this kind became from year to year looser, as he succeeded in the assiduous cult of his own uniqueness. Up to 1902 we even find him quite often speaking publicly as the mouthpiece of such movements and groups; the phrase 'we moderns' ('wir Moderne') comes easily to his pen. In his very beginnings he is an adherent of German Naturalism, a movement in which influences from the English-speaking world count for very little, and it is of decisive importance that he never to the last rejected Naturalism on principle, that a certain unbroken naturalistic strand, usually indeed very much subordinated to other tendencies, still connects his latest work with the crudities of his early proletarian drama, *Now and at the Hour of our Death*.[1] But his development takes an immense stride forward, when, in the years 1896 and 1897, he begins to associate himself with those anti-naturalistic stirrings in German literature which are now as a rule referred to under the comprehensive term Neo-Romanticism ('Neuromantik'), taking over from them nearly everything in their programmes, except their doctrinaire repudiation of the naturalistic principle as such. He marched more or less shoulder to shoulder with these Neo-Romantics for six or seven years, at the end of which time he was almost able to get on without any groups, colleagues or programmes. But his Neo-Romantic years, 1896 to 1903, brought him again and again face to face with English art and literature.

The term 'Neo-Romanticism' is for our purposes to be taken in a comprehensive sense as including the new conception of lyric most impressively represented by Stefan George and Hofmannsthal, together with the decadent aestheticism underlying it; furthermore the school of painters which had its centre at Worpswede, near Bremen, and divided its attention between dream-like, idyllic landscape and wistful visions of mediaeval young men and maidens, or at least of young men and maidens in mediaeval costume; furthermore the revolution in actual book-production and typography, whose ideal was the 'beautiful book' —or perhaps one might say, 'the book beautiful'; and finally, in the field of applied art, the supplanting of the German ('Wilhelmine') equivalent of the Victorian style of dress, furniture and house-decoration with hand-produced articles of new design, characterized above all by one special kind of recessive, sweeping curve, which was supposed to be based on water-lilies, twining tendrils and kindred phenomena of the vegetable kingdom, and appealed to the taste of that age as the quintessence of beauty, though to our disillusioned eyes it chiefly suggests a limp duster attempting unsuccessfully to sit down on nothing in particular. These tendencies found their most memorable collective expression in a number of influential periodicals, the chief amongst them being *Pan* (beginning 1895), *Jugend* (beginning 1896) and *Die Insel* (beginning 1899), to all of which Rilke was a regular contributor. From the most popular of these periodicals, *Jugend*, the new movement came to be called by the name which is still chiefly used for it, when the emphasis is on the aspect of it concerned with the visual arts, handicrafts, house-decoration and book-production: 'der Jugendstil.'

With this movement, then, Rilke associated himself extremely intimately from about 1896 to about 1903—he even married into it. It is as an apostle of this new cult of loveliness that he paces solemnly, like Reginald Bunthorne, through the most densely crowded streets in the heart of Prague in summer 1896, 'wearing an old-world frock-coat, black cravat and broad brimmed black hat, clasping a long-stalked iris and smiling, oblivious of the passers-by, a forlorn smile into ineffable horizons.'[1] It is in the same capacity that he writes letters in white ink on sky-blue paper to Ernst von Wolzogen[2] in the following winter—a practice ridiculed four years earlier by George and Weedon Grossmith in *The Diary of a Nobody*.[3] The chief inspiration of this new movement came, as it quite openly professed, from England,[4] from Pre-Raphaelite painting and poetry, from Ruskin, from William Morris with his Kelmscott Press and the handicrafts revival, from the aestheticism of the still comparatively well-behaved 'eighties and of the naughty 'nineties. It can be fairly claimed that all these various English developments were much more than the unconnected, echoless outbreaks of a few quite unrepresentative and isolated eccentrics; they constitute collectively one single, powerful movement with considerable unity of purpose and method, with considerable continuity and duration, and with a very large following. Nevertheless it was inevitable that this movement should remain confined to a minority, however important and numerous a minority, that it should be looked upon with suspicion, contempt or at best with good-natured amusement by the majority not only of the British nation as a whole, but also of the educated classes. To that Gilbert and Sullivan's *Patience* (1881) and Robert S. Hichens' *Green Carnation* (1894) bear witness. It is open to question, then, how far it can be regarded as a *representatively* English movement, and in its later *Yellow Book* stage it hardly regarded itself as such. Nevertheless an English movement it was, and in a certain sense it did represent England abroad in aesthetically-minded circles.

The German 'Neo-Romantics', who derived so much of their impetus from the English movement we have been considering, and who recognized in its poets and artists the pioneers of their own aspirations, were after all, in spite of their importance for the age's culture, also an opposition minority group, looked on with hardly less derision, distrust or positive dislike by the bulk of the upper classes in their own country than their prototypes and fellows in Victorian England. Since the later eighteenth century, what posterity, in Germany and in England alike, has come to regard as the nation's cultural heritage has as often as not been something that the majority even of quite educated contemporaries rejected. The Pre-Raphaelites and their aesthetic successors were at least as representative of Victorian England as the Neo-Romantics were of Wilhelmine Germany; the point for us is not whether they were typically Victorian or typically English, but that there was so much going on in England at that particular juncture that could stimulate a ponderable number of the most gifted minds in contemporary Germany to enthusiasm and emulation.

Stefan George began his life as a traveller with some months spent in London at the age of twenty-one (1889) and revisited England in 1898 specially to meet Ernest Dowson. He translated not only Shakespeare's sonnets, but also, characteristically, poems of Rossetti, Swinburne and Dowson. Swinburne, in particular, was of the greatest importance to him in his early writings, up to 1894, most conspicuously in *Algabal*. English influence is, indeed, in George's case, early blended with French, and both are from about 1899 onwards (*Teppich des Lebens*) largely overlaid by the monumental mannerism of his own massive, despotic and arrogant personality. The precocious Hugo von Hofmannsthal who, without apparently so far having visited England, had somehow acquired a precise and subtle understanding of the language, was in his youth an enthusiastic reader of Shelley, Swinburne and Rossetti, and also, under Swinburne's influence, of Webster, Ford, Massinger and Otway. In 1896 he discovered for himself Otway's *Venice Preserved,* of which he was later to write a German adaptation, and the most successful of his dramas, *Jedermann,* was also inspired by an English model. Between 1891, when he was still a schoolboy of seventeen, and 1896 he published some five brilliant essays on English life and on recent developments in English literature and art. Specially noteworthy amongst these essays, which show how well qualified this gifted adolescent was to speak on the subject, and how much the new English aestheticism meant to him, is that on Walter Pater, published in 1894 over the pseudonym: 'Archibald O'Hagan, B.A., Old Rookery, Herfordshire.'[1] The most important of all Hofmannsthal's prose writings takes the form of an imaginary letter from Philipp Lord Chandos to Francis Bacon, dated 1603, the true theme being Hofmannsthal's suffering under a sudden cessation of his poetic creativity. Hofmannsthal, like George, aimed early at a certain universality of culture, in which his acquisitions from England were only one strand, but an extremely important strand.

Such German aesthetic periodicals of the 1890s as *Pan, Jugend* and *Die Insel* (out of which that great publishing firm, the Insel-Verlag, that was to deal so munificently with Rilke, arose) were all of them closely and avowedly modelled on publications like the *Yellow Book*, the *Savoy* and the *Studio*, and regularly contained translations from the English and reproductions of contemporary English pictures, especially of Beardsley. This general pre-occupation with the English aesthetic movement was the first inducement for Rudolf Kassner to travel to England in 1897, though he soon became even more interested in other, less specialized phenomena of English life and culture.

When Rilke identified himself for six or seven years with German Neo-Romanticism and its 'Jugendstil', it was imperative for him, as an adherent and often a public advocate of this movement, to know something about contemporary and near-contemporary English culture, or at least to speak as though he knew something about it. In these years he did indeed frequently speak as though he knew quite a lot about it—nay more, he actually did know quite a lot about it, though rather on the side of the visual arts than of literature. It was the most natural thing in the world that he should have been amongst the first and most attentive readers of Kassner's book on the English poets of 1900.

In April 1898 Rilke went to Florence, remaining in Tuscany for about two months. It was one of the decisive experiences of his early development—quite as decisive as the Russian journeys of the two following years, to which, in later life, he was alone willing to attach great importance. What was it that had taken him to Florence? What was he looking for there? It was above all Rossetti and Burne-Jones who had sent him there. He had come to take a survey of fifteenth-century Italian art, and the greatest impression, from which his poetry was to draw sustenance for years to come, was made upon him by Botticelli, by Botticelli as seen through eyes prepared by nineteenth-century Pre-Raphaelite painting. In his remarkable 'Tuscan Diary' Rilke defends the Pre-Raphaelites, with whom he feels himself completely at one, against the indictment of standing for nothing more than a 'whim' ('Laune'), of only 'seeking a recondite kind of beauty' ('die mühsame Schönheit') because they had become bored with the smooth, obvious kind,[1] 'It was not chance or whim that led us to those before Raphael,'[2] he insists. The highest praise he can bestow on a painting of Carpaccio's that delights him in the Pitti Palace is that 'one could take it for a good picture of Rossetti's, so fairytale-like and mysterious is it in form and colouring'.[3] As late as 1902 Rilke refers twice deferentially in articles to Ruskin,[4] of whom he is hardly likely to have read any more than of Shaftesbury or Knight (presumably Richard Payne Knight, 1750–1824) whom he similarly cites in giving a list of writers on aesthetics in an article 'On Art' published in 1899. In writing on 'The New Art in Berlin' in October 1898 he praises Kurt Stöving's portrait of Stefan George as 'a kind of Lorenzo il Magnifico in a dream of Burne-Jones'.[5] In 1902 he lauds Rossetti—and here the influence of Kassner's book is particularly recognizable—as a 'painter and as the poet of unforgettable sonnets', the secret of whose 'fine and passionate art' lies in his 'combination of the Italian with the English spirit'.[6] In his monograph on the Worpswede School, written during the same year, he speaks of Rossetti as having 'acquired an idiom of his own through Elizabeth Ellinor (sic) Siddal' and in another passage dwells admiringly on Rossetti's Madonnas.[7]

There are few indications of Rilke's having taken any interest in English painting of an earlier date than the Pre-Raphaelite movement. In May 1896 he appeals once in passing to Hogarth as an

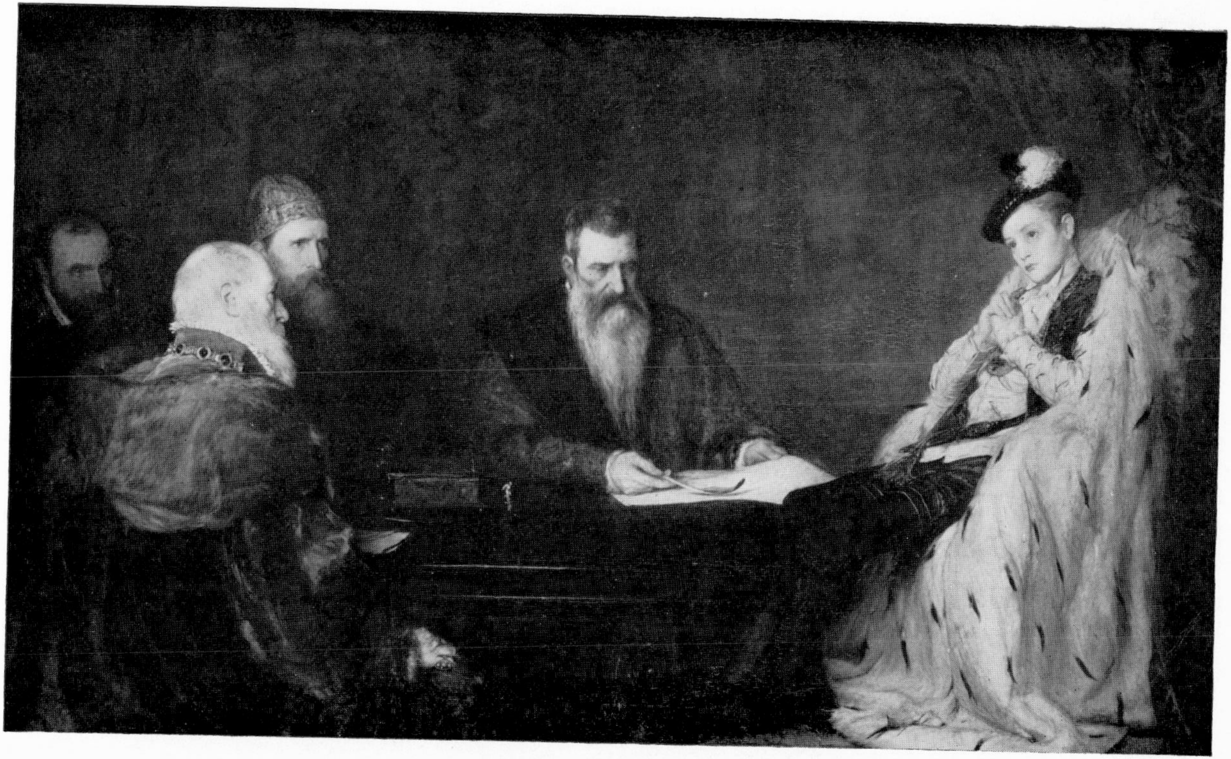

The Death Warrant by John Pettie. This painting inspired Rilke's 'Der König' of 1 July 1906 (See text p. 73.)

example of unsophisticated realism—'Hogarth'sche Natürlichkeit'.[1] In 1901 he mentions the English portrait-painters of the late eighteenth century as having influenced contemporary Russian art, and on 22 January 1901 he urges Otto Modersohn, when visiting Berlin, not to miss some paintings of Reynolds then on exhibition there.[2] It is more interesting to find him quoting in his monograph on *Worpswede* (1903) from a letter of Constable's: 'The world is wide; no two days are alike, not even two hours; neither were there ever two leaves of a tree alike since the creation of the world.'[3] This quotation Rilke, of course, gives in German. Such evidence as there is of his having been interested in Blake's paintings belongs to the later phases of his development, and will concern us in one of the following chapters. In April 1900, in writing of his compatriot and friend the painter Emil Orlik's technique as an engraver, Rilke has occasion to say: 'his eager admiration led him to the Scots, particularly to Whistler, and to the English masters.'[4] In December 1898 he had occasion to refer to 'James Paterson of Glasgow' (landscape-painter 1854–1932), but only because Paterson had happened to exhibit in Berlin together with Félicien Rops, and in January 1901 to Lavery (later Sir John Lavery), whose pictures he recommends to Modersohn at the same time as those of Reynolds just mentioned. Another Scottish painter who receives Rilke's notice is John Pettie (1839–93), whose historical painting *The Death Warrant*, seen by him in the Hamburg Kunsthalle about 1905 or 1906, served as model for the poem 'Der König' in the first part of *New Poems*.[5] G. F. Watts is another British painter whom Rilke once refers to, the occasion being an article on Segantini of March 1902.[6]

In Florence in spring 1898 Rilke made the acquaintance of a young German artist, Heinrich Vogeler (1872–1942), who was instrumental in bringing about extremely important new developments, both in Rilke's outward fortunes and in his poetic growth, by introducing him to Worpswede and its school of painters. Vogeler, himself one of the Worpswede group, was not, like the rest of them, primarily a landscape-painter, but a depicter of legendary and fairytale scenes. In the years when Rilke knew him,

Vogeler owed nearly everything he had to Rossetti and Burne-Jones, when he used oils, and to Aubrey Beardsley in his far more convincing and accomplished pen-and-ink drawings, vignettes and arabesques, some of which decorate the first editions of Rilke's work. The other Worpswede painters owed comparatively little to England; they were conscious, indeed, of their ultimate debt to Constable, but the Barbison school had come in between and meant more to them. Throughout his connexions with Worpswede, however, from Christmas 1898 to the end of 1902, Rilke was never really so much interested in the landscape-painters, who constituted the original Worpswede school proper, as in Vogeler, who counted a good deal with him, both as a personal friend and through his art. This association with Vogeler meant, amongst other things, that Rilke was brought still more closely face to face with the English inspirers and sources of the 'Jugendstil'. Some examples of how this worked itself out in his journalistic writings of these years have already been cited. He refers twice also to Aubrey Beardsley's drawings, on both occasions in studies on Vogeler. One of these studies forms part of the monograph on Worpswede, which was designed by the publishers to appeal to as wide a circle of readers as possible, and it is interesting to see how Rilke accommodated himself to this policy by giving pride of place in the entire world and history of art and culture to Germany at the expense of the rest of Europe, and also by avoiding, as he nowhere else does, anything that might offend the respectable citizen's sense of what is normal, healthy and proper. Thus, in admitting Vogeler's debt to Beardsley, Rilke is here careful to deprecate and dissociate himself from Beardsley's 'decadence'.[1] A few months earlier, however, in writing on Vogeler for a select aesthetic periodical, and therefore under less cramping conditions and more directly from his heart, Rilke simply tells, without any apparently disapproving reservations on the score of 'decadence', how Beardsley's drawings had been 'a revelation'[2] for Vogeler, when he first came across reproductions of them in *Die Insel*. The term 'decadent', in its German and French connotation,[3] is, as Rilke well knows, just as applicable to Vogeler in his best work as it is to Beardsley. It is just as applicable, for the matter of that, to Rilke himself,[1] whose whole life and art are inconceivable without the myth and pathos of decadence attending them. In 1911 Rilke has occasion to refer to Beardsley again on two occasions; firstly to acknowledge a copy of Katharina Kippenberg's translation of Beardsley's letters[2] which she had sent to him, and secondly in recommending to Anton Kippenberg the Hôtel du Quai Voltaire[3] in Paris as one where he himself has often stayed and which is proud of having numbered Beardsley and Pissarro among its guests.

Vogeler devoted a considerable part of his energy to handicrafts, especially to metal-work and to designing furniture, fabrics and house decorations in general. His inspiration here is, of course, derived ultimately from William Morris and his school. Rilke attaches great importance to this side of Vogeler's activities, and knows, too, something of its English prototypes. As early as October 1898, in an article on 'The New Art in Berlin' he speaks of 'what Liberty's ('Libertyhaus') has done for London' as a great precedent for what still remains to be attempted in Berlin and Vienna.[4]

In two outstanding figures of English decadent aestheticism Rilke took much more than a perfunctory interest, in Walter Pater and Oscar Wilde. On 27 July 1902 he reviewed at length and with genuine enthusiasm Pater's *Renaissance* in the German translation of Wilhelm Schölermann, with whom he had corresponded about Pater shortly before[5] and whom he praises for having perfectly reproduced in German 'that equivalence of form and content which is so important to Pater and which characterizes both his style and his mode of vision'.[6] It is in this review that Rilke praises Rossetti for having enriched the 'lofty culture' of the English ('ihre hohe Kultur')—a phrase to be lingered on, for we shall never again find him saying anything like it—by bringing it into touch with 'the great age and best painters of Italy'. He ranks Pater's study amongst 'the best and most living books on art, those that stimulate in the reader a need for great works of art'. He praises Pater not only for his evocation of individual figures, but also for his 'exceptionally precious general reflections'. On 5 July 1902, in one of his letters to Schölermann, Rilke says of Pater's book: 'The essays on Leonardo da Vinci, Luca della Robbia and the School of Giorgione will remain amongst the few things that I shall read again and again, whenever a quiet hour comes, demanding the voice of a good book.'[1] He remained sufficiently interested in Pater to read his *Imaginary Portraits*[2] (also, presumably, in translation) in the following year. When, just at the time of his first reading Pater's *Renaissance*, Rilke speaks in his *Worpswede* monograph, which was completed eight weeks before his first journey to Paris, of the profound wisdom required to express the 'smile of Mona Lisa'[3] in words, probably Pater's famous prose-poem is quite as much his point of departure as the painting itself. The same is true of the long passage on the Mona Lisa beginning: 'As though all humanity were contained in her infinitely tranquil portrait...' in Rilke's fragment 'On Landscape'[4] written in the same weeks and originally intended to form part of the *Worpswede* monograph. On going to Paris at the end of August 1902 and actually seeing the 'Mona Lisa' in the original for the first time, Rilke at once commences an elaborate cult of it, which continues intermittently throughout the following twelve years; and it appears likely that the meaning it has for him is in a considerable measure determined by Pater's seductive dithyramb.[5] As a piece of writing this could hardly fail, even in translation, to make a great impression on Rilke as he was in 1902. The phrase 'and the eyelids are a little weary' might easily have been coined by the early Rilke himself; 'müde' was then one of his favourite, much overworked epithets, and 'Augenlid' is an image that constantly recurs in his writings, down to the mysterious epitaph he composed for himself shortly before his death. The purple passages in Rilke's monograph on Rodin, written in autumn 1902, especially the one on the 'Man with the Broken Nose', probably owe something both in tone and in conception to Pater. Rilke's great interest in Michelangelo's poetry, to which he refers in letters in 1906 and 1912, and much of which he himself translated into German between 1913 and

1921, was presumably in considerable part aroused by the essay in Pater's *Renaissance* on 'The Poetry of Michelangelo'.[1] When Jessie Lemont gave him a copy of *Studies in Seven Arts* by Pater's disciple, Arthur Symons, at Christmas 1908, Rilke wrote to her that he intended to study carefully 'poor Arthur Symons' beautiful book, which promises so much illumination, even when one only glances furtively through its pages'.[2] Symons' essays on Rodin, Beethoven and Eleonora Duse were by their themes particularly calculated to interest Rilke at this time, but he had by winter 1908–9 quite outgrown the Pateresque stage of his development, and it is to be presumed that the difficulties he had with the language prevented him from ever going much beyond his first 'regard furtif' in Symons' pages.

The earliest evidence so far available of Rilke's interest in Oscar Wilde is not before 1905, when his Neo-Romantic phase was over and done with. In that year the publication of *De Profundis* had revived general interest in Wilde, making of him once more a topical subject. In October 1905 Rilke wrote his lecture on Rodin, with whom he was at that time living. In that lecture, which was delivered at various places in Germany and Austria during the following winter, and was published, together with the original Rodin monograph of 1903, as a second part, in 1907, the following passage[3] (an addition of 1907) occurs:

It was ordained that he (Rodin) should work as nature works, not as human beings work.

Perhaps Sebastian Melmoth felt that when, solitary, he went out on one of his sad afternoons, to see the *Porte de l'Enfer*. Perhaps some hope of making a fresh start quivered once more in his half-shattered heart. Perhaps, if it had been possible, he would have liked to ask the man, once he was alone with him: What has your life been like?

And Rodin would have answered: Good.

Had you any enemies?

They have not been able to prevent me from working.

And your friends?

They demanded work of me.

And women?

In my work I have learnt to admire them.

But wasn't there a time when you were young?

I was nobody in particular then. One understands nothing, when one is young; that comes later, slowly.

What Sebastian Melmoth did not ask has perhaps passed through the minds of many on gazing at the master, again and again, and marvelling at the inexhaustible strength of this man of almost seventy....

Sebastian Melmoth is, of course, the name assumed by Oscar Wild after his release from prison. On 1 May 1898[1] Wilde praises, with characteristically flippant undertones, the 'Balzac' of Rodin; in June or July 1900 Kassner[2] saw Wilde, half a year before his death, in the Rodin Pavillion at the Place d'Alma, where the 'Porte d'Enfer' was publicly exhibited for the first time. Presumably Rilke had heard from Rodin himself about Wilde's having come to see the 'Porte d'Enfer'. The conversation between Wilde and Rodin that Rilke gives us is, however, quite certainly, as it professes to be, purely imaginary. Nothing could be more unlike Wilde, who was out to shine in all conversation and to score over his *vis-à-vis,* even on his deathbed, than that he should ever tamely have allowed Rodin to talk down to him. What Rilke here gives us is simply the gist of some of his own conversations with Rodin,[3] what he felt to be the lesson, so to speak, that he, that every modern artist had to learn from Rodin. Wilde symbolizes here for Rilke the dangers of a too exclusively aesthetic attitude towards life and art, dangers which he felt, *mutatis mutandis,* threatened himself also. Rodin seemed to Rilke at this time—he was to think very differently later—a great example of how the inherent dangers of the artist's life might, by the doctrine of 'Work', be overcome, of how art might be reconciled with life and so bring about the salvation of the artist himself, instead of betraying him, one way or another, into downfall and disaster. Certainly Rilke, like Hofmannsthal,[4] saw Wilde as a victim not so much of society, fate or some psycho-physiological kink, as of art itself, of his own specifically poetic genius with its inherent dangers. In April 1906[5] Rilke cites Wilde as an example of overweeningness ['Prätension'], as opposed to the legitimate pride of the artist in his work.

Everything points to Rilke having been interested in Wilde's legend, but hardly at all in his work. In the Wilde legend, however, he was deeply interested. In February 1908 he wrote to the publisher S. Fischer, asking him for a free copy of the German edition of *De Profundis*, which had just appeared.[1] He went on to say that he would like to write something on the subject—'über das ich schreiben möchte.' We know that he received the book, but no further direct comment on it from him has so far turned up. It can be taken as certain, however, that he read it, and it probably contributed something to those experimental, heterodox interpretations of the person and teaching of Christ which so much occupied his mind throughout his life.

We have some faint indication of what impressions *De Profundis*, coupled with the Wilde legend, must have made on Rilke, from an unpublished list which he jotted down, presumably in autumn 1908, of possible themes for treatment in his great prose work, *The Note Books of Malte Laurids Brigge*.[2] The first four themes in this list, each given in a separate line, are: 'The neighbour / Luxembourg / Mont Saint-Michel / Sainte Geneviève'—of these only the first was actually worked out and incorporated in the final text of *Malte Laurids Brigge*. At some later date, as is shown by the different, much more hasty character of the handwriting, Rilke added here, in brackets: '(Wilde, Verlaine).' It is impossible to recognize from the manuscript whether these two names have been jotted down on the same line as 'Mont Saint-Michel' because of some inner connexion which Rilke here conceived of, or merely because there was more space for them there than anywhere else on the small page. What is certain is that Rilke contemplated writing about Wilde and Verlaine in the *Note Books of Malte Laurids Brigge*, either by themselves, or in connexion with the theme of 'Mont Saint-Michel'. It is, indeed, difficult to think how such a connexion could have been established, unless Rilke had in mind here the Boulevard St Michel district of the Latin Quarter, where the Luxembourg and Sainte Geneviève are also situated, instead of the little rocky island off the coast of Normandy and Brittany,[3] which we know he had visited and been much impressed by five or six years previously. Some light is thrown on the way in which Rilke probably intended to treat Wilde and Verlaine in *Malte Laurids Brigge* by his marginal notes on Xavier Bichat's *Recherches Physiologiques sur la Vie et la Mort*[1] of winter 1908–9. In developing certain speculations about the distinction between sheer, undilutedly intense experience and what is merely habitual and therefore dull, Rilke quotes Bichat's words: 'The sensation which affects us most is that which has never touched us before.' Rilke comments on this: 'Thus it is that God touches those who have never before felt him fully: as a new sensation: Verlaine, Wilde: but they get used to him.' What interests Rilke about Wilde, and what Wilde has in common with Verlaine, is that the shattering ordeal of imprisonment led to his experiencing religion, of which he had previously known next to nothing, 'absolutely', as an entirely new sensation—Wilde's *De Profundis*, Verlaine's *Sagesse*. (Shortly before in the notes on Bichat, Rilke had been concerned with the problem of whether imprisonment brings 'only relative sufferings, which custom reduces to indifference . . . or absolute suffering . . .'.) That Wilde, like Verlaine, died as a penitent Catholic, Rilke must have known—and this must, in the one case as in the other, have disappointed him and aroused his disapproval; thence the phrase; 'but they get used to him (i.e. God).' Here again it is clear that Rilke's interest was in Wilde after the catastrophe, imprisoned in Reading and exiled in Paris. It is likely that André Gide,[2] with whom Rilke was on friendly terms probably from 1908 onwards, told him something about his meetings and conversations with Wilde. It is to be regretted that Rilke never wrote the projected section of *Malte Laurids Brigge* in which Wilde would have appeared.

VIII

RILKE AND ENGLISH LITERATURE AFTER 1902

When Rilke left Worpswede for Paris in August 1902 he was turning his back for good on the phase of his closer association with German Neo-Romanticism, particularly as manifested in the field of the visual arts as 'Jugendstil'. It was a phase in his development that he soon became ashamed of,[1] and one of the results of his breaking away from it was that the indirect and tenuous link with the English prototypes of the 'Jugendstil' which it had involved was also broken. Only his interest in Pater and Wilde seems to have outlived this transition, and Pre-Raphaelitism ceased to exist for him. His attention was henceforth focussed on the Impressionists and Post-Impressionists,[2] especially on Cézanne, on French Symbolist poetry and, of course, on Rodin.

But even in Paris, in this new phase of his development, he was still from time to time brought face to face with works of literature and of the visual arts from the English-speaking world which his new, austerer mentors took seriously, and expected him to take seriously. What he would encounter ranged from eager, well-informed, sympathetic but not uncritical interest in particular English writers and works, to vaguer, old-style, naive Anglomania or to the most superficial Anglicizing snobbishness; but in one way or another Rilke was, as a proselyte of French culture, constantly being compelled to take cognizance of English books, English authors, English traditions, above all during the last seven years of his life, whether it was in 1920 through Charles Vildrac's *Paquebot Tenacity*,[3] in 1923 through Valéry Larbaud's *Barnabooth*[4] or Maurois' *Colonel Bramble* and *Dr O'Grady*,[5] in 1924 through Paul Morand's *Lewis et Irène*[6] or in 1925 through St Jean

Perse's *Images à Crusoé*[1]—which last inspired Rilke's own poem of this year, 'Robinson nach der Rückkehr.' Baudelaire, Verlaine, Laforgue, Mallarmé (of whose having taught English Rilke expressly 'did not disapprove'),[2] Gide, Valéry and Rodin all had important connexions of one kind or another with the English-speaking world and its culture. Even Maurice de Guérin, who was to mean so much to Rilke in the years 1910 and 1911, had occasionally introduced into his diary such words as 'at home (délicieuse expression anglaise)', 'strange dream', and 'silver-sweet sounding'.

The American painter James McNeill Whistler, of whom Rilke had (as has been seen above, page 73) heard enough to allude to him as one of Orlik's masters in 1900, had died in 1903, leaving an enduring impression both as a painter and as a personality in the Paris art world. In 1904 Rodin had travelled to London to be installed as Whistler's successor in the office of President of the International Society of Sculptors, Painters and Engravers. One of Whistler's best pupils was in winter 1905–6 to become an intimate friend of Rilke's (see below p. 122). Rilke had probably therefore plenty of material to go by, when he cited Whistler together with Wilde in April 1906 as an example of 'overweeningness'.[3]

Thanks to W. E. Henley, Rodin was early accorded ampler recognition in England even than in France, and from 1884 onwards the relationships of Rodin (who never learnt a word of English or of any other foreign language) to Britain and to the United States became more and more important. Rilke, as an admirer of Rodin and a writer on him, soon became aware of this, and it was brought still more forcibly home to him, when, from September 1905 to May 1906, he acted as Rodin's unofficial secretary—a post in which he was, it may be noted, succeeded by an Englishman with the curiously un-English name of Anthony M. Ludovici. In March 1903, within a few weeks of the publication of Rilke's own monograph on Rodin he was approached by an English publisher who wanted to produce an English translation[4] of it. It was in England that a monopteros was to be built in

1905 to provide the best possible setting for Rodin's 'Baiser'.[1] All through January and February 1906 Rilke was busy with correspondence in connexion with Rodin's journey to London for the great banquet and exhibition of the International Society of Artists. He finds particularly troublesome a letter which he has to write on this occasion to John Lavery[2] of the Glasgow school, whose paintings had impressed him five years earlier in Berlin. In December 1913, when the first illustrated edition of his Rodin book is being prepared, Rilke successfully insists, against the proposals of his publisher, that the only suitable portrait of Rodin for his purposes is that of the Anglo-American painter Sargent. (Letter to Anton Kippenberg of 5 December 1913.)

To one writer of the English language whose fame, thanks to Baudelaire, was greater in France than in his native land, Edgar Allan Poe, Rilke's attention had been drawn in his Worpswede days by the musician Egon Petri. 'I recall an excellent conversation with him (Petri) about Edgar Allan Poe,' Rilke writes to his wife from Sweden in 1904.[3] Probably Kassner's valuable pages on Poe[4] in his book about the English poets also made some impression on Rilke, when he read that book in 1901. A reference on 12 August 1904 in a letter to Kappus to 'the prisoners in Poe's tales, feeling the shape of their fearful dungeons and the unspeakable terror of their abode', suggests that Rilke had read, with all the appropriate horror, such stories of Poe's as *The Pit and the Pendulum* and *The Premature Burial.* The impression Poe made on Rilke was lasting enough for him to refer to him again twenty-one years later, as a master of horror.[5] When, however, Robert Musil[6] would apparently, by implication, attribute to Poe (and also to Walt Whitman) a decisive influence on Rilke, one must agree with J. R. von Salis that he is mistaken.

It was in Paris and as a result of his association with Rodin that the more important of Rilke's only two personal encounters with living men of letters from the English-speaking world took place—that with Bernard Shaw in April 1906. It is difficult to think of any writer more different in every respect from Rilke than Shaw, and it is a curious irony that circumstances should have brought him together with Shaw, of all men, rather than with Yeats say, or D. H. Lawrence, who had each of them, in their own so dissimilar ways, much in common with him, and whose paths might well have crossed his. Even with James Joyce or T. S. Eliot, whom he might also easily have run into, Rilke had a little more in common than with Shaw. It is remarkable, however, that Rilke, while at once feeling this difference, was neither repelled nor scared by Shaw. On the contrary, he felt greatly attracted by him and at ease with him.

The occasion was the modelling of Shaw's bust by Rodin, which Shaw himself sometimes referred to later as the most important event in his life. Rilke wrote to S. Fischer, the publisher of the German edition of Shaw's works:

> Shaw's personality, and everything about him makes me want to read more of his books, of which I only know *The Man of Destiny*, I think. Would it be justifiable for me to ask you to let me have some of his books, if I were to say (without rashly committing myself to it) that I hope to write some little thing about him?[1]

Rilke then goes on to praise Mrs Shaw as a 'good wife, whose eagerness for and delight in beautiful things caresses her husband as the breezes of spring caress a billy-goat'. On the same day, 19 April 1906, Rilke writes to his own wife, herself a sculptress, about Shaw and the modelling of his bust. In doing so he specially speaks of Shaw as being 'Anglo-Irish'—it is one of the rare occasions on which Rilke is found taking such distinctions into account.

> Bernard Shaw, he writes, comes every day, with his wife; we meet quite often and I was present at the first sittings, seeing for the first time how Rodin sets about his work.... Yesterday, at the third session, he placed Shaw (to the extreme delight of that ironical and, by the way, not at all unsympathetic mocker) in a nice little nursery chair and cut off the head of the bust with a piece of wire. Shaw, to whom the bust already bears a remarkable, as it were enhanced resemblance, looked on at this decapitation with indescribable delight.

A week later Rilke says that Shaw has a special faculty for standing for his portrait, 'like a thing endowed with the *will* to stand, over and above being naturally adapted for doing so.... And everything, right from the depths of his long legs, concentrates itself in his head and neck.' (26 April to Clara Rilke.) 'This bust of Shaw's', he writes on the same day to Elisabeth von der Heydt, 'seems to excel in expression and masterliness the most perfect of Rodin's portrait-busts.' This he attributes to Shaw's being so 'indescribable a model'. He goes on to characterize Shaw as 'a man who has quite a good method for keeping on friendly terms with life,—for bringing himself into harmony with it (which is worth something). He is proud of his works, like Wilde or Whistler, but without their overweeningness, just as a dog is proud of its master.'

Rilke did not forget Shaw. He mentions him again in passing a year later, when Shaw's German translator, Siegfried Trebitsch, a young author whom Rilke had known since 1896, calls on him at Capri.[1] Early in the 1914 war Rilke was delighted to hear that Bernard Shaw, together with Romain Rolland and other enemy aliens, had offered to collaborate in an international pacifist journal, which a number of Munich intellectuals, Rilke himself apparently amongst them, were, in defiance of the German government, trying to launch.[2] In October 1924 Rilke spoke with evident pride and somewhat misleadingly to his Polish translator, Witold Hulewicz, of having in his old Paris days been 'on friendly terms with Verhaeren, Shaw and Rodin'.[3] His very brief encounter with Shaw belongs, of course, to quite a different category from his year-long friendship with Rodin and Verhaeren. Within less than a year of his death Rilke writes quite enthusiastically about Shaw's *St Joan,* in connexion with a production of it by the Pitoëffs of Geneva:

What a pity that you won't see Mme Pitoëff in the part of St Joan. Luckily it has been possible for her to take it seriously, as the mocker Bernard Shaw concentrates all his irony—which is, in any case, quite respectful, this time—in a kind of epilogue. In the main body of the play the figure of St Joan stands out in simple purity; but Ludmilla Pitoëff has succeeded in investing this purity with unforgettable radiance.[4]

It is natural for us to wish to know something of the other side of the picture. What did Bernard Shaw think of Rilke? Professor E. M. Butler put this question to him about 1939—and put it, one may be sure, with some persistency. All she could get out of him, however, was apparently that he remembered Rilke perfectly well; but as to Rilke having been present in the studio, when Rodin modelled his bust, he simply couldn't believe it. Which is rather meagre and disappointing. However, the *Wiener Journal* for 12 January 1935 gives the following report of what Shaw said about Rilke shortly before that date in a conversation with the well-known Austrian elocutionist, Margaret Bach:

Grete Bach, in enumerating the items in her repertoire, happened to mention Rilke. 'A strange man,' said Shaw, interrupting her, 'a genius in working clothes. I often met him at Rodin's, when Rodin was modelling my bust. Rilke was the maid of all work. If it came to the point, he had to push a figure weighing several hundredweights out of the way. There was nothing at all fastidious about Rodin's choice of assistants when occasion arose. Whoever happened to be passing had to give a hand in pushing about the huge figures in his studio. Once it was the postman, another time it was the tax-collector. But usually it was Rainer Maria Rilke. He never looked as though he would or even could write poetry. His works are splendid in their simplicity. It is a pity that so few of them have been translated into English.'

(After a description of how Margaret Bach read the story of Samson and Delilah to Shaw the newspaper report goes on:)

Of his own accord Shaw asked for further specimens from the artist's repertory. 'Something of Rilke's', he begged. Grete Bach gave him in English the essential outlines of the poem about the 'Blind Girl', before reciting it to him in German. Shaw does not understand more than a few words of German . . . But now he read the words from the lips of the young woman who was sitting with closed eyes before him and unfolding the drama of what it means to be blind. 'The end is touchingly beautiful,' he said with emotion, 'I never knew that Rilke had written anything so fine.'

(Miss Bach, to whom I would here express my sincere gratitude for lending me this cutting and allowing me to quote it here, has told me that Shaw had tears in his eyes when he spoke these last words. The poem in question is in the *Book of Images* and was written in November 1900. Shaw stands almost alone in finding that Rilke did not look as though he were a poet. It is difficult to understand what he meant by describing him as a 'genius in working clothes' (ein Genie im Arbeitsrock), unless Rilke was still in the habit of wearing his Russian peasant's blouse in Rodin's studio. That Shaw was so much more communicative and genial on the subject of Rilke on this occasion than a few years later, when Professor Butler wrote to him, is probably due to his attention having in the meantime been drawn to the references to himself in Rilke's published letters. It is likely to have surprised and perhaps also annoyed Shaw to find that the apparently so meek and diffident Rilke had commented so freely and uninhibitedly upon him.)

Rilke's only other encounter with an English-speaking literary contemporary of note took place in Cairo or Heluan, early in 1911. It was Algernon Blackwood, writer of fantastic novels with a streak of mysticism and spiritualism in them, whom he ran into there through their common friends, Baron and Baroness Knoop. Blackwood, though six years Rilke's senior, had only recently begun to write. He knew German well, and presumably it was in that language that he and Rilke conversed. The enthusiasm would seem to have been less on Rilke's side than on that of Blackwood, who went on for some time sending presentation copies of his new books to Rilke as soon as they appeared. Rilke grew impatient with this in the end, and sent the books straight on to his friend Fürstin Marie Taxis, with the excuse that he did not know English and so could not read them.[1] Of the frequent references to Blackwood in Rilke's correspondence with the Princess one is particularly interesting for its malicious humour. In spring 1912, just at a time when he was tormented by an apparent cessation of his own creative powers, Rilke had run into Blackwood, evidently dressed in some curious way (possibly in a pith helmet), in Venice.

And who do you think was there? he writes to the Princess: —Blackwood, in his ownest, extremely convincing person. My God, Princess, these coming men look like Arctic explorers or lion-hunters—they are right too. People are finding out at last that this trade of writing calls for some such equipment. And what is more, he is at present writing three books all at once, the beast ['die Bestie'], and still has masses of time for the most delectable idling around. But we established an excellent contact in our brief meeting, that is to say we sincerely marvelled at one another.[1]

Evidently Rilke took Blackwood very much less seriously as a fellow-author than he had taken Shaw. Yet Blackwood was occupied with just the same kind of problems, ideas and experiences as Rilke—with the invisible world, with strange modes of consciousness and with the overcoming of time, at all of which Shaw would only have scoffed. But a first-rate positivist and sceptic ranked higher in Rilke's eyes than a minor mystic, any day —little though most of his worshippers realize it. One of Blackwood's books at least Rilke must, however, have managed to read, probably with the help of Princess Marie Taxis, and in the original English too, since it had not been translated—*The Education of Uncle Paul* (1909). This book is based on the playful conception of there being

a tiny crack between yesterday and to-morrow. They don't join as they once did, and if we're very quick, we can find the crack and slip through.... And once inside, there's no time, of course. Anything may happen and everything may come true.[2]

The recollection of this passage came in very handy for Rilke some ten years later, when he had to write a birthday letter to a little boy who had had the misfortune to be born on 29 February. 'My dear friend Balthusz,' he writes (in French)—

years ago I knew in Cairo an English author, Mr Blackwood, who in one of his novels propounds a very pretty hypothesis. He assumes that always, at midnight, a minute crack opens between the day which is finishing and the one which is commencing, and that an extremely agile person who could manage to slip through it would leave time behind him, and find himself in a realm independent of all the changes which we undergo. In that place all the things are accumulated that we have lost . . . the dolls broken by children etc. It is there, my dear Balthusz, that you should slip through, on the night of February 28th, to take possession of your birthday, which is hidden there, only emerging into the light once every four years.... Only I advise you, out of consideration for your dear mother and your brother Pierre, not to disappear into it altogether, but only to take a peep at it in your sleep.[1]

Something, at least, Algernon Blackwood had been good for. He had enabled Rilke to write a charming and whimsical birthday letter.

One writer of the English-speaking world whom he could hardly have helped admiring Rilke came near to meeting, but just failed to meet. In July and August 1922 the New Zealander Katherine Mansfield, in her vain search for healing from the tuberculosis which was to put an end to her life in the following January, was staying at Sierre in the Hotel Bellevue. In this hotel Rilke regularly took many of his meals and often spent his nights during the period of his residence in the nearby Château de Muzot. During July 1922—in August Rilke was in other parts of Switzerland—the two writers must often have seen one another without any knowledge of one another.

There are quite a number of English books which Rilke is known to have read with enthusiasm in German translation in his earlier and middle years, but nearly always in French translation in his later years. There is something exasperatingly haphazard about this selection, when one thinks of all the English books he never heard of that would certainly have been far more congenial to him. He seems chiefly to have relied on various literary periodicals, especially on the *Neue Rundschau* in Germany and on the *Nouvelle Revue Française* and *Commerce* in France, to draw his attention to such books—far more, at least, than on the recommendations of his friends which, if too pressing, as they often were, could easily put him off.

Of decisive importance for Rilke in his early years were quite certainly the essays of Emerson, which he variously quotes and refers to, and which helped to confirm him in his bent towards a quasi-mystical individualism, and possibly also contributed some elements towards his religious ideas. That he prefixed the phrase from Emerson's *Considerations by the Way*, 'The hero is he who is immovably centred,' as a motto to his monograph on Rodin in winter 1902–3 has already been mentioned. (See above p. 37.) In 1902, in an article on Maeterlinck, he speaks of Emerson together with Marcus Aurelius.[1] Still more interesting are the two quotations from Emerson, which occur at the beginning of Rilke's very important 'Tuscan Diary' of spring 1898.[2] On this occasion he quotes in German, not, as in the motto to the Rodin book, in English. The one quotation is from Emerson's *Love*: 'All mankind love (sic) a lover.' The other is from *Circles*: 'I simply experiment, an endless seeker, with no Past at my back.' Emerson was in vogue in Germany at that period, otherwise Rilke would certainly never have read him. A curious item in Rilke's library at the time of his death is Washington Irving's *The Alhambra* in a French translation of 1921.

With few exceptions Rilke confined himself in his desultory dealings with the literature of the English-speaking peoples to books not dating much further back than the middle of the nineteenth century, the time, that is to say, of Edgar Allan Poe, Emerson and Elizabeth Barrett-Browning; and the great bulk of his reading was contemporary. This applies, however, to his dealings with German and French as well as with Anglo-Saxon literature. Lefèvre's[3] statement that he had 'read all our classics from Ronsard to Chénier and from Montaigne to Bossuet' is simply a wild and completely inaccurate guess. Nearly all Rilke's reading was contemporary or near-contemporary. It cost him an immense effort, at the age of thirty-five, to go so far back as to Goethe and his period, and that effort, kept up with highly important results for about five years, was then relaxed, so that from the age of forty or so till his death he was again substantially a reader of books of the day only. Old chronicles, memoirs and letters he could, indeed, at all times read with delight, probing about in them for evidence in support of his curious speculations on love, death and the invisible, but the actual great literature of the past more than one or two generations removed from his own day was strangely difficult of access to him,[4] and he could certainly never see it as a variegated but continuous texture, closely related to the rest of the outward and inner history of humanity. This was due in considerable measure to the unfortunate circumstances which had attended his education—'I am almost without culture,'[1] he says of himself in a letter to Lou Andreas-Salomé of 10 August 1903; but still more it corresponded to the inmost laws of his genius that he should never have acquired the scholar's way of approaching literature. He could only pick things out here and there, isolating them from their historical context and making, as far as possible, something quasi-contemporary out of them. Much as he loved to brood upon the past, history had only a curiously shadowy reality for him, and such access as he had to it was rather through the dream-like contemplation of old pictures and statues, old buildings and ruins, old artefacts of every description, from harness or armour to lace, than through the written word. This gives to his most deliberate and sustained excursion into the world of history,[2] the *New Poems* of the years 1906–8, with their approximately chronological arrangement, a strangely distorted quality—recorded historical causes and circumstances are quietly ignored, and their place is taken by an erratic, penetrating, but quite unsystematic psychology, which turns out to be Rilke's own, very modern psychology. Rilke is concerned with catching history at points where it is, so to speak, behaving unhistorically. The same would appear to apply also to such rare attempts at more sustained historical reading as Rilke is known to have made, that is to say above all to his researches in Venetian history for the projected book on the fourteenth-century admiral, Carlo Zeno, and to his intermittent browsing (no doubt at Rodin's recommendation) in Froissart's *Chronicles* from 1902 onward, which is of some interest to us, as it brought him face to face with mediaeval England. In connexion with Rodin's group of the 'Citizens of Calais' Rilke narrates at some length in his *Rodin* monograph the story of Edward III's cruel conditions at the siege of Calais, and how he relented at the petition of his pregnant wife. On two other occasions Rilke touches upon English history: in the poem 'Der König' which refers to Edward VI (see above p. 73) and in the description of how the unfortunate Danish Countess Leonora

Christina Ulfeldt, authoress of *Jammersminde*, was abducted from the court of Charles II, where she had sought refuge. (See letter to Hermann Pongs of 21 October 1924.)

The disproportion between Rilke's reading of older and of contemporary literature is quite startling, as is also the enormous, but usually short-lived enthusiasm which he is often able to generate for comparatively mediocre modern publications. The breadth, range and variety of literary impressions which most educated readers normally gain from a more or less systematic study of the literature of the past, thereby avoiding the parochialism of not being able to see beyond their own age, Rilke gained for himself by acquiring many different languages and reading extensively the books—but still in the main contemporary or near-contemporary books—of different countries and peoples. Here, as elsewhere all along the line, he made, or strove to make, extension in space serve as a substitute for extension in time.

There is something astonishingly naive in a poet of Rilke's stature exclaiming with reference to the Sonnets of Louise Labé, which he had himself translated: 'It is extraordinary ('alles Mögliche'), for poems published in 1555 to interest and move us so much at the present time!'[1] A great poet himself, and forty-two years old—and yet he finds it almost incredible that poems written 360 years earlier should be able to move us powerfully! If he had such difficulties in dealing with the older poetry of France or Germany, what is to be expected when it comes to England, to which he had in any case no connexion?

But then, of course, there is always Shakespeare, and even a Rilke cannot quite manage to ignore Shakespeare completely for the whole of his lifetime.

Rilke's father gave him a copy of Shakespeare's works (in German, of course) for his eighteenth birthday.[2] In his first *Story of Prague*, 'King Bohusch', written about 1897, a Czech actor, Norinski, arguing with a critic, insists that he will continue to act *Hamlet* in his own way, not in the German way: 'My dear fellow,' he cries, 'what is a German Hamlet to me? You don't mean to declare that we can't have an opinion of our own? Well then, what have the Germans to do with it? I take my conception direct from the English.'[1] This conversation is only meant to illustrate how the tension between Czechs and Germans in Prague enters into and poisons everything, including even the arts. On two other occasions in these early years Rilke similarly takes up the name of Shakespeare when he wants to appeal to some representative great poet of whom everybody has heard, without there being any need for us to suppose that he was really interested in Shakespeare or knew anything about him. 'The same applies to Shakespeare,'[2] he says in the course of a most un-Eliot-like argument in the 'Tuscan Diary' on the theme of tradition and individual talent. Again four years later, in *Worpswede*, Rilke declares: 'Shakespeare made his own language.'[3] These three meagre allusions, which are all that has so far come to light regarding Rilke's attitude towards Shakespeare up to his thirty-fifth year, amount to nothing. In April 1910, on the occasion of his first visit to the Castle of Duino, Rilke gave a shock to Rudolf Kassner and Geheimrat Bode by declaring that he had never read Hamlet.[4]

It was in the following year, 1911, when he had embarked, chiefly under the guidance of Anton and Katharina Kippenberg, on his tardy attempt to acquire some knowledge of Goethe and of the great German literature of the Goethe period, that Rilke at last, as a part of the same educational programme, tried to do something about reading Shakespeare. On 23 June of this year he asked Anton Kippenberg to send him a few volumes of Shakespeare in the best translation, together with instructions as to the right 'place for me to burgle my way into him'. The way in which the Kippenbergs react to this request shows clearly that they must shortly before this have been exerting themselves in conversations with Rilke to infect him with something of their own enthusiasm for Shakespeare. On 30 June Katharina Kippenberg answered at great length in the tone which she easily fell into on such occasions and which can hardly have failed to irritate Rilke a little, or rather would have irritated him, if the writer had been anybody but Katharina Kippenberg, a woman, as he well knew, of genuine intelligence and ability, his publisher's wife and *née* a von Düring. 'And you really want to read Shakespeare? How marvellous! marvellous!' she begins. She then gives the reason why she and her husband have decided in favour of presenting him with the standard German translation of Shakespeare's works by A. W. Schlegel and Dorothea Tieck, rather than any other. She continues: 'I have pondered a great deal what it would be best for you to read first, and think it is right . . . to get the full impact of him at his most stupendous straight off, instead of working up to it gradually.' She suggests, accordingly, that Rilke should begin with *Hamlet*, or, better still, with *Macbeth* or *King Lear*:

In that way you will receive the most colossal impression of him. If, then, you feel the need for some relief, you might turn to the *Merchant of Venice* with the Fifth Act that begins so enchantingly, or to the *Tempest*, which I cannot remember exactly, but which I see before me as everything that is sweetest, and as though it were in some way endowed with wings.

Then she runs with brief comments through *Coriolanus*, *Richard II*, *Richard III*, the Sonnets, *Julius Caesar*, *Romeo and Juliet* and the *Winter's Tale*. After this Katharina Kippenberg goes on to speak of Rilke's impending visit to Leipzig some six weeks later, when he was to be her guest for about a month:

Could we not have a go at Shakespeare together in one way or another, when you come here? What a pity that he has been translated already! otherwise I could stammer him out to you in German straight from the English original, while you would quickly turn him back into poetry.

In Rilke's answer of 3 July there is something of that very faint, indeed evanescent irony, which often characterizes his relationship to Katharina Kippenberg. He compares her letter to a sea breaking, wave upon wave, against the shore:

thus you have lifted, wave upon wave, the powerful visions of the inexplicable poet up against me, and there was always still one more wave to follow. . . . How long and with what freedom must you have lived beside that sea, to be able to give such a feeling of it to one who does not know it! I have now indeed a regular devil-may-care eagerness in me to have a go at Shakespeare ['nun hab ich freilich eine förmliche Ausgelassenheit in mir, Shakespeare zu betreiben'], and when I consider it, the *Richterstrasse* is the only possible place where he can be given birth to within me. We must manage it between us.

Rilke goes on to say how much he looks forward to the promised copy of Shakespeare's works, which has evidently not yet arrived—and then he remembers that he has at least a copy of Hamlet amongst his books in Paris, and says he will at once sit down and read it.

These two letters of Katharina Kippenberg of 30 June and of Rilke of 3 July 1911 set the entire pattern for Rilke's experience of Shakespeare, such as it is. There is a close parallel between what happens to Rilke here in respect of Shakespeare and what happens to him in the same months in respect of Goethe, with the one highly important distinction that whereas, in the case of Goethe, Rilke's initial irony at the expense of the portentousness of the Kippenbergs, especially of Katharina Kippenberg, is soon superseded by unconditional and quite independent enthusiasm, Rilke to the last never brings himself to take Shakespeare quite seriously.

On 2 August 1911 Katharina Kippenberg writes to Rilke, who is now in Bohemia, imploring him not to read *Macbeth* before his arrival in Leipzig:

I must be near you, when you read it, when it comes streaming out of you again. You will see how you will be caught up in the orbit of the very forces of Nature, and rotate with them, to be set down again at some other point than that where you entered: 'What fair and foul a day is this'—divine line!

Which is all very well, except that Shakespeare did not write, and for linguistic reasons could not have written, 'What fair and foul a day is this!' The 'divine line' which Katharina Kippenberg has in mind is presumably: 'So foul and fair a day I have not seen.' There is no record of Rilke ever having looked at *Macbeth* or gone through any of the exhausting experiences which Katharina Kippenberg not altogether encouragingly foretold for him.

From 23 August to 8 September 1911 Rilke was the guest of the

Kippenbergs in Leipzig, and during these weeks[1] Katharina Kippenberg carried out the plan she had thought of, to read parts of Shakespeare to Rilke in the English original, translating it literally into German as she went along. 'It was wonderful,' she records, 'how he apprehended the original right through this disintegrating process, and how his sensibility even responded to the sound of the English language, which he did not know.'[2] (Rilke seems to have allowed Katharina Kippenberg to suppose that he was far more ignorant of the English language than he really was.) It was her object, she explains, to lure Rilke into improvising a more poetic German version of the text, with her own baldly literal translation as a point of departure, thus reconstructing what she conceived must have been the situation in April 1907 at Capri when he read Elizabeth Barrett-Browning together with Alice Faehndrich. How far she succeeded in this she does not indicate. These Shakespeare sessions with Katharina Kippenberg in August and September 1911 cannot have been very long or very frequent. We know that they read together in this way the Hubert and Prince Arthur scene in *King John*, which he was interested in because of an allusion to it in Goethe's *Euphrosyne*, and also parts of the *Tempest*—and that was pretty certainly all. This is the 'narrow segment' of Shakespeare's work which Katharina Kippenberg speaks of Rilke having known and venerated. (See above p. 39.)

Two weeks after this stay in Leipzig when Katharina Kippenberg did so much for his education, Rilke, wanting an image to express the tempestuous, uncontrollable temperament of his *protégée*, the young French girl Marthe Hennebert, described her as 'a Shakespearean world'.[3] On 31 October 1911 he wrote to Katharina Kippenberg, at the beginning of his momentous long winter in the castle of Duino, that he was having his copy of Shakespeare's works sent to him from Paris. There it was that he made his one serious effort to read Shakespeare, shortly before the writing of the first two *Duinese Elegies*. But it did not go well. 'I feel a great desire to do a lot of reading now,' he writes on 30 December 1911 to Fürstin Marie Taxis; 'I have been inside

Shakespeare a little, whom I hardly know—, but he is too much of a mountain-range for me, too steep, too amorphous ['zu amorph']; I climb and slip down and never know what is happening to me.' This image of being 'inside' Shakespeare stands, it may be noted, in a direct line with that which he had used seven months earlier in writing to Anton Kippenberg of 'burgling his way into' Shakespeare ['an welcher Stelle ich in ihn einbrechen soll']—and suggests something forbidding and peculiarly inaccessible.

A few weeks later Rilke comes upon something even more 'mountainous' than Shakespeare, which nevertheless pleases him better. His friend, the poet Alfred Heymel, has sent him a copy of his newly published translation of Marlowe's *Edward II*, and from the letter in which he acknowledges this gift one can gather how much progress he has made during the preceding nine months since he began his attempt to 'burgle' his way into Shakespeare.

I don't know Shakespeare, he writes on 27 February 1912 to Heymel, and as there is hardly any prospect of my ever learning English, that entire vast world will in all likelihood remain remote from me. But I probably owe the most powerful notion of its powerful existence to your *Edward II*. That is how I had imagined Shakespeare, I now realize, and I was put off at not finding him like that in the little I have read of him in Schlegel's translation. Here, in this play of Marlowe's, is the savour I had foretasted in my imagination. I have read it with great willingness to respond to it, marvelling at the authority to which the unhappy king rises; that is amorphous misery, misery in fragments hewn from a mountain-range of misery, misfortune hard and sterile and sharp at all its edges. . . .

Marlowe's *Edward II* in Heymel's translation is the nearest Rilke can come to appreciating Shakespeare, and the experience, so far as it goes, is gloomy but impressive, and also much in keeping with the more conventional German way of seeing Shakespeare. Stefan George, for example, sees Shakespeare as 'The foggy island's gloomy prince of ghosts'—surely too uncheerful a view both of Shakespeare and also, even, of our much maligned climate.

The result of Rilke's bout with Shakespeare in 1911 was then quite negative; he comes back again and again to such terms as 'amorphous' and 'an unscalable mountain-range'; he sees Shakespeare as French critics had seen him in the middle of the eighteenth century. When one considers what kinds of incoherency, wretchedness and horror Rilke could, if it came to the point, thoroughly relish in French, German, Russian and Scandinavian literature, and could also produce with great force in his own work, it is hard not to feel that he is here straining at a gnat, after having swallowed a whole drove of camels without being any the worse for it. His Shakespeare experience is, however, still not quite over. There is a pleasanter epilogue to follow. We do not, indeed, hear much of his ever actually trying to read Shakespeare again. The most there is to record in that respect is that a copy of George's translation of the Sonnets was lent to him by Elsa Bruckmann in Munich in October 1912,[1] and that he unfortunately mislaid it. Much more important than this was a conversation which he had in Venice in August 1912 with the Austro-Italian actor Alexander Moissi (1880–1935), a native of Trieste. Moissi as a rule got on Rilke's nerves—only a month earlier, in July 1912, he had caustically remarked of him: 'My God, what an *acteur* he has become!'[2] and in February of the following year he finds him deficient in 'sensibility, discernment and intelligence'.[3] But on 6 August 1912 Moissi contrived for once to make a more favourable impression on Rilke:

> Moissi called on me here on Tuesday evening, he writes, and spoke curiously about Shakespeare. I was afraid he had become nothing but an *acteur*, but then, for a single moment, something surged up within him again, giving him a pure impetus, the vocation which there is no withstanding burst forth at every point of his whole being.[4]

Possibly Rudolf Kassner's statement that 'Rilke was brought to Shakespeare by Moissi's *Hamlet*'[5] should be interpreted as going back to this conversation and to what Moissi may have said about *Hamlet* in the course of it, rather than to any actual performance of *Hamlet* by Moissi seen by Rilke, of which we have otherwise no record.

The following winter, 1912–13, Rilke spent in Spain, and it was there that the little he had been able truly to assimilate of Shakespeare in his various attempts of the preceding year and a half crystallized into poetic form. What above all, perhaps alone, turned out to have been congenial to him was *The Tempest*, which he had read, as we know, in August or September 1911 together with Katharina Kippenberg. It looks very much as though he had taken at least the one volume of the Schlegel-Tieck translation of Shakespeare containing *The Tempest* to Spain with him and actually re-read the play there. But that is not completely certain. What interests him is Prospero forswearing magic—he sees this situation as symbolically akin to that in which he had been himself two or three years earlier, when he had seriously thought, or had at least said that he seriously thought of giving up poetry altogether and becoming, of all things, a country doctor. What had been involved then, after the completion of *Malte Laurids Brigge*, was, in a peculiarly acute form, the central problem of Rilke's entire existence, the conflict between art and life, the sense that art is impotent to modify real life for the better, that it cannot 'heal wounds',[1] as he himself puts it, and the doubt whether it might not be his true duty to abandon so questionable a calling and adopt something practical and salutary, or at least safe and innocuous instead. His answer to these misgivings, which came upon him often throughout his life, is really always the same:—that it is after all his highest duty to remain true to his poetic vocation which, although it cannot 'heal wounds', must nevertheless surely in some mysterious way be destined to serve a lofty cosmic purpose. To turn one's back on art, if one really is a true artist, as Tolstoy, for example, had done, to 'forswear magic', as Prospero does and as, for the matter of that, Goethe's Faust also does, is, Rilke now thinks, to betray what is highest in oneself, to sell one's birthright for a mess of pottage. With these thoughts in his mind Rilke wrote at Ronda in January or February 1913 his one poem with a Shakespearean theme, 'The Spirit Ariel—on reading Shakespeare's Tempest.' Ariel has here become one of Rilke's many symbols for the sense of poetic vocation, of creative power as distinct from merely human consciousness. The point of departure is Prospero's 'But this rough magic / I here abjure' and the Epilogue:

> Now my charms are all o'erthrown,
> And what strength I have's my own;
> Which is most faint....

The circumstance that Rilke quotes this last phrase literally in August Wilhelm Schlegel's translation, 'Und das ist wenig', strongly suggests that he had the book actually before him at the time, and was not relying only on his memory. The point of the poem is in the concluding verses, which are given by Rilke in brackets:

> Ließ ich es schon? Nun schreckt mich dieser Mann,
> der wieder Herzog wird. Wie er sich sanft
> den Draht ins Haupt zieht und sich zu den andern
> Figuren hängt und künftighin das Spiel
> um Milde bittet.... Welcher Epilog
> vollbrachter Herrschaft. Abtun bloßes Dastehn
> mit nichts als eigner Kraft: 'und das ist wenig.'

This may be translated:

> Have I already cast it loose? This man,
> turned duke again, dismays me now. So meekly
> dangling by wire himself threads through his crown
> beside the other puppets, begging henceforth
> mild usage of the piece.... What epilogue
> to wielded sway. Renouncement, bare existence,
> with only his own strength, 'which is most faint.'

This poem of January or February 1913 marks the end of Rilke's encounter with Shakespeare. We find him, indeed, in July 1914 praising Gundolf's newly published *Shakespeare and the German Mind* as a book which has enriched his experience with 'an entirely new phenomenon' and revealed to him 'the most far-reaching relationships'.[1] This belongs, however, to the chapter of Rilke's dealings with German, not with English literature and culture; above all it has a bearing on his partial *rapprochement* with the circle of Stefan George, to which both Gundolf and the brilliant young man to whom he thus praises him belonged. In 1915, when some woman who felt an urge to go on to the stage, instead of working in an office, wrote to Rilke, as such women were apt to do, asking him for consolation and advice, he recommended her to 'venture that in her, which is an urge to act, on the reading of Shakespeare'.[1] In 1916 Rilke energetically refused an invitation from Princess Marie Taxis to see *Twelfth Night*: 'But as for *Twelfth Night, no,* thank you very much. No theatre.'[2] This is not the only record we have of his *not* going to a Shakespeare play—whether he ever did go to one remains uncertain, Kassner's reference to the impression made on him by 'Moissi's *Hamlet*'[3] presenting various difficulties. In November and December 1920 he writes to three friends[4] about a performance of *Hamlet* in Geneva which he is greatly interested in, though more on account of the Russian producer Pitoëff, whom he immensely admired (see above p. 85) than of the play itself. He cannot attend this performance, because he is living at the time in the opposite corner of Switzerland. On 13 December 1921, in sending his poem 'The Spirit Ariel' to his publishers, for inclusion in the *Inselschiff*, Rilke ordered himself a volume of the new Insel edition of Shakespeare's works.[5] The learned comparison between Shakespeare's and Racine's treatment of Plutarch attributed by Carl J. Burckhardt[6] to Rilke in a conversation supposed to take place in Paris in 1924—a year in which Rilke never left Switzerland—is quite certainly apocryphal. There is no reason at all for supposing that Rilke ever went appreciably further with his study of Shakespeare, such as it was, after February 1913. Rilke in his dealings with Shakespeare behaves somewhat like a nervous non-smoker badgered against his own better judgment into sampling a heavy Brazilian cigar and inconspicuously laying it aside after the first two or three puffs, apprehensive of the worst.

Seventeenth- and eighteenth-century English literature would seem scarcely to have existed for Rilke, who does not even allude anywhere to Milton. At the age of seventeen, in a still unpublished diary, he notes down immediately after one of his private lessons that the standard English translation of Homer is that of Pope. Of

Young he must have been made aware about 1911 by Klopstock's ode 'An Young'[1] of 1752, which impressed him, as he was in 1914 made aware of Sterne by Kassner's admirable dialogue, 'The Chimaera' (written in London in 1912). Of this dialogue, in which visionary metaphysics go hand in hand with rich humour, Rilke wrote, immediately after his first reading of it, to Magda von Hattingberg on 17 February 1914: 'Here Kassner makes a probably imaginary uncle of an imaginatively heightened Lawrence (sic) Sterne expatiate with eccentric oddity and grandeur just on this very question of what it would be like "to be inside, deep down inside".'[2]

Kassner sees Rilke as historically belonging to and terminating the series of European 'visual' (as opposed to 'auditive') lyrical poets of the nineteenth century which begins with the 'never sufficiently to be praised John Keats'; only with the important difference that in Rilke this specifically visual lyric has undergone a 'marked deepening' ('eine deutliche Vertiefung'), not to be traced in Keats himself or in any of his successors hitherto.[3] This view is substantially right, if it be taken (as it is intended) to imply only a fundamental affinity between the two poets, and not any direct *influence* of Keats on Rilke, which, as Kassner very well knows, is out of the question. That Rilke seems to have regarded Keats as a true poet only so long as he did not know his work and had nothing to go by but his legend, his general reputation and the portrait of him on his deathbed, has already been mentioned in connexion with Rilke's attitude towards the English language. (See above pp. 41–45.) There is no need to look for any further explanation of Rilke's attempt to appreciate Keats ending in disappointment and disrelish than that it was probably undertaken just as half-heartedly as the similar attempt to appreciate Shakespeare two or three years earlier, and that Rilke still could not muster up a really earnest and effectual desire to overcome his long-standing prejudice against everything English, particularly the English language. If, beyond this, he lighted first on 'Endymion' or on some of the other immature poetry which necessarily occupies more than half of every volume of Keats' collected works, the chances of his being favourably impressed were slight indeed. One should, however, be on one's guard against a misunderstanding which can easily arise in this matter, and has indeed sometimes arisen,[1] the misunderstanding, namely, that Keats may have been too sensual, too fleshy, not aethereal enough for Rilke. That Keats himself clearly recognized the danger of a too obvious, cloying sensuality marring his art, and that he substantially overcame that danger in the brief year and a half of mastery granted to him from spring 1818 to autumn 1819 is well known and concerns us little here. What does concern us is that Rilke himself is through and through, in his very essence, one of the most sensuous, if one will, one of the most 'fleshy' of poets, that everything aethereal and spiritual in him and his art is, demonstrably and perceptibly, sensuality volatilized or, to use Kassner's phrase, 'deepened' from within. One of his favourite watchwords is 'sensualité de l'âme'.[2] On one occasion he writes: 'For spiritual begetting too is derived from physical, is of the same essence, and only like a gentler, more enraptured and more eternal repetition of bodily voluptuousness.'[3] Kassner is absolutely right, when he says: 'Rilke is a completely un-Platonic person.... Or if one may speak of Platonism in the case of Rilke, it is a Platonism of the flesh....'[4] This is one of the things Kassner has in mind, when he speaks of a far-reaching affinity between Rilke and Keats. Keats *ought* to have appealed to Rilke, if he had ever really apprehended him—certainly more than Shelley or Wordsworth who, in the opinion of Mr J. B. Leishman,[5] would have stood a better chance. Even after his unsuccessful excursion into Keats' poetry Rilke continued to take an interest in his legend. This is shown by his jotting down in February 1922 the title of a publication he evidently hoped to consult: 'J. Keats—*Lettres à Fanny Brawne—N(ouvelle) R(evue) F(rançaise)*.[6]

There are three other English Romantic poets, besides Keats, in whom Rilke took some interest—and all three of them are touched upon in Kassner's book on English poetry which he had read in 1901. André Maurois' light-hearted Shelley biography *Ariel*

(1923) was one of his favourite books during the last years of his life. He read it again and again, gave away several copies of it, and recommended it enthusiastically to his friends. 'With how unconstrained and light a hand he [Maurois] has contrived to mould this airy subject, never weighing down or impeding its movement!'[1] Rilke writes. An inscription in his own copy records that it was his friend Baladine Klossowska who had first introduced this book to him, and that he read it together with her on the 9, 10 and 11 November 1923. He also brackets his own Christian name, in its original form 'René'[2] with the name 'Ariel', thereby identifying his own youthful self with Shelley. It makes no impression at all on him when Baladine Klossowska herself only one month later changes her opinion of Maurois' book and writes to him: 'I have re-read *Shelley* on my own account and no longer believe in Maurois. He ought to have sided with this delicious Shelley, who becomes more and more living and impalpable.'[3] In this same year, 1923, it happened that a volume of French translations of Shelley's poems (*Odes, Poèmes et fragments lyriques choisis*) by André Fontainas was published. Rilke was sufficiently stirred by Maurois' *Ariel* to procure for himself a copy of these translations—possibly it is to them, and not to Maurois' book that Baladine Klossowska refers when she says: 'I have re-read Shelley on my own account....' Early in 1924 Rilke received an invitation from Duchess Aurelia Gallarati Scotti to be her guest at Viareggio, a place which had been extremely important for him in his youth, when he wrote parts of *In my own honour* there in 1898 and the third section of the *Book of Hours* in 1903, but which now interests him even more because of its proximity to the spot where Shelley was drowned—'cette mer amie et divine—tombeau de Shelley'.[4] Rilke felt it impossible to accept the invitation, but he sent to the Duchess on 2 March 1924 his own copy of Shelley's poems with the comment: 'I add to this letter my copy of a recent translation of Shelley, to be your companion during your days at Viareggio; one of the agreeable things about it is that it contains all the little *fragments*, which are often delicious!'[5] The Duchess replied on 25 March, expressing great enthusiasm for Shelley, whose tomb she had just visited in Rome and a biography of whom she was just reading. On 28 March Rilke replies:

As for the volume of Shelley's poems—I shall be delighted, if you will consent to keep it: it is a pretty wretched copy, but I spent hours and hours over it before sending it to you, and now you have definitely ennobled it, since it has been privileged to be your companion during such happy weeks, full of sublime harmonies and inexhaustible influences. And is that 'Life' of Shelley to which you refer in your letter by any chance the delightful *Ariel* of André Maurois, which really enchanted me when I read it last autumn and which, moreover, was the occasion of my ordering those translations?[1]

The copy of Fontainas' Shelley-translations which Rilke sent to Duchess Aurelia Gallarati Scotti and which still remains in her possession, exhibits 'numerous indications of what he had read and of what he preferred'.[2] On the following day he ordered himself another copy, which, however, remained uncut at the time of his death. In addition to three passages in the 'Lines written among the Euganean Hills' and to the fifth section of the 'Ode to the West Wind' ('Make me thy lyre, even as the forest is—') Rilke marked in Fontainas' translation the following fragments: 'Fragment to Music' ('Silver key to the fountain of tears ...'); 'To William Shelley' ('Thy little footsteps on the sands ....';) 'Epitaph' ('These are two friends, whose lives were undivided ...'). He also marked the last two lines of the poem 'To Jane: The Recollection': 'Less oft is peace in Shelley's mind, / Than calm in waters, seen.' (These particulars were kindly communicated to me by Duchess Aurelia Gallarati Scotti.)

What most interested Rilke in Shelley was evidently his legend, as Maurois presents it in whimsical, novellistic guise, rather than his actual poetry. It was a similar interest in the poet's destiny, as distinguished from his actual poetic achievement, to that he had shown in Keats and in Wilde. Even what had attracted him to Elizabeth Barrett-Browning, making him perceive in her Sonnets 'one of the great bird-songs of the heart in the landscapes of love,'[3] had been, in a considerable measure the poetess's strange situation—fading, bed-ridden and cut off from all hopes of normal happiness, up to the age of forty, and then suddenly finding herself loved and hardly able to believe it. It is thus that Rilke portrays her in the dedicatory sonnet of 3 November 1919, 'O Wenn ein Herz, längst wohnend im Entwöhnen',[1] the third set of verses in his later work with an English poet for its theme. Similarly the one passage in all Shakespeare's work that means something to him is the one which can be, and often is interpreted as throwing some light on the mystery of how Shakespeare came to give up writing some years before his death. Rilke, who so often maintained in principle that one should not inquire after the personality or the private destiny of the poet, and who particularly discouraged all too searching interest in his own person and fortunes, was himself always in practice very much concerned with the biographies of all the poets and artists who appealed to him, and in the case of English literature his interest lay mainly on this side.

The two other English Romantic poets in whom Rilke showed some interest were Wordsworth and Blake—though the evidence we have to go by here is very meagre. On the back of an envelope which he cannot have received before 11 June 1922 he jotted down two lines of the opening stanza of Wordsworth's 'To the Cuckoo':

O Cuckoo! shall I call thee Bird,
Or but a wandering Voice?

in French translation, as follows:

Wordsworth dit du
Coucou

'O! Coucou! Est-ce oiseau
qu'il te faut appeler, ou
bien chanson que la
brise remporte?'[2]

I have not so far succeeded in finding out where Rilke came upon these lines. The translation, which is very free and not particu-

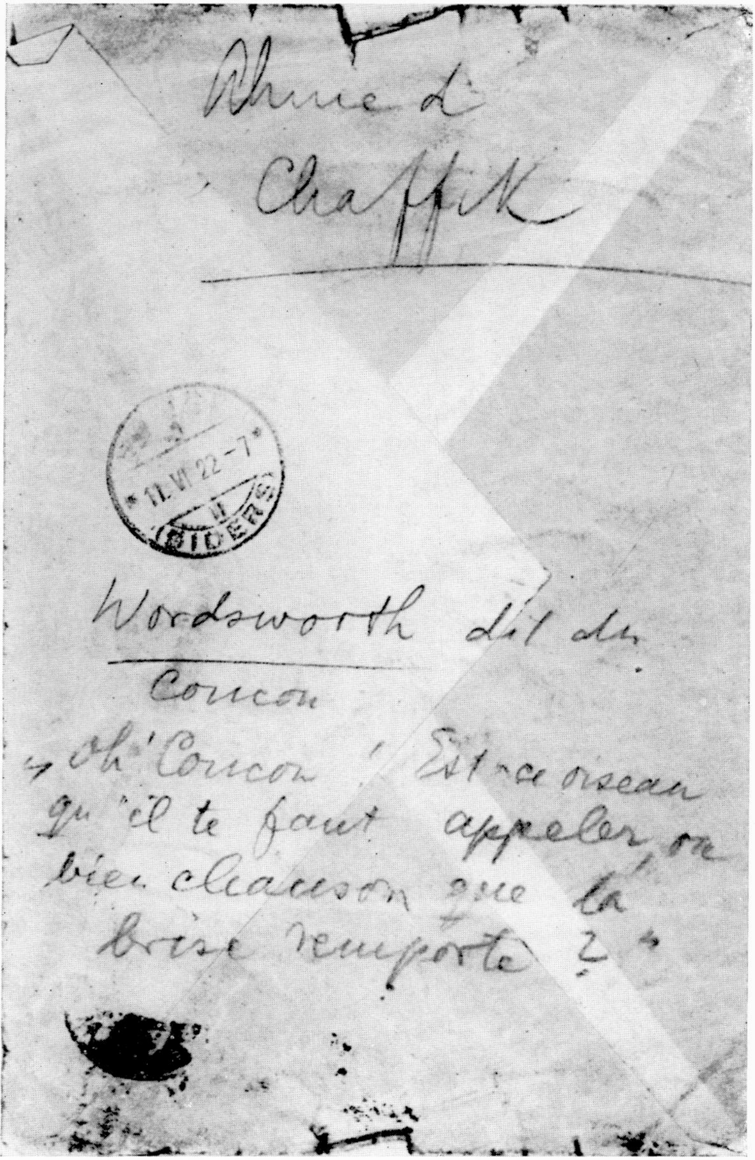

An envelope on which Rilke jotted down a quotation from Wordsworth about 1922. (See text p. 106.)

larly skilful, differs completely from the official French version of Émil Legouis.

In 1912 Rilke writes in a letter: 'Sometimes I ask myself if yearning cannot surge from one like a storm, so that nothing can make headway against this outward current to come towards one. Perhaps William Blake has somewhere made a drawing of that.'[1] So Rilke did know something of Blake, at least as a painter, if not as a poet. In Kassner's book on the English Poets of 1900 he had seen at least one reproduction from the Prophetic Books. One can be certain that he did not miss André Gide's translation of Blake's *Marriage of Heaven and Hell* in the *Nouvelle Revue Française* in summer 1922. At the beginning of Maurois' *Ariel* he had also before him in English the lines from Blake's *Songs of Experience:*

> So I turn'd to the Garden of Love
> That so many sweet flowers bore;
> And I saw it was fill'd with graves.

When he was staying in Paris in 1925 Rilke had with him a *de luxe* volume of reproductions of Blake's pictorial work (presumably *The Drawings and Engravings of William Blake,* edited by G. Holme in 1922), which had been lent or given to him by Princess Bassiano and which he sometimes took with him on his evening visits to the Klossowskis, showing much enthusiasm for Blake as he turned over the pages together with them.[2]

Thus Rilke did after all take some interest in the four most important figures of English Romanticism, above all in Shelley. To Byron, who is so much overestimated on the continent, and to Coleridge who is so much overestimated in England itself, he would appear to have paid no attention. He makes his Malte Laurids Brigge record in his *Note-Books* that he read in his boyhood 'whatever there was of Walter Scott'[3] in his father's library. Whether there is any reference here to Rilke's own early reading is uncertain.

Just as Rilke had found the English scholar Ralston useful in 1899, when he was engaged in his Russian studies, so also he was glad of the American Breasted's *History of Egypt from the Earliest*

Times to the Persian Conquest when he was amassing information about Egypt in 1910 and 1911. This book, which he recommends to Princess Marie Taxis[1] as 'the best preparation for a voyage to Egypt', appeared in 1910 in German translation. Rilke speaks as though both the English original and the German translation were known to him.

In September 1913 in Munich Rilke began to take an interest in Tagore's *Gitanjali,* and three months later, in Paris, this interest was temporarily converted into something like enthusiasm by a lecture of André Gide's. He would seem to have looked at the *Gitanjali* in the English version of 1912, as well as in Gide's translation.[2] Twelve years later, however, shortly before his death, when Duchess Aurelia Gallarati Scotti had asked him what he thought about Tagore, he replied:

> Tagore: . . . I did once to begin with like him, when—many years ago—Gide sent me his so sensitive translation of the *Gitanjali*; subsequently I have, from work to work, moved further away from this poet—whom, it is true, I have never read in any language but French; for some time now I have forgotten my English.[3]

Tagore is not the only case in which Rilke was brought up against English as the *lingua franca* of Asia, used for literary purposes by orientals. On 5 August 1913 Katharina Kippenberg wrote to him: 'I have been reading a charming book by a Japanese, written in English. There is a chapter in it that I should like to translate to you.' This book was Kakuzo Okakura's *Book of Tea* (1906). Some seven years later, in Switzerland, Rilke bought himself a copy of this book on the recommendation of another friend, Frau Gudi Nölke, who had just returned to Europe from Japan. He speaks with much enthusiasm of this book[4] in his letters to her, especially of the chapter on 'Flowers'. Probably he read it in the German translation, which was published in the Insel-Bücherei about December 1919.

In his dabblings in the occult Rilke appears to have glanced sometimes in the years 1911–14 at the publications of the Society for Psychical Research, of which Princess Marie Taxis was a member, and he certainly knew in the same connexion something (probably not very much) about William James.[1] (He ought, of course, to have come across the brother, Henry James, instead, who would have been altogether after his heart.)

One of Rilke's favourite books in his last years was an abridgement in German translation of George Henry Lewes'[2] *Life of Goethe* (1855), which he read again and again, specially admiring the style.

On 2 July 1917 Rilke wrote to Sophie Liebknecht about an English novel which she had presumably lent him—fairly certainly in German translation: '"Irene" did indeed touch me, but the novel as a whole seems to me after all only mediocre and, like everything English, it is extremely alien to me.'[3] It is not clear whether *Irene* here is the actual title of the novel in question, or only the name of the heroine. It seems possible that the novel was Galsworthy's *Man of Property* (1906), out of which the *Forsyte Saga* later developed. Soames' wife Irene would have been likely to touch Rilke, and the novel is certainly mediocre enough. On 26 May 1925 Rilke had occasion to refer to Galsworthy in his capacity as President of the Pen Club. Rilke had been invited to represent Czecho-Slovakia officially at a great banquet, and this had led to attacks upon him with various misrepresentations in the German nationalistic press. Rilke writes to explain to his publisher that he had in any case refused the invitation, and to correct some of the misstatements: 'for example, the person who sent out the invitations', he writes, 'was not an American, but the great English novelist Galsworthy.' This does not, of course, imply that Galsworthy was known to Rilke by anything more than his name and general reputation.

In his Swiss period, when Rilke had finally expunged England from his map of Europe and decided no longer to allow his attention to stray outside the European area, he still went through a number of quite lively and enthusiastic contacts with English books. They were for the most part works of the day, to which his attention had been drawn by reviews in French periodicals or by French friends, and he read them in French translation. Thus on 30 October 1922 he writes to Princess Marie Taxis:

Do you know *The Man who was Thursday* by Chesterton—one of the most glorious books and at the same time also one of the most mysterious—which I have just discovered? Do you know the remarkable writings of George Moore? They are now at work on the first edition of them in French, on which, knowing no English, I must depend.

There were amongst Rilke's books at his death copies, in French translation, of Logan Pearsall Smith's *Trivia* (read 15 December 1921), of Chesterton's *Orthodoxy* (uncut), of David Garnett's *Lady into Fox* (of which he spoke with great enthusiasm to Marga Wertheimer[1] in September 1924), of George Moore's *Confessions of a Young Man* (bought in October 1925 in Zürich) and of Clemence Dane's *Legend* (read at Valmont in April 1926). In a letter to his booksellers of 6 October 1922 Rilke ordered a copy of Larbaud's translation of Samuel Butler's *Way of All Flesh*, which had just been reviewed enthusiastically in the *Nouvelle Revue Française*. On 8 November of the same year, in acknowledging some books just received, he wrote: 'How delightful that book of George Moore's is'—probably the reference here is to the *Confessions of a Young Man*, the copy bought in October 1925 replacing an earlier one which Rilke had meanwhile given away.[2] One of the surprising items in his Muzot library is Logan Pearsall Smith's *Trivia* in Phil Neel's translation, which Rilke 'received on December 15th 1921 and read the same evening'. What had attracted him to this book was undoubtedly the strong recommendation of Valéry Larbaud, who had written the introduction to it and compared it with Baudelaire's *Poèmes en Prose* and Rimbaud's *Illuminations*, also declaring that it was 'contrary to the very genius of the English language'.[3] Rilke was fascinated too by the figure of Joseph Conrad,[4] whose experience with the English language had been so very different from his own, and who was specially recommended to him by the interest taken in him by his great hero, Paul Valéry. In this connexion it may also be noted that he admired the French writer of American extraction, Julien Green,[5] whose *Mont Cinère* he owned, and of whom he said: 'ce sera un grand poète.' In his declaration to Claire Goll of 11 April 1923, 'Your American Anthology has given me much pleasure',[1] there is probably more politeness than genuine enthusiasm.

Particularly interesting items in Rilke's Muzot library are a volume of essays by Valéry Larbaud on English Literature, a number of *Commerce* for summer 1924 containing a specimen of Joyce's Ulysses in translation, and also the French edition of Joyce's *Dubliners,* which is, however, not cut much beyond Larbaud's excellent introduction. Rilke was then aware of and interested in James Joyce—though it is impossible to determine how far this interest went. On 18 May 1922 he ordered from his bookseller the number of the *Ecrits nouveaux* for the previous February, particularly, as he said, because it contained an article on James Joyce. On 22 April 1924 he ordered the French translation of the *Portrait of the Artist as a Young Man*—'Dédalus'.[2] There is a phrase which Rilke uses of Mussolini in his important letter to Duchess Aurelia Gallarati Scotti of 14 February 1926, 'ce forgeron d'une conscience nouvelle' which curiously recalls the famous conclusion of the *Portrait of the Artist as a Young Man*: 'to forge in the smithy of my soul the uncreated conscience of my race.' But after all, no special literary stimulus was needed to designate Mussolini as a 'forgeron'. Presumably Joyce in this phrase uses the English word 'conscience' in the French sense of 'consciousness'.

Rilke also owned Synge's *Aran Isles* in French translation. His pencil marking shows that he read this book with careful attention, and it is characteristic that he specially marked the passage about the Connaught parricide being sheltered for months from the police by the islanders, who say: 'Would anyone kill his father, if he was able to help it?' Rilke went twice to Pitoëff's production in French of the famous drama that Synge constructed out of this anecdote, *The Playboy of the Western World*—once in Winterthur, once in Zürich.[3]

It is remarkable that Rilke knew of and took some interest in George Moore, Oscar Wilde, Bernard Shaw, John M. Synge and James Joyce. Only one name is missing here to complete the list of the six most important Irish writers of the age—that of W. B.

Yeats. But Rilke did take some interest in Yeats too, though we have but meagre information on the point. On 15 September 1916 Katharina Kippenberg wrote to Rilke, sending him a list of about fifteen books just published or on the point of publication by the Insel-Verlag, and asking him to say which of them he would like to receive copies of. One of these titles was *Stories and Essays* by Yeats, in German translation. In his reply of 18 September (addressed to Anton Kippenberg) Rilke selected the volume of Yeats as second in order of preference only to the newest book of Carossa's, with Spinoza's letters in third place. In conversation with Miss Harriet Cohen (see below p. 142) in September 1926 he showed himself fully aware of Yeats' importance.

In view of the haphazard manner in which Rilke was contented to let English books come his way, more anxious to keep them off than to attract them, such completeness in this one case of the modern Irish writers can hardly be a mere coincidence. One can only conclude that he took some special interest in Ireland—an interest aroused perhaps in the first place by his memorable encounter with Bernard Shaw in 1906 and then reinforced by his growing antipathy to England, in keeping with the common and not unnatural phenomenon that those who take a dislike to England tend to feel some kind of attachment to Ireland and also, though more rarely, to Scotland. Some confirmation of this supposition may be found in one of the French poems in the volume *Vergers*, 'Le Drapeau', written in May 1924 and occasioned by Valéry's visit to Muzot of the preceding month (6 April 1924) when Rilke had obtained a French tricolour in honour of his guest:

> Et pourtant quel fier moment
> lorsqu'un instant le vent se déclare
> pour tel pays: consent à la France,
> ou subitement s'éprend
> des Harpes légendaires de la verte Irlande ...

('And yet how proud is the moment when the wind declares itself fleetingly in favour of one particular country: decides for France, or suddenly falls in love with the legendary Harps of green Ireland.')

This emphatic and affectionate evocation of Ireland is noteworthy, when one considers how indistinct all the other English-speaking countries remain for Rilke. In this connexion it may be noted that Rilke in December 1923 praised Maurois' *Dr O'Grady*[1] in which the Irish are presented in a particularly attractive light.

In August 1938, six months before his own death, Yeats read an essay by Professor William Rose on *Rilke and the Conception of Death*[2] which, in his own words 'annoyed' him. 'I wrote in the margin,' he goes on:

'Draw rein, draw breath,
Cast a cold eye
On life, on death.
Horseman, pass by.'[3]

These words, which were by Yeats' own directions used as his epitaph, formed the germ of his last poem but one, 'Under Ben Bulben'. One of Rilke's favourite doctrines, that of 'the unity of life and death' or that of 'dying one's own death', had met with Yeats' disfavour. In December 1938, about a month before he died, Yeats talked of Rilke and Stefan George at a dinner-party with Lady Gerald Wellesley, W. J. Turner and Schnabel. The statement of Edmond Jaloux[4] that Yeats visited Rilke's last residence, Schloss Muzot, is erroneous. Little though he himself realized it, Yeats was, of all contemporary poets employing the English language, the one who stood nearest to Rilke in his art and in his outlook on existence—excepting perhaps D. H. Lawrence.

The affinity of D. H. Lawrence with Rilke is perhaps even closer than that of Yeats—only one must try to conceive here of a Lawrence whose raw, impatient, slapdash qualities have been eliminated and replaced by something of Yeats' meticulousness, polish, dignity and elusiveness. One of the first persons to recognize this remarkable resemblance (beyond all glaringly obvious superficial differences) between the two poets was Rilke himself. The role of intermediary was played here by Katharina Kippenberg, who says of herself, not without complacency, in a letter to Rilke of 6 October 1924: 'I have read . . . one, two, three—seven

American books and two by Conrad . . . and I know pretty well what is going on in Anglo-Saxon literature.' She was proud of being the first German publisher to discover Lawrence and of having secured his works for the Insel-Verlag. As early as 6 April 1921 she wrote to Rilke:

But there is another book which we are absolutely delighted with, the *Rainbow* of Lawrence, probably the most important work written in England for decades. O if only you could read English! The translation can't reproduce it properly. It penetrates into regions of which I doubt whether anybody has hitherto penetrated to them. The marriages of three generations. . . . Here those things are touched upon of which Malte Laurids Brigge says that they have never yet been put into writing. If only I could translate it to you!

In his reply Rilke quite ignored all this, as he normally did with so much that Katharina Kippenberg wrote to him. Owing to the great difficulties of the inflation, it was not till over a year later, in summer 1922, that the *Rainbow* was actually published by the Insel-Verlag in German. A copy of it was sent to Rilke shortly before Christmas 1922, and it is clear that he had quite forgotten what Katharina Kippenberg had told him about it in April 1921. On 10 January 1923 he wrote to her:

With an astonishment about which I could say quite a lot in detail, and often with the most uncanny agitation I have read this *Rainbow* of Lawrence; totally unacquainted with English literature as I am, I did not know so much as the name of this author! Was it you who discovered this very exceptional book and secured it for the *Insel*? This and two or three other books have recently moved me indescribably, and also alarmed me with a fruitful kind of alarm.

About the same time Rilke jotted down for Katharina Kippenberg the words: 'This book—the *Rainbow*—will mean a turning-point for me'[1] ('wird einen Abschnitt für mich bedeuten').

Katharina Kippenberg was delighted at Rilke's response to the *Rainbow*, but meanwhile she had herself come to have misgivings about Lawrence, chiefly on account of *Women in Love*, which she describes as 'the most perverse, godless, almost devilish thing I have ever read'. She finds traces in it of such inner emptiness and disillusionment as only an Englishman, I believe, is capable of, when he has outgrown the consolations of *sport* and *five o'clock tea*. The most terrible thing about it is that it seems to be written not just by an onlooker on hell, but by one who is himself damned....[1]

Instead Katharina Kippenberg now recommends to Rilke her latest discovery, Sherwood Anderson: 'I have now got hold of a wonderful young American, younger and healthier than Lawrence.'[2] She returns to this theme of Sherwood Anderson and Lawrence at great length in a letter of 21 May 1926, again insisting on the devilishness of *Women in Love*, which the Insel-Verlag was now on the point of publishing. Rilke took no notice of all this in his replies, and it is unlikely that it made any impression on him. But something else did make an impression on him, and a very considerable impression. Shortly before Christmas 1924 he received a copy of the *Insel-Almanach* for the following year, which contained, in addition to five poems of his own, an essay by D. H. Lawrence 'On Being Religious', that Katharina Kippenberg had found in the *Adelphi* and had had translated into German by Philipp Lehrs. It is an insouciant, slangy little hastily dashed-off sketch, and shows Lawrence at his most characteristic and his best—all genius and next to no talent. On 5 December 1924 Rilke wrote excitedly to Anton Kippenberg from his sanatorium above Montreux: 'I have read Lawrence's essay out loud again and again; it is strange, it contains sentences which I know exist almost word for word the same in my own papers.'[3] Rilke was probably thinking here above all of his *Letter from a Young Artisan* of 1922, which was only published posthumously (in 1933) and which contains the most concise, challenging and unambiguous statement of his religious views, especially of his detestation of *every* form of Christianity and of his desire to see phallic mysteries once more established as the true centre of religious experience.

One would need to write at considerable length to[4] work out adequately the parallels between Rilke's and Lawrence's mode of seeing and feeling, and of apprehending spiritual symbols in material things, especially in plants, animals and buildings;

between their strivings after a new relationship of man and woman, in which the self would remain inviolate, their desire to re-animate pre-Christian religious cults and their speculations and intuitions regarding death. What concerns us here is that Rilke was involuntarily forced to recognize, at the last stage of his life, so closely kindred a spirit in an Englishman, and in one who, despite all conflicts with his native land, still felt himself 'English in the teeth of all the world, even in the teeth of England'.[1] I know of no recorded utterances of Lawrence on Rilke—he may well have heard something about him through his German wife and his other German connexions. Most likely, however, he would have been too irritated by his first impressions ever to penetrate to what Rilke had in common with himself. After all, it is on the strength far less of what Rilke himself published during his lifetime than of what has appeared posthumously since 1930, especially of the letters and of the phallic poems, that we are able to recognize his affinity to Lawrence.

IX

RILKE AND THE ANGLO-SAXON ABROAD

RILKE was, like D. H. Lawrence, though within a narrower orbit, a feverish traveller—travel was a part of his vocation, he travelled with genius. His travels were too, like those of Lawrence, above all a search for himself *and* a flight from himself, rather than an attempt to see the foreign lands he visited in their objective, prosaic reality. His travels gave him the material for his writing, the true theme of which was nevertheless always himself, his inner problems, the depressions and belts of high pressure in his interior climate. In fact, he experienced the various countries he visited as so many projections or embodiments of his own fluctuating temperament, and he never seriously asked himself whether those countries might have some other meaning or function, some other justification for their existence. He may even have obscurely dreaded that England or America, if he had visited them, would have led to certain repressed elements within his own nature embodying themselves in definite form and becoming articulate. Travel was for him applied symbolism.

There were, however, always considerable numbers of people travelling about Europe at the same time as Rilke was, but for other, less cosmic reasons, and although he did his best, it was not always possible for him to avoid seeing them and being forced to react to them in some way, usually with distaste. In particular Europe was swarming with travellers from Great Britain and America, who as a rule disturbed his equanimity almost as much as his principal bugbears, the German tourists. Italy, in particular, was largely spoilt for him in this way. He managed in spring 1903 to escape from the almost ubiquitous German tourists there by going to Viareggio, but not from the still more pertinacious British tourists. He wrote to his wife:

> Now certain difficulties arose again at meals. The dining-room is small and unfortunately the tables are round. I was given a place next to an old Scotswoman, who insisted on talking to me at all costs, first in Italian, then in French. That was awful. I constantly underlined my taciturnity with the thickest possible strokes, but it was no good, she began again and again, and would not give over.—And all about me, at the two other round tables, there were English people, talking and laughing from one table to another, so that I had to pass the dinner-hour in the midst of brisk English conversation, bombarded at the same time with questions by my aged Scotswoman. Yesterday evening therefore I at once had the table laid for me in my own room, where it is also not very agreeable to eat, but at least quiet. . . . As soon as one of the old horrors from England goes away, I shall take a seat at one particular table and decline all advances.[1]

A week later Rilke has become somewhat hardened: 'At present,' he writes, there are only a few English people here, but one can get used to them, as one does to the striking of a clock; at first it disturbs one, but later one only notices it when it fails to occur.'[2] There is still, however, one way in which Rilke is disturbed, and that is when he is bathing. The chief thing about bathing is, for him, not so much actually going into the water, at least above the knee, as divesting himself of his bathing costume altogether, to take the air more unimpededly. When this is not practicable, he makes a point of not putting on the top half of his striped black and red bathing costume except 'in case of emergency, the emergency being the Englishwoman who suddenly pops up somewhere.'[3] It was under these very trying circumstances that Rilke wrote the third part of his *Book of Hours,* one of his most important cycles of religious lyric, terminating with the famous hymn to St Francis, 'the most loving of all.'

Experiences of this kind repeat themselves again and again throughout Rilke's life, and are certainly not without some influence on his general attitude towards the English-speaking world. In 1910 in Venice he complains that the pens in the writing-room in his hotel 'scratch so noisily that one can do nothing but listen to them the whole time, except when one is exasperated by the American who can't find room for his feet anywhere, and looks across every now and then to see if he could not perhaps rest them on the writing-table'.[1] In May 1914 Rilke's hopes of developing the appropriate Franciscan mood and feelings within himself in visiting Assisi were frustrated by all the 'merely inquisitive persons' he saw around him; 'and even if they didn't give me the horrors,' he writes, 'I should still not be able to assign any appreciable degree of inward fervour to such expressions as "*lovely*" and "*charming*".'[2] (This is interesting as one of the very few occasions on which Rilke actually cites English words untranslated.) No sooner was the 1914 war over, than the Anglo-Saxon tourists once more deployed over Europe. In November 1922 Rilke's friend Frau Gudi Nölke informed him that there were 'lots of English people'[3] at Meran, in December 1923 Frau Baladine Klossowska of 'quelques Anglais . . . venus au Régina Palace [Beatenberg, Berner Oberland] faire du ski'.[4] In 1925 Paris, when Rilke was on the last of his travels, he yet again went through the old irritating experience. Maurice Betz records how, on his calling upon Rilke for the first time at the Hotel Foyot, 'a travelling Englishwoman was writing letters behind us; we spoke in undertones. The presence of the foreigner disturbed us both, and Rilke soon suggested that I should go out with him.'[5] Not, of course, that Rilke was anything like alone in sometimes finding Anglo-Saxon tourists irritating. His friend Baladine Klossowska, on returning to Paris from Sierre after being together with him for the last time, in September 1925, wrote:

My journey was tiring, I was sorry not to be travelling first class. In addition to certain Englishwomen ('women anglaises'), who exasperated me with their chattering, there was a fearful draught. . . . I was furious and in despair at one and the same moment, and I could hardly understand Valéry Larbaud. For a moment I had to think of Queeny. At Vallorbe . . . we were all taken *en bloc* for English, and my passport was not examined.[6]

The 'Queeny' here referred to is Queenie Crosland, the English heroine of an excellent, lascivious story of Valéry Larbaud's

Beauté, mon beau souci, which Baladine Klossowska and Rilke had read together with great enthusiasm. It will be seen that Rilke was well aware that there existed, besides the frumpish or gushing Anglo-Saxon female tourists who got on his nerves, the attractive and impressive Englishwoman typified by Larbaud's Queenie, and that he was sometimes even on the look out for her, and found her too.

The travelling habits of the Anglo-Saxon race occasionally brought with them some slight material advantages, even to Rilke. In Spain, in winter 1912–13, when the discomfort of the indigenous hotel at Ronda, near Gibraltar, became too much for him, he was glad to move into the Hotel Reina Victoria instead, of which he writes:

Ronda ... would be just the place to live and make oneself at home in in true Spanish style, if it were not for the time of year ... and on top of everything else, the devil has put it into the heads of the English to build a really excellent hotel here, in which, of course, I am now staying, neutrally, expensively and in the way that would be just to the taste of any ordinary person. And yet I am brazen enough to give people to understand that I am really travelling in Spain.[1]

The following day he complains of the typically British open fire in this hotel: 'unfortunately I can never stand an open fire very well.'[2] Eight years later, however, in winter 1920–1 at Schloß Berg in Switzerland, he was to become a great lover and advocate of open fires, which he celebrates in one of his *Sonnets to Orpheus*.[3]

The Queen Victoria at Ronda was only one of the hotels with an English or American name to which Rilke was conducted by his flair for the exquisite, luxurious and exclusive. His first meeting with Fürstin Marie Taxis took place at the Hotel Liverpool[4] in Paris on 13 December 1909. He considered booking rooms for the Kippenbergs in Paris in May 1911 in the Hotel Roosevelt.[5] In the previous winter he had himself stayed at Shepheard's Hotel[6] in Cairo. Even private persons of his own circle were liable to give to their own houses such names as 'Haus Amerika'.[7]

At Venice in 1912 Rilke managed to get on sufficiently good terms with some of the English residents to be allowed freely to visit the gardens of their villas on the Giudecca. He complains, indeed, that these gardens have 'unfortunately come into casual, ignorant hands',[1] which have ruined them, but still he is very pleased to be able to walk about in them and show his friends over them. One of them belongs to a family called Johnston,[2] who seem also to have lent Rilke the key to their house, 'Casino dei Spiriti', on the Fondamente Nuove; but the one Rilke is fondest of is that of a Mr Eaden, 'a crotchety old Englishman whom nobody ever sees, but who admits into his garden the few strangers who know about it, if they hand in their visiting-cards.'[3] After the war Rilke revisited this garden on his last stay in Venice, in June 1920. Mr Eaden seems to have been dead by then, but Rilke mentions 'old Mrs Eaden'[4] now as the owner. On this occasion he writes of the 'giardino Eaden' at much length—it is one of his finest letters,[5] and admirably illustrates his way of finding symbols for his own states of feeling in the external world. He is once found paying a tribute to English landscape-gardening[6] as a valuable achievement, though on the whole his own taste favoured rather the earlier formal French and Italian type of garden.

A long list could be made of the persons of half-German and half-English or half-American extraction, and of the Anglo-Saxons well acclimatized in some part of the European continent, with whom Rilke was on comparatively cordial terms. As early as 1896 we find him speaking familiarly of a certain Friedrich Graf Jenison-Wallworth,[7] who, born in 1842, was the last representative of an old English noble family which had established itself in Bavaria, Saxony and Austria after 1777. How well he knew this old nobleman is uncertain—well enough, at least, to dedicate to him the poem on Venice, 'Ave weht von den Türmen her', which was written on 31 March 1897 and published in the volume *Advent* of the same year. On 21 May 1896 Rilke wrote from Prague to Laska van Oesteren of a projected journey to Hungary: 'On the way back from Budapest I intend to stop in Vienna; especially if *my dear uncle Graf Jenison-Wallworth* is there.' That the Graf was his uncle turns out to be a little invention on the part of the youthful Rilke, dictated perhaps by the circumstance that he imagined he was corresponding with a Baroness. If there had been any validity in this claim of Rilke's to be related to Graf Jenison-Wallworth, we should be able to establish some sort of link by blood between him and the English nation which he so persistently dismissed as alien to him.

At the age of twenty-one, in April 1897, Rilke was taken to Venice for the first time as the guest of an American of German extraction called Nathan Sulzberger, to whom he dedicated a poem as a mark of gratitude.[1] The collaborator of his last year in Prague and his first year in Munich, 1896–7, was a young poet, Harry Louis von Dickinson, an Austrian of English descent. Rilke specially insists on Dickinson's 'englische Abkunft', when reviewing his poems in October 1896.[2] His hosts at Jonsered near Goteborg in 1904, Jimmie and Lizzie Gibson,[3] whom he particularly liked, must have belonged to one of the innumerable Scottish families which have settled in Sweden since the days of Gustavus Adolphus, and of whom one or two other traces appear in Rilke's letters, in such Swedish names as Luise Nyström-Hamilton[4] and Montgomery.[5] The Tweeds whom Rilke refers to evidently as old Paris acquaintances in a letter to his wife of 19 April 1906 must have come from Great Britain or America.

Far less casual than these encounters, however, was his friendship with Gwen John (1876–1939), of which, unfortunately, nothing is so far known beyond the somewhat meagre references in *Chiaroscuro*, the autobiography of her celebrated brother, Augustus John. A painter, like her brother, Gwen John had gone to Paris to study under Whistler and remained there after Whistler's death, becoming friendly with Rodin, for whom she often posed. It must have been during the months from September 1905 to May 1906, when he was living at Meudon as Rodin's unofficial secretary, that Rilke came to know Gwen John. 'Gwen's friendship with Rainer Maria Rilke was also warm and close,' writes Augustus John; 'The poet used to lend her books and help her with his sympathy and understanding.'[6] It is to be presumed, in the absence of any concrete evidence, that Rilke continued to see Gwen John from time to time so long as he and she were both living in Paris, that is to say until summer 1914. Whether Rilke resumed relationships with her after the war or met her on his last stay in Paris from January to August 1925 remains uncertain. From the deep impression which the news of his death made upon her, it seems probable that he did. Four months after Rilke's death Gwen John wrote in her diary: 'I accept to suffer always, but Rilke! hold my hand! You must hold me by the hand! Teach me, inspire me, make me know what to do. Take care of me when my mind is asleep. You began to help me, you must continue.'[1] In the view of Augustus John, Rilke was one of the very few who really sympathized with and understood her.

In this same period, 1906 and the following years, falls Rilke's friendship with the partly English, partly German student of sculpture, Dora Herxheimer, together with whom he began his work on Elizabeth Barrett-Browning's *Sonnets from the Portuguese* and who has already been spoken of above in Chapter V.

In Rodin's studios Rilke was always being brought together with Americans—far too much for his liking. He thought Rodin wasted too much of his creative power on the lucrative business of modelling portrait-busts of wealthy American travellers—'Rodin is for ever making his Americans,' he complains in a letter of 3 November 1909 to his wife. His indignation was, however, much greater in the following year, when the seventy-year-old Rodin allowed himself to be twisted round the fingers of the unprepossessing adventuress Lucy Mary Tate from the United States, who had become by marriage the Marquise de Choiseul and about whom one can read sensational things in Judith Cladel's biography of Rodin. This Marquise de Choiseul was just the person to reinforce Rilke in all his prejudices against the English-speaking world, especially because he had to look on helplessly at her demoralization of his great artist-demigod. There is evidence that this was one of the worst shocks ever given to that faith in the redemptive powers of art which Rilke struggled to maintain throughout his life, and of which Rodin had for a time seemed to him the supreme confirmation. In spring 1911 Rilke unburdened his heart on these matters to Katharina Kippenberg as follows:

What a petty and wretched end to his life after such great things! I had built up my own life on all this, I have passed right through it with my entire body as through a bath. It cuts me to the heart to see what has come of it. Rodin is now under the thumb of a good-for-nothing woman, and when he works, it is money that he is out for.[1]

It was directly out of this crisis that Rilke's *Duinese Elegies* arose in January 1912. He writes frequently about this American Marquise de Choiseul with considerable bitterness, calling her 'dreadful' ('fürchterlich') and hoping that she may be 'left without a roof over her head'.[2] Her strong American accent in speaking French[3] probably did not commend her any more in his eyes.

A more pleasant and valuable American acquaintance made by Rilke through Rodin in summer 1908 was that with Jessie Lemont who, although far from proficient in the German language, was, with the help of her German-born husband Hans Trausil, to translate a considerable number of his poems into English in 1919 and his monograph on Rodin in 1920. Jessie Lemont, who culturally had her roots in the later nineteenth-century aesthetic movement, had apparently come to Europe chiefly to meet Rodin, on whom she was planning to lecture in America. It must have been in August or September 1908 that she met Rilke in Rodin's studio. Rilke was sufficiently interested in her to order a copy of his *Rodin* specially to give to her. In sending it to her on 30 September 1908 he expressed 'the liveliest good wishes for her lectures', saying: 'I am sure that you will prepare victories for the genius of Rodin in your country, whose long future you will courageously reinforce by conveying such a message to it.'[4] This is noteworthy as being one of Rilke's few friendlier references to the United States of America. At Christmas 1908 Jessie Lemont sent Rilke a copy of Arthur Symons' *Studies in Seven Arts* (see above p. 77), which he did not acknowledge till 15 January 1909. Two important passages from this letter have already been quoted in other connexions (see above pp. 37 and 77). Together with it Rilke sent to Jessie Lemont the two volumes of his *Neue Gedichte* —a gift which he would certainly not have made to anybody to whom his feelings were indifferent. About this time, if not earlier, Jessie Lemont must have returned to the United States, touring around there in 1909 and 1910 with her lecture on Rodin. In June 1911 she published in *The Craftsman* an article, 'Auguste Rodin: A visit to Meudon', in which a description of her own visit to Rodin of summer 1908 is followed by ample excerpts from Arthur Symons' essay on Rodin in his *Studies in Seven Arts*. A copy of this article she sent to Rilke and he acknowledged it from Venice on 8 June 1912, saying that he has read it 'with the liveliest pleasure—but above all I am touched by your kind remembrance of me' ('par votre si gracieux souvenir'). There must have been some further correspondence between Jessie Lemont and Rilke about 1919 or 1920, when copies of her translation of his poems and the Rodin monograph were sent to him, and it was almost certainly Jessie Lemont or Hans Trausil who invited him to come to New York for a holiday (see below p. 171). Jessie Lemont, who was only able to read and translate Rilke's books with much outside help, regarded her meetings with him as 'one of the most vital experiences of her life'.

Another American Rilke met in Paris in these same years was the authoress Edith Wharton (1862–1937)[1] who in the winter of 1915–16 collaborated with Romain Rolland and André Gide in their unsuccessful efforts to prevent the sequestration and compulsory sale of the books and other property which Rilke had left behind him in Paris in summer 1914.

One of Rilke's neighbours in the Hotel Biron in Paris from 1909 to 1911 was an American woman who had qualities that Rilke could have admired, the dancer Isadora Duncan.[2] She felt at this time that it was her mission to produce the superman, and being assured that she could make herself responsible for his perfect physique, she was on the look out for a great poet to provide, as sire, for the qualities of his mind. The present writer has in familiar conversation sometimes yielded to the temptation to suggest, when recounting this episode, that her eyes lighted on her frail and retiring neighbour Rilke as the best candidate. Actually they did not. Her attention was mercifully drawn further afield to Maeterlinck, who politely refused the honour on the grounds of connubial felicity. Rilke was content to look on at Isadora Duncan from a distance, not altogether approving of the noise and commotion which her temperament and sociable disposition created in his quiet world.

Besides Paris, Venice, with the not distant Castle of Duino on the Istrian coast, was a place where Rilke could not help running into Anglo-Saxons. In his memorable solitary winter at the Castle of Duino in 1911–12 he was looked after by a housekeeper called Miss Greenham, who was, however, half-Italian, and who ever after referred to him as 'l'indimenticabile' ('the unforgettable one').[1] When he moved in May 1912 into the *mezzanino* of the Fürstin Marie Taxis in Venice, he was badgered by a man called Vincent,[2] apparently an architect who was hoping to be employed by her. From Rilke's report of this encounter in his letter to the Fürstin of 14 May 1912 it seems certain that this Vincent, whom he had evidently met before (probably in the previous summer at Lautschin—see below p. 131), was British or American:

Near here Vincent came up to me yesterday, anxious about his model. I told him it had only recently arrived at Duino and was undamaged, so he could set his mind at rest. I said to him, however, that nothing would be altered at Duino, that for the time being all thought of having anything done to it had been abandoned, which is true enough. He is here with his colleague Scott and very much wants to introduce me to him. He is living next door, almost in the same house, but thank goodness only for a few days.

Nothing more is heard of this Vincent and Scott, whom Rilke was obviously anxious to avoid. But it was during this same Venetian spring and summer of 1912 that he saw much of a certain Horatio Brown, who has the distinction of being the man of English-speaking race who knew him best. This Horatio Brown, a man of fifty-six when Rilke first met him as a fellow-guest at Duino in October 1911, but looking a good deal older, had been living in Venice for over thirty years. He was a well-known figure in the drifting, largely foreign intelligentsia of the place, but was so uncommunicative that few people there seem to have known whether he was English or American. Certainly some thought he was American, and that would appear to have been Rilke's belief. Brown did not know much German, and in his conversations with Rilke he presumably spoke Italian, or possibly French—and spoke them too with that Anglo-Saxon accent which Rilke found it hard to endure. Princess Marie Taxis, who had a great liking for Brown, describes him as an 'exceptional being, more fitted than any other to understand and love Rilke'.[1] From May to September 1912 Rilke was in Venice and must have seen a fair amount of Brown during these months. On 26 June he wrote to Princess Marie Taxis:

I see Brown from time to time. Yesterday I had breakfast with him, then he rowed me in a *sandalo* (a kind of punt) towards San Nicoletto. (So there still are people who row, people who work, I say to myself, and feel ashamed once more.)[2]

In this same month Rilke presented Brown with a copy of Hofmannsthal's recently published *Gedichte und kleine Dramen*, with the dedication:

Al Signor Horatio F. Brown
omaggio e simpatia
del suo R. M. Rilke
(Venezia, Giugno 1912)[3]

A pencil reference '(vedi pag. 12)' draws attention to the well-known purple patch in the 'Ballade des äußeren Lebens' ('Ballad of External Life'):

Und dennoch sagt der viel, der 'Abend' sagt,
Ein Wort, daraus Tiefsinn und Trauer rinnt
Wie schwerer Honig aus den hohlen Waben.

Translated:

Yet who says 'evening', much, indeed, has said,
A word whence plaints and pensiveness exude
Like heavy honey from the hollow comb.

From this one can form some idea of the lines on which Rilke's conversations with Horatio Brown in June 1912 must have run.

It can also be inferred that Brown must have had at least some smattering of German, enough for Rilke to think it not impossible to initiate him into those aspects of Hofmannsthal's poetry which have most in common with his own.

On 17 November 1913 Princess Marie Taxis wrote to Rilke:

I am sending you two remarkable poems in Italian by Brown. He assures me that it was not *he* who wrote them, and considering what his Italian is like, one can well believe it. He has the feeling that they were dictated to him. I find them . . . really beautiful.

Rilke concurred in the Princess's judgment, particularly praising one of the two poems, 'though one can see that it was only an accident.'[1] This poem evidently struck him as being, if not exceptionally good by normal standards, at least too good for Brown's Italian, or for Brown himself. We have Kassner's very dependable word for it that 'Brown greatly loved Rilke, loved him without being able to read his poems, because he knew just as little German as Rilke did English'.[2] Brown, like scores of others who met Rilke without, for one reason or another, knowing anything about his poetry, was immediately aware of and attracted by his genius. He talked much about him to Princess Marie Taxis, sent greetings to him through her and also inquired eagerly about him after the war.[3] Here was friendship, inarticulately proffered and manifesting itself more readily in such bodily services as oarsmanship on the lagoons than in words. Rilke's response would appear to have been lukewarm and perhaps also a little distrustful. We have the record of one conversation in which both Rilke and Brown were involved, and in which Brown appears in the role of the blunt, common-sense, unimaginative Anglo-Saxon on whom the more exquisite things of the mind are wasted. This was about the end of April 1914, when Rilke and Brown were once more both guests of Princess Marie Taxis at Duino. Rilke's mind was at this time chiefly taken up with the problem of how to break off his relationships with Magda von Hattingberg, whom he had met a month or two previously and had just imprudently asked to marry him. Magda von Hattingberg was now with him at Duino and records in her diary how 'the American' (i.e. Brown), in opposition to the rest of the company, maintained that 'the only true art is that which everybody can understand'.[1] The Princess herself tried to put him right on this point, but 'the American would not allow himself to be converted, and said it was after all not quite just to credit only one particular class of mankind with culture'. Horatio Brown got the worst of the debate. In deploring that the chief effect practically brought about by art and culture in the modern world has been more and more to engender exclusive côteries of supercilious intellectuals complacently segregating themselves from the rest of mankind, the usually untalkative Brown was really only advancing a view which many great modern poets and artists of various nationalities have also at times expressed; only he was advancing it too abruptly and crudely, and above all at the wrong time and in the wrong place, amongst people to most of whom art would have meant very much less than it did, if they had not been able to regard it as the exclusive prerogative of their own higher type. Brown had simply proclaimed himself a philistine, and that seems to have been the view of him to which Rilke had all along inclined. This emerges from another entry in Magda von Hattingberg's Duino diary:

Yesterday the Princess and her son, Prince Pascha, went with the American to Grado. The old man's Christian name is Horatio, 'instead of William or John, which would suit him a good deal better,' says Rilke, who thinks he is a crank. One doesn't know what to make of this Horatio; he usually just sits there saying nothing, sucking at an English pipe stuffed with pungent honeydew tobacco. The Princess thinks the American has a great admiration for Rilke, 'although he doesn't let it show.' Prince Pascha, however, is of the opinion that the old man doesn't understand the first word about poetry.[2]

This taciturn, puzzling old American crank with the pipe, who ought in Rilke's opinion to have been called William (like Shakespeare) or John (like Milton or Keats) rather than Horatio, was in reality a Scot and the Laird of Newhall and Carlops in the Pentlands. He was an Oxford greats-man and an Honorary

Doctor of Laws of the University of Edinburgh. In his earlier days he had mixed in Pre-Raphaelite circles and known John Addington Symonds, whose biography he wrote, and also Browning. He was himself a man of letters, with many books, including a volume of poems, to his credit. He was one of the outstanding authorities of his age on the history, topography, art-treasures and antiquities of Venice.[1] Very likely it was he who drew Rilke's attention to the old gardens on the Giudecca and introduced him to their English owners. The simple people of Carlops, when he returned there, as he did for a month or so from time to time, seem to have known as little of what they should make of him as the distinguished people of Venice and Duino, and to have been just as ready to assume the worst—that is to say, for them, that he might have become a Roman Catholic out in those foreign parts where he was continuing his 'schooling' for such an inordinate number of years.[2] Of the whole circle at Duino, probably only Rudolf Kassner knew who and what Dr Horatio Brown really was, and how little true ground Prince Pascha, Magda von Hattingberg or Rilke himself had for looking down upon him superciliously as an outsider. To Kassner Brown once haltingly confided what was at the back of his taciturnity, the thwarted feeling: 'I have not lived.' Kassner, no friend of such indiscreet intimacies, answered:

> Brown, it isn't English to talk like that. An Englishman doesn't say such things, still less a Scot. That is phrase out of a novel, a German, Scandinavian or Russian novel. What is more, the times are over when such a phrase still had any meaning.[3]

It was a rebuff, though a very friendly one. If Brown had confided his depression to Rilke instead, the result would certainly have been very different. The ice would have been broken between the two men, Rilke would have been in his element proffering ghostly counsel and consolation, and might even have come to suspect that at least the Scots (or the Americans) are, after all, human.

It appears probable that Rilke saw Brown once more, on his

last visit to Venice in summer 1920—we know at least that Brown was there a fortnight before Rilke arrived, and that he was eagerly inquiring after him. On 4 June of this year Rilke wrote to the Princess: 'I thank Horatio Brown cordially for bearing me in mind, and ask in return to be kindly remembered to him.' Exactly one week later Rilke was himself in Venice and stayed there for a month.

Princess Marie Taxis regularly filled her various mansions with English guests and persisted in believing that Rilke would be delighted to meet them, from which one may perhaps infer that he spoke less freely to her of his prejudices against everything British than he did to his other intimate friends. She says herself: 'I made a point then of only inviting people fitted to appreciate and understand him.'[1] We know that Rilke actually did in this way meet quite a number of the Princess's English friends[2]—amongst others a Captain Barton and his wife, and a 'very gifted young English architect' (probably identical with the 'Vincent' who turned up in Venice in May 1912—see above p. 126) at Lautschin in Bohemia in August 1911, and a certain 'Mary C—' at Duino in October of the same year. Captain Francis Rickman Barton (1865–1947) was, at the time when Rilke met him, Financial Minister of Zanzibar, and had from 1905 to 1907 been Administrator of Papua. He had been educated partly in Germany and knew the language well. Twenty years later he had still not forgotten Rilke. On seeing a Cambridge undergraduate reading something of Rilke's at a hotel in the Bregenzer Wald in 1933, he remarked: 'I knew that fellow. Met him before the war at Prince Taxis' place in Bohemia. Went there for the hunting.... Queer sort of fellow. Didn't seem to have much to say for himself.'[3] What impression this Captain Barton made on Rilke is not recorded. But indirectly he did play some part in Rilke's destiny. Princess Marie Taxis relates how, at Duino in October 1912—

> we had been telling Rilke that one of our English friends, a very intelligent and cultivated man, formerly the Governor of a great colony in the Pacific Ocean [i.e. Captain Barton] had, during his stay at Lautschin that same summer, insisted on trying an experiment with the

planchette, by means of which one can make a pencil write 'automatically' and establish communications with the occult world.... Thereupon Rilke wanted to try it too.[1]

This was the beginning of those séances with the *planchette* in which Rilke received mysterious messages from the 'Unknown One' ('die Unbekannte') and which have already been touched upon in this study, in connexion with his relationships with the English language (see above pp. 51–2). A year later Rilke records how, encouraged by him, the authoress Annette Kolb of Munich ordered a *planchette* from London: 'Annette ... faisait venir une très aimable planchette de Londres.'[2]

It is to be regretted that Rilke did not meet two other English guests of whom Princess Marie Taxis wrote to him at some length in 1912 and 1913 as an inducement to him to come to Lautschin in Bohemia once more. One of them was A. G. B. Russell, a leading authority on Blake and a friend of Kassner's. The Princess, however, finds him '*entre nous* rather hard going, because he is such an island-dweller—and one would like also to massage away the very bitter line about his mouth'.[3] The other is Dame (then Miss) Ethel Smyth, now famous as a musician, then better known as a very militant suffragette. She declared that she thanked God every day on waking up that she was a woman, and that on her return to England she would at once throw another bomb into a theatre or set a house on fire. 'Only,' the Princess adds, she is, 'like many Englishwomen, quite without instinct.'[4] Miss Smyth asked Rilke through the Princess for permission to set one of his unpublished poems to music. He replied, 'Let Miss Smyth have a free hand in the matter, if it pleases you and her.'[5] Rilke always disliked having his poems set to music—only in the case of Ernst Krenek did he once willingly depart from this principle.

Another English guest of the Princess's, even more interesting than A. G. B. Russell or Dame Ethel Smyth, Rilke just missed when he left Duino early in May 1914. If he had only stayed on a few weeks longer, he would have met Lord Kitchener,[6] who broke his journey from Egypt to London there for a day or two.

Even during the war years Anglo-Saxon names occasionally turn up in Rilke's letters. Marianne Mitford,[1] who lent him a house in Berlin in December 1914 and January 1915 had only come to her English name by a marriage to an Englishman which had been dissolved after two months; she later married a Goldschmidt-Rothschild and was by birth a Friedländer-Fuld, and we have already come across her under her nickname 'Baby Friedländer' (see above p. 48). On 4 December 1916 Rilke heard a certain Sibyl Vane[2] give a public recital from the poetry of the 'Activist' Gottfried Kölwel in Munich. In September 1918 he speaks of a Lady Blennerhasset, regretting that he had not made her acquaintance, as he is sure that she would have 'done him good'.[3] This Lady Blennerhasset was, however, only British by marriage. By birth she was Gräfin Charlotte von Leyden, and on becoming a widow in 1909 she had settled down in her native Munich, remaining there at the outbreak of war and dying there at the age of seventy-four in 1917.

During the first year and a half of his residence in Switzerland after the war Rilke only found one place to live that anything like satisfied his complex needs for aristocratic seclusion, and that was the Palazzo Salis at Soglio in the Grisons, where he spent about eight weeks from late July to late September 1919. This palace, now let to a contractor as a hotel, really belonged, as Rilke liked to explain in his letters of the time, to 'Count John von Salis of the branch of the family at Soglio that became Anglican, who is at present British ambassador at the Vatican'.[4] One of Rilke's fellow-guests at Soglio was a young American schoolmaster (since university professor) of German extraction, Dr Henry Lüdeke. With him Rilke had some interesting conversations about Paris, Rodin and the literature of German-speaking Switzerland.[5] It was presumably at Soglio that Rilke first met the young Frau von Salis[6] whom he describes as 'page-like' ('pagenhaft') and whom he was pleased to see again when he read publicly from his works at Winterthur on 28 November 1919. This Frau von Salis was a native of Cardiff; her maiden name was Dorothea Parker.

At Christmas 1921, the first that Rilke spent at Muzot by Sierre in the Valais, his friend Frau Wunderly-Volkart gave him much pleasure with the present of a box with 'a charming English colour-print of Syon mounted under glass in the lid'.[1]

In April 1923 and again in April 1924 a young Australian violinist, Alma Moodie,[2] visited Rilke at Muzot. She came at the suggestion of Dr Werner Reinhart, the owner of Muzot, who played a leading part in the musical life of Switzerland. The chief purpose of her visit was to play Bach privately to Rilke. It was one of the several attempts made to convert him to music, which never succeeded in evoking more than a short burst of enthusiasm. Rilke was not on much better terms with music than with the English language. But he liked Alma Moodie and enjoyed her playing. She had spent so much of her life in Austria and Germany as fully to have acclimatized herself, so that Rilke, in hearing her speak, was no more conscious of her being really Australian than he had been of Henry Lüdeke being really American.

There is a puzzling unsigned and undated entry in Rilke's Muzot guest-book between 21 March and 6 April 1924, just before Paul Valéry's memorable visit of the latter date: 'As the blackest sky foretells the heaviest tempest.' Whether the unidentifiable visitor in question was of English-speaking nationality or not—the handwriting looks English—it seems as though the conversation had turned upon some points of English literature, culture or language. I have not so far been able to trace the source of the quotation. It is conceivable that Alma Moodie, who came to Muzot on 20 April 1924, may have had something to do with this entry in the guest-book.

The most important event in Rilke's Swiss years was the completion of the *Duinese Elegies* and the composition of the *Sonnets to Orpheus* in February 1922. Amongst his manuscripts of these and the following weeks there is a jotting which is of peculiar interest because it is in the English language and belongs furthermore to a period at which Rilke himself constantly declared that he had forgotten every word of English he had ever known. It runs as follows:

The photographs of Mrs Eyre Macklin and Miss Nicola Blake which attracted Rilke's attention in the *Queen*. (See text pp. 135–6.)

Mrs Eyre Macklin. The first woman publisher to set up business on her own account. Under the name A. M. Philpot Ltd she has edited and published the famous series of translations known as *Les Fleurs de France.*

(portrait très accueillant)

There is no indication of where this excerpt is taken from. I searched for it for years, to begin with in such publications as *The Bookman*, eventually tracking it down on page 428 of *The Queen* (*Lady's Newspaper and Court Chronicle*) for 8 April 1922. There was clearly much to interest Rilke about this British woman-publisher who, as the accompanying article in *The Queen* explained, had laboured so much towards 'making the French novel better known in England', and whose face furthermore struck him as 'très accueillant', which in this context can probably be understood as meaning something like 'responsive', 'sympathetic' or 'attractive'.

In April 1924 Rilke wrote a French poem which was first published posthumously and without any superscription in 1935:

Comme tel dessin de maître accapare
le vide du papier entre les traits
tant que son blanc paraît précieux et rare,
ainsi décide le dessin parfaït

de tes sourcils et de ta bouche pure,
de ces distances et de la matière
qui entre ton menton et tes paupières
se vantent, belle, d'être ta figure.

Translated:

As on some drawings, by the master's care
enhanced, white paper in between the lines,
blank though it be, seems wonderful and rare,
so too this perfect contour that defines

your eyebrows and pure mouth governs the space
and moulds the substance whose proud boast it is,
between your gentle chin and gentle eyes
to constitute, o lovely girl, your face.

In the second volume of Rilke's complete works, published in 1956, the editor, Ernst Zinn,[1] supplies the original superscription of this poem, 'À Miss Nicola B . . .' and gives the following explanation of it in his notes:

These verses refer to the photograph of an actress which Rilke had seen in an English periodical. At the end of the note-book containing the draft there is the following entry: '*Miss Nicola Blake* (*Photos Hay-Wrightson*) "*Cinema-Queen*" *in* "*Chiquita*". *The Queen* / *No du* 2 *avril* (*page* 7) (*4032—Vol. CLV.*)' The cutting with this photograph has turned up amongst the papers of Katharina Kippenberg, to whom Rilke presumably gave it when she visited Muzot at the end of April 1924.

The circumstance that Rilke is thus on two occasions, in April 1922 and again in April 1924, found making excerpts from *The Queen,* and in each case from almost current numbers too, suggests that he must have seen it fairly regularly, probably having it sent on to him by a friend who was a subscriber. After all his disappointing and estranging experiences with the English language and English literature, even when they were represented by such figures as Shakespeare and Keats, he would appear here at last, in this British *Lady's Newspaper and Court Journal,* to have found something more congenial to him. It need not surprise us to find Rilke interested in ladies' society and fashion journals (which are occasionally elsewhere referred to by him) or even in film-stars. Through Claire Goll, authoress of *Lyrische Films* (see above p. 47), he came from 1918 onwards to be much interested in and eventually also, in 1925, to meet Elisabeth Bergner[2] (before the days, however, when she left the stage for the screen), and the Egyptian Nimet Eloui Bey[3] to whom he was so much attached in the last months of his life, adored Greta Garbo and was consumed with the ambition to emulate her as a film-star. There are moments when Rilke in his evaluation and presentation of the erotic comes much nearer to the spirit of Holywood with its pin-up beauties than one might at first expect.

A central factor in all Rilke's experience, especially during the last sixteen years of his life, was his unremitting and never successful search for the ideal woman who would be able really to understand him and to love him in the way in which he wanted to be loved. In a letter of 21 October 1913 to Lou Andreas-Salomé he ironically describes himself as 'always standing at the telescope, ascribing to every approaching woman a bliss which was certainly never to be found with any one of them: my own bliss, the bliss, in times past, of my most solitary hours'. Again and again he thought he had at last found this visionary happiness, again and again these hopes gave way to bitterness and revulsion. His motherly friend, Princess Marie Taxis, in whom he confided these troubles of his in May 1921, commented on them as follows in her diary:

Will they never leave him in peace? Will there never be a woman who will love him enough to understand what a being of such genius and such capacity for suffering needs, and to live for him alone, without thinking about her own little life, which is probably stupid and of no importance whatsoever? ... It is difficult to reply. The woman who gives her entire heart without ever asking for anything for herself—that is what it amounts to.... Such a woman might exist, indeed, but the problem is, how to find her.... And yet he cannot live without the atmosphere of a woman around him. Yes, I have often been startled at the extraordinary attraction that women have for him....[1]

In this connexion the question arises for us, whether Rilke's avowed antipathy to the English-speaking peoples was strong enough to prevent him from ever feeling attracted towards women belonging to those peoples. Apparently it was not: the way in which he speaks of the 'page-like' Frau Dorothea von Salis, *née* Parker, the way in which, when reading *The Queen*, he singles out the face of Mrs Eyre Macklin as 'très accueillant' and writes an entire poem on that of Nicola Blake, suggests that he is no less susceptible to British feminine charm than to that of other nations. This is borne out by a little incident of summer 1922 or 1924 communicated to me by Fräulein Frieda Baumgartner, who kept house for Rilke at Muzot.

During his Muzot years Rilke often lived in the attractive old hotel *Château Bellevue* in Sierre instead of in Schloss Muzot. In May and June of the year in question his attention was caught by an English couple also living in this hotel, a Mr and Mrs Perry. In particular Rilke was interested to overhear Mrs Perry say in German to another lady in the Library of the Hotel: 'O wie gut, dass niemand weiß, daß ich Schneewittchen heiß.' This is an adaptation to the story of *Snow-White* of the well-known verse of Grimm's *Rumpelstiltzchen*:

Little does my lady dream
Rumpel-Stilts-Kin is my name.[1]

In confiding this to Fräulein Baumgartner, Rilke also remarked how admirably Mrs Perry spoke German. In the course of time Mr and Mrs Perry left Sierre and went to the Hotel Palace in Lausanne. Shortly after this the cherries in the orchard of Muzot were harvested, and Rilke packed some of the choicest of them in a little basket and posted them to Mrs Perry in Lausanne. The following day the parcel was, to Rilke's great disappointment, returned unopened. Mr Perry had energetically refused this present to his wife, because it came from a German or a Czech. One might recognize in this little incident the germs of such a situation as that between Detlev Spinell and Anton and Gabriele Klöterjahn in Thomas Mann's *Tristan*.

In Paris in 1925 an experience was in store for Rilke with regard to America, not dissimilar to that which he had had in December 1924 with regard to England, when he read D. H. Lawrence's essay 'On Being Religious'. He had, probably at Paul Valéry's recommendation, read a book called *Pensées d'une Amazone*, in which he was amazed to find again and again his own feelings, his own thoughts, his own experiences. The authoress of this book was, however, an American, Natalie Clifford Barney,[2] the friend not only of Paul Valéry, but also of Rémy de Gourmont and indeed of many of the outstanding French writers of the age. She was a great literary hostess, and well acclimatized in France, most of her books having been originally written in French. Rilke was anxious to meet her when he came to Paris in 1925, and above all to speak with her *tête-à-tête* and not just at one of her famous Friday evening crushes. He wrote her a little note in French, expressing this wish, one of the most tortuously phrased of his never very forthright letters, a kind of travesty of the later Henry James:

Passing before your door yesterday morning, I was seized with the audacity to try whether the god of that little, unknown temple would permit me to exchange the hundred negations of a dreary winter's day for the dateless grace of a consenting moment. Nothing came of it, the face of the god was turned elsewhere....

Miss Barney, not *séduite* by this style of letter-writing, nevertheless arranged a small dinner-party for Rilke, which he attended, but still gave him no opportunity for the kind of conversation he had in mind. He declined various further invitations to the crowded Friday gatherings, with more and more preciously phrased notes of apology, speaking of the *Pensées d'une Amazone* and promising Miss Barney a copy of his own *Notebooks of Malte Laurids Brigge,* as soon as the French translation should appear. He left Paris without having seen Miss Barney under favourable circumstances and so also without having established those sympathetic relationships with her on which his heart was set. In her salon, it is interesting to reflect, he might have met James Joyce. When *Malte Laurids Brigge* at last appeared in French, in June 1926, he sent Miss Barney a copy with a dedication in French verses

> O le temple défait ou jamais terminé.... Comment
> adorer un Dieu qui tant se plaît aux ruines!
>
> Les offrandes usent l'autel et le sel de nos larmes marines
> ronge les dalles. Et quant aux colonnes: à deux
> on les soutient; c'est leur beau fût qui sépare
> les amants.... Aussi l'entrainent-ils avec eux
> dans la lente chute de leurs étreintes avares.[1]

Translated:

> O the temple dilapidated or never finished.... How
> can one adore a God who delights so much in ruins?
>
> The offerings wear away the altar, and the salt of our briny tears
> eats away the flag-stones. And as for the pillars: it is in pairs
> that we support them; their beautiful shaft it is that separates

the lovers. . . . So they drag it down along with them
in the gradual downfall of their covetous embraces.

Miss Barney put *Malte Laurids Brigge* away without looking at it, and it was not till some time after Rilke's death (which had made no impression on her) that she took the trouble to read it and found out at last what it was that had drawn him towards her, the affinity between his and her mode of sensibility. 'Why were we either too discreet, or too inattentive, or too awkward, Rilke and I?' was her final comment. Neither here nor in the case of D. H. Lawrence did differences of nationality or language seem to count for so much at bottom, where the finer things of the spirit were concerned. Nevertheless such differences could lead in practice to Rilke's being underrated or misjudged until it was too late—and also to his misjudging or underrating others.

There is another encounter of Rilke's in Paris in 1925 to be recorded, with a young Northern Irishman, William McCousland Stewart,[1] now Professor of French at the University of Bristol. By Professor Stewart's kind permission this can here be reported in his own words:

I met him at the flat of André Germain, Director and editor of the *Revue Européenne,* who gathered European figures, and invited some of us whom he had met at the *Groupe Internationale* of the *École Normale* (where I was then *lecteur d'anglais*) to come to some of these evenings of his. . . . Rilke was very correctly dressed in tails on that occasion. He was glad, I think, to find someone who was fond of poetry and was at the *École Normale,* where he had known Hellingrath. I think I accompanied him back from the Île Saint-Louis to the Hotel Foyot where he was staying . . . and he promised to look me up.

He did this somewhat later, at the *École Normale*—partly I think in memory of Hellingrath, who had been killed in the first world war . . . and who is known as editor of Hölderlin; but Rilke said Hellingrath showed him good poems of his own—which Rilke admired and wanted him to follow up with more.

Though I know German well (and speak it as one who has known it from early childhood) and knew Rilke's poetry—he always, or practically always, spoke French—whether out of a habit contracted during his French years, or as his automatic response to his environment or as the simplest means of avoiding misunderstandings and even, perhaps, minor incidents (we were still under the shadow of World War I). But he did speak about his method of bringing an audience to the point where he felt he could say or read some of his poems.

He greatly admired—indeed almost venerated—Valéry. . . . As you know, he published a little volume of poems he wrote in French under the title *Vergers*. . . . He told me he was very glad that Valéry had said that he liked them.

He fell very quickly into the rhythm and feel of a people and/or language. He told me that had happened for him with Russian, though he later forgot much. In this connection he spoke of his translation of the *Sonnets from the Portuguese*. This he had made with the help of a friend. . . . He said he had felt himself at the time completely immersed in and at home in the English language, enjoying its rhythms, and yet later forgetting it completely. He promised to send me his version. . . . And he was as good as his word and did in fact send them from Muzot, with the inscription:

À Monsieur William Stewart
ce petit livre promis naguère,
très cordialement donné
R. M. Rilke
(Muzot s/Sierre, en Novembre 1925)

This is the amplest firsthand account that we have of an encounter between Rilke and a member of one of the English-speaking peoples. Rilke's health was, as he himself knew, already seriously undermined, when he went to Paris in 1925. One of his principal objects in making that journey was to escape his present suffering self and recapture some of those older Parisian experiences which he had had in pre-war years, together with the sense of buoyancy which, as it now seemed to him, had attended them. Such an old experience he did recapture, evidently, in meeting this young Northern Irishman with his intelligent interest in poetry, who was English lector at the École Normale; it brought back to him the days when he had been on friendly terms with the promising young Norbert von Hellingrath,[1] who from 1910 to 1911 had been German lector at the same institution. William Stewart entered, almost as last, into the long series of promising young men after his own heart whom it delighted Rilke to befriend, encourage and confide in, together with Norbert von Hellingrath, Thankmar von Münchhausen and Bernhard von der Marwitz.

The first five months of 1926, the last year of his life, Rilke spent in the sanatorium of Val-Mont near Montreux, where he was to die in the following December. On 1 May of this year he wrote two poems,[1] the one ('Wer kann Amber schenken! ...') dedicated to 'Madame P. Verrijn-Stuart', the other ('Bruder Körper ist arm,' inscribed in a copy of the *Book of Hours*) dedicated 'Für Herrn und Frau Verrijn-Stuart'. The name suggests that the husband was Dutch or Flemish and that the wife was, by birth, British. Possibly they were fellow-patients of Rilke's at Valmont.

In late summer 1926, four months before his death, Rilke was staying at the Hotel Savoy at Ouchy-Lausanne, where, about 12 September, he made the acquaintance of the Egyptian Nimet Eloui Bey. (See above p. 136.) In these weeks Miss Harriet Cohen,[2] now so well-known as a pianist, was staying at Evian on the south shore of Lake Leman, but crossing by motor-boat every day to Lausanne for treatment which she was receiving from a specialist in Geneva. Through Swiss friends who also knew Nimet Eloui Bey Miss Cohen was introduced to Rilke, meeting him three or four times at Ouchy between 14 and 23 September, and also visiting Geneva with him. 'We spoke French, and my German was not so rusty as it is now,' Miss Cohen records, adding, however, that Rilke 'had a few words of English'. Clearly Rilke was much attracted by Miss Cohen. He showed understanding when she spoke enthusiastically of Yeats, though smiling at something that evidently struck him as extravagant in her admiration. It much interested him to hear that she was a favourite of Bernard Shaw's, and still more that D. H. Lawrence had some years before written verses for her autograph album. What is most remarkable is that he gave her an autograph copy of his own verses:

> Du im voraus
> verlorne Geliebte, Nimmergekommene,
> nicht weiß ich, welche Töne dir lieb sind.
> Nicht mehr versuch ich, dich, wenn das Kommende wogt,
> zu erkennen. Alle die großen
> Bilder in mir, in Fernen erfahrene Landschaft,

Städte und Türme und Brücken und un-
vermutete Wendung der Wege
und das Gewaltige jener von Göttern
einst durchwachsenen Länder:
steigt zur Bedeutung in mir
deiner, Entgehende, an.

Ach, die Gärten bist du,
ach, ich sah sie mit solcher
Hoffnung. Ein offenes Fenster
im Landhaus—, und du tratest beinahe
mir nachdenklich heran. Gassen fand ich,—
du warst sie gerade gegangen,
und die Spiegel manchmal der Läden der Händler
waren noch schwindlig von dir und gaben erschrocken
mein zu plötzliches Bild.—Wer weiß, ob derselbe
Vogel nicht hinklang durch uns
gestern, einzeln, im Abend?

Translated:

You, beloved, who were
lost in advance, who have never come,
I do not know what sounds delight you.
No longer do I try, when the future surges,
to recognize you. All the vast
images in me, landscapes, far off, that I have felt,
cities and towers and bridges and the unexpected twist of the pathways,
and the immensity of those countries
permeated once with living gods:
all this converges to a symbol within me,
the meaning of which is you, elusive one.

Ah! you are the gardens,
ah! I saw them with so much
hope. An open window
in a country house—, and you were almost
approaching me, pensively. I came upon lanes,—
it was as though you had just passed through them,
and often the mirrors in the shops of the merchants
were still dizzy with you, and startled at having to reflect
my too sudden image.—Who knows, if the same
bird was not perhaps singing through both of us
yesterday, separately, in the evening?

It was only several years later that Miss Cohen discovered, not, as she herself admits, without some disappointment, that these verses were not written specially for her by Rilke in September 1926. At that time they were still unpublished, not appearing until April 1927 in the Rilke memorial number of the *Inselschiff*. Rilke had, however, written them twelve years earlier, in winter 1913–14. The most probable explanation for his happening to have a copy of them with him in his hotel at Ouchy—for he can hardly have written them down for Miss Cohen from memory alone—is that they had been selected for inclusion in the collected edition of his works, about which he had been negotiating with his publishers for years. The chief point about the verses is that they express so intensely and with unusual directness that yearning for the ideal woman which, as has already been shown (see above pp. 136–7) was a central factor in Rilke's experience and work. That Rilke transcribed this particular poem for Miss Harriet Cohen does, however, suggest that he did, for the time being, see in her, as he had done in Magda von Hattingberg, Lulu Albert-Lasard, Claire Studer, Baladine Klossowska and others, the realization of his dreams. Miss Cohen herself writes:

> The description of looking in antique shops in the old city (Geneva), the description of my coming from far away lands (England), of my antiquity (Jewish), made the poem absolutely perfect for the occasion. We looked at an old antique shop in the old part of Geneva. There was a special mirror there.

Rilke certainly came in contact with more persons from the English-speaking world than those whom it has here, in the light of the evidence now accessible to us, been comparatively easy to trace. In the nature of things it will never be possible to compile a list of such meetings of which we could say with absolute certainty that it was complete; nor would there be any point in trying to compile such a list. It is enough for our purposes to have shown that Rilke did come across quite a considerable number of British and American citizens, apart from Germans and others of partly Anglo-Saxon extraction, like Harry Louis von Dickinson, Dora Herxheimer, Gräfin Luise Schwerin and Frau

Alice Faehndrich, and that at least fourteen of these personal encounters were of more than superficial importance to him: those with Gwen John, Bernard Shaw, Algernon Blackwood and Horatio Brown from Great Britain and with Nathan Sulzberger, the Marquise de Choiseul and Jessie Lemont from America before the war; and those with Mr and Mrs Perry, William Stewart and Harriet Cohen from Great Britain and with Henry Lüdeke and Natalie Clifford Barney from America after the war. Most of these encounters were agreeable and cordial, and only one was distinctly unpleasant and calculated to confirm Rilke in the unfavourable estimate of the English-speaking world that he often professed—that with the Marquise de Choiseul. It seems legitimate, therefore, to ask whether his unfriendly utterances on these matters should really be accepted at their face value.

X

RILKE'S REAL QUARREL WITH THE ENGLISH-SPEAKING WORLD

But the English invented political economy, and that is something for which the genius of humanity will never forgive them.

Naphta in THOMAS MANN'S *Magic Mountain*

RILKE'S prejudice against the English language, with all the elaborate and far-reaching consequences he derived from it, was, at bottom, not different from the kind of prejudice that many people of all countries easily have against a language of which they know very little. Thus English and also French people are readily prejudiced against the 'guttural' German language, which is not in reality so guttural as all that—nothing like so guttural, for example, as Dutch or Danish or braid Scots. Rilke's prejudice was of the same category as the aversion which English people and Americans easily entertain against one another's mode of speaking. That Rilke should have thought he could afford, in the one single case of English, to indulge, not without something near to affectation, so parochial a prejudice, and even to pride himself on it, is likely to trouble us a good deal more in our sensitiveness as admirers of Rilke than in our sensitiveness as champions of our mother tongue.

If the type of person with whom Rilke everywhere came in contact had been less interested in and less well-informed about the English language and English literature and culture, it is likely that he himself would have taken more interest in them. Here was a wide range of topics which were always liable to turn up, and confronted with which Rilke, through the unfortunate circumstances of his education, was always at a disadvantage. It has already been seen (above p. 37 and p. 40) that Rilke allowed people to suppose that he knew much more than he really did know in this field (as indeed also in certain other fields) before his reputation was fully established, and much less than he actually knew after it was established. From about 1910 onwards he not only frankly admitted that comparative ignorance of everything connected with the English-speaking world which previously he had as a rule tried to conceal; he very much exaggerated it and even in a sense almost boasted of it. He was here in a situation not unlike that of the fox with the grapes: his knowing so much less about things English and particularly about the English language, than everybody expected him to know, seemed to prove that there must be something wrong here either with him or with everything English; and the decision which his unconscious mind arrived at in this dilemma was probably in the first place determined quite as much by the desire not to feel himself in the wrong as by any definite, arguable criticisms that he had to advance against the English-speaking world and its works. Where a total ignorance that saves one all sorts of complications and embarrassments can be more or less deliberately cultivated, an antipathy which cuts off all discussion may also be half-consciously fostered and encouraged, until it becomes second nature and really invincible. Something of this kind would seem to have happened in Rilke's dealings with the English language, and with various other things too. Rilke indulged in irrational antipathies against music, mountains, Austria, Germany, Switzerland, Goethe and the Christian religion, as well as against all things English; and that he could, if it came to the point, overcome such prejudices without too much effort, is shown most strikingly in his conversion to Goethe and in his partial conversion to music in the years immediately before the 1914 war, when he for a time set about broadening the basis of his cultural attainments on comparatively traditional lines.

It is not suggested here that Rilke had no serious, genuine and arguable quarrel of his own with the English-speaking world, but only that there is a strange discrepancy between this real quarrel and the vague, often trite and stereotyped anti-English sentiments which he habitually utters—sentiments which in any case seem in a considerable measure belied by the cordial relationships unobtrusively existing between him and quite a number of British and American people and books. It is noticeable that in all his derogatory utterances on this subject he hardly ever indicates what it is that he objects to; instead he produces a long series of variations on the word 'fremd' (alien), of which there can be no doubt that it here always expresses disapprobation and distaste. J. R. von Salis writes in this connexion:

Alien to him were all environments that owed their character too perceptibly to the Reformation—for example, North Germany and Zürich; and it was undoubtedly in the first place Puritanism that estranged this otherwise so cosmopolitan-minded man from England and from everything Anglo-Saxon.[1]

There is certainly something in this, though it must be remembered that Rilke loved such emphatically Protestant lands as Denmark and Sweden and was not unduly repelled by the Puritanism of Kierkegaard. Ultimately, of course, Puritanism is thoroughly odious to Rilke, and that is a consideration that may well have played some part in determining his unfavourable attitude towards the English-speaking world. But the only occasion on which this particular sentiment is expressed by him is in the early *Two Stories of Prague*, where there is mention of a 'stiff and horrified English governess'. (See above p. 62.) I would suggest that the decisive factor in Rilke's attitude should be looked for elsewhere. One can at least be certain that the parliamentarian system of democracy of which we are so proud would rather have repelled than attracted him, despiser as he was of 'ce parlementarisme vide et vaniteux' (17 January 1926 to Duchess Gallarati Scotti). That opposite feature of our character, however, that we 'love a lord', might well have attracted him, for nobody ever loved a lord more dearly than he did.

It has already been suggested above (see pp. 63–4) that Lou Andreas-Salomé's anti-British sentiments and particularly her fierce outbreak against England of March 1904 on the occasion of the Russo-Japanese war probably influenced Rilke profoundly and may well have led to his seeing England as the enemy and, still more important, as the exact opposite of his beloved Russia. A passage in one of the *Two Stories of Prague* particularly clearly illustrates what this would involve. Rezek, as representative of the Czech people, says:

> Our people are like a child. I often realize that our hatred of the Germans is not at bottom anything political, but something—how shall I put it?—something human. Our grievance is not that we have to share our native land with the Germans; but having to grow up in the midst of a nation that is already so very grown up—that is what makes us sad. It is the story of a child that grows up amongst adults. . . .[1]

Peter Demetz comments on this: 'To see in the Czechs a naive, still immature people, was by no means Rilke's own personal and original idea.'[2] Whether it was 'original' or not matters little—but it certainly was 'personal', in the sense that Rilke was here operating with conceptions that belong very much to his own peculiar mode of experiencing and interpreting life. That he happens to be speaking about the Czechs here is the least important point in what he says—for he never really loved the Czechs very warmly for their own sake (see above pp. 13–14 and 23) and even in the brief year or so, 1895–6, when he more or less fraternized with them, he tended to make them symbols for private visions and aspirations of his own. What is important and remains important throughout Rilke's life is the distinction here made between 'childlike' and 'grown-up' nations. In Rilke's experience and work everything turns—as was pointed out with admirable discernment and penetration by Rudolf Kassner[3] as early as 1927—upon partisanship for the child against the adults. He imagines and also, as far as possible, puts into practice paradoxical new ways of growing up, so to speak, without really growing up. 'I am a child who would like to be surrounded by nothing but more and more adult childhoods,'[4] he writes in 1915. These aspirations of Rilke's are indeed counterpointed all along by others of just the opposite kind, which manifest themselves, for example, in his devotion to Rodin, Kassner and Valéry as masters of grown-up maturity—but that does not concern us here. What does concern us is that Rilke projects his partisanship for the child against the adults into the relationship between the nations. The classification of nations as childlike or adult, formulated in so many words as early as 1897 in the *Two Stories of Prague*, underlies tacitly all Rilke's later judgments on national characters and traditions, down to his death—and the nations he loves are, in his eyes, all of them childlike ones. That he sees the Russians as a childlike people is so obvious that there is no need to cite special evidence for it. But the same is true of the Scandinavian peoples: Denmark is for him above all the land of Jacobsen who 'had no experience, no love, no spiritual adventure and no wisdom, nothing but a childhood';[1] Sweden is for him the land of Ellen Key's *Century of the Child*; 'these Nordic men and women seem to have bright childhoods,'[2] he writes in 1902; Denmark lives in his work above all in the childhood memories of Malte Laurids Brigge, Sweden in his essay on the *Samskola*, that reform school in which childhood is treated not as a mere prelude to adult existence, but as a state with its value and justification within itself. And—strangest paradox of all—so it is also even with Rilke's way of seeing France and the French. When Rilke had been violently attacked by the German nationalistic press in 1925 for having said, 'all the nuances of happiness or unhappiness or solitude I discover only in the faces of the people of Paris,' Friedrich Märker shrewdly defended him with the assertion that one might just as well say: 'Rilke has gone into raptures over the French in just the same way as Gauguin went into raptures over the negroes.'[3] It is quite true that just what delights Rilke about the French, the way in which, according to him, everything they feel at once appears in their faces, is the token of a comparatively primitive, childlike people and would be disclaimed as a weakness by a nation that prided itself on its adult maturity. Few may perhaps concur in Rilke's estimate of the French people as comparatively childlike—he himself, in that very passage in his early story of 1896–7 in which he speaks of the Czechs as childlike, had cited the French, whose 'culture is the last word in refinement', together with the Germans as examples of an adult nation. That, however, was long before he had been to France or begun to feel any enthusiasm for French culture. There are plenty of indications that he soon after 1902 began to think of the French as comparatively primitive and childlike, and that this endeared them to him—one has only to read, for example, his delightful description of his hopelessly inefficient and old-fashioned post office in Paris, in the letter to Magda von Hattingberg of 19 February 1914, beginning: 'You have no idea how—what shall I call it?—how home-made ['hausgemacht'] such post offices are here, with their constantly hotted-up penholders and blotting-paper....' A certain measure of inefficiency commends itself to Rilke as naive, childlike, guileless, while all smart and ostentatious efficiency is suspect to him as grown-up, dictatorial, insensitive and ruthless. Only in the case of his own native Austria was his resentment too strongly engaged from the outset for inefficiency to charm him as a mark of childlike ingenuousness.

Whether it is in the Czechs, in the Russians, in the Danes, in the Swedes, in the French or in the Valaisans that Rilke finds something that strikes him as being in its own way comparatively childlike and therefore attractive, one factor remains constant: the comparison is always, if not explicitly, then implicitly, with Germany, or rather with Prussia as the quintessence of ruthless grown-up German efficiency. Germany, at least post-1870 Germany under Prussian hegemony, is for him the adult nation *par excellence*—that constitutes a barrier still, even when he comes closest to a complete reconciliation with German culture in the years 1911–14. The specifically grown-up mentality, as Rilke sees it, is, of course, although efficient, by no means always in any deeper sense intelligent, still less wise—indeed, it is quite compatible with abysmal stupidity.

The question that arises for us out of all this is whether Rilke sees the English-speaking peoples as childlike or as grown-up—and although he makes no explicit statement in these terms, there can be no doubt that he saw them as, in his sense, grown-up. The somewhat sulky evasiveness with which he speaks of them is exactly the same as that with which, in his frequent role of the eternal child, he speaks of the 'grown-ups'. If he had seen anything childlike in them, they would not have been 'alien' to him. It was probably never brought home to him how much British literature has been taken up with the mystery and magic of childhood, from Blake's *Songs of Innocence* and Wordsworth's *Immortality* ode to *Alice in Wonderland* and the sugariness of *Peter Pan*. One English writer representative of such tendencies in whom he took an interest was G. K. Chesterton, while Shelley, particularly as portrayed by André Maurois, delighted him as a childlike type—but these two, whom he in any case only encountered shortly before his death, obviously could not be expected to determine his conception of the British peoples in their totality. At most one could suppose that he may have thought of the Irish as a childlike nation by comparison with the other inhabitants of the British Isles—a view in which above all Synge's *Playboy of the Western World* could have encouraged him. Least of all is it to be supposed that the often insisted on 'youthfulness' of the American peoples ever struck him as having anything in common with that childlikeness which attracted him in the Russians, the Scandinavians and the Latin races. On the contrary, the Americans, with their cult of efficiency, smartness and success, could not fail to strike him as being outstandingly and objectionably adult (in *his* sense), much like the Prussians. In fact, his amplest and most explicit indictment of Prussia culminates, as we have already seen (p. 24) in the phrase: 'I have always detested German nationalism as the pretentiousness of *a vaguely Americanized parvenu*.'[1] In his eyes America and Germany belong closely together just at that point where Germany is most offensive to him. That these are no mere vague and abstract considerations which lead nowhere in particular becomes clear when we see them in relationship to the highly important problem of Rilke and the machine.

In Rilke's world, which was a world beyond good and evil, the role of the old diabolical principle was chiefly played by the machine, by the whole mechanizing process of modern technical civilization. Just as, in his judgement, the principal manifestation of the abhorred adult mentality on the spiritual plane was Christianity, so also its principal manifestation on the physical plane was the machine. The machine, however, in its modern form, with the industrialism which it gave rise to, had its birth in England and came to its fullest unimpeded development in the United States. Probably few of us would nowadays claim that the industrial revolution has proved or is ever likely to prove an unmixed blessing either for our own land, where it was begotten, or for the rest of the world. Whether or not we are prepared to admit that it has contaminated our cultural tradition with a somewhat broader and drabber streak of materialism and philistinism than is to be observed in most other countries, it should at least be intelligible to us that many foreign onlookers and critics in all good faith regard it as having done so. Considerations of this kind lead to Oscar Wilde's feelings about England, as formulated in one of his American lectures, being so mixed: 'This dull land of England, with its short summer, its dreary rains and fogs, *its mining districts and factories, and vile deification of machinery*, has yet produced very great masters of art, men with a subtle sense and love of what is beautiful, original, and noble in imagination.' In much the same way Arthur Symons, in his *Studies in Seven Arts*, which Rilke, as we have seen, happened to possess, raises and answers the questions:

Has the sense of beauty, the sense of proportion, gone completely out of the modern English mind? . . . Are we wholly deficient as a race in any fine sense of beauty outside picture frames and the covers of books? By no means. . . . (But) modern craftsmanship is the *craftsmanship of the machine, those deadly pistons and hammers have got into our very brains*. . . . We pride ourselves on being a *business nation*: look at the result. The Americans pride themselves on being *an even more business-like nation*; and has any beautifully made thing come out of America since we colonized it?

These are considerations which count also for a great deal in Rilke's hostile estimate of Great Britain and of the United States.

We naturally find ourselves wishing that we could only once have got Rilke on to the shores of this country. We think of all the things we would eagerly have shown him and of which he appears to have known nothing—though Princess Marie Taxis, Rudolf Kassner and many others quite certainly talked to him about them. We would have shown him Oxford and Cambridge—but should we have let him see the Black Country and the Potteries? We would have shown him villages in Suffolk and Devon—but should we have let him see a typical London suburb? We would have shown him Edinburgh—but should we have let him go near Glasgow? We can feel fairly confident that he would have been delighted by many of the old country mansions[1] with their parks and their social life, as they were before 1914—and furthermore that he would somehow have gained admission to them as a favoured guest in less than a fortnight. It is even conceivable that he might, instead of being simply revolted by the worst London slums, have come to adore them with a perverse adoration, as he did the slums of Paris. What would have been really unendurable to him is our streets full of smart, standardized multiple shops, the grossness of our restaurants, the uninspired, ready-made cheery-and-brightness of our popular holiday resorts at the height of the season. One would have had to shepherd him through the land as Quaker delegates are shepherded through the Soviet Union. There are forms of sheer vacuity and shoddiness, of blatant good-natured bad taste spread far and wide and taken universally for granted in this country, for which it would be difficult to find any parallels elsewhere in Europe. There is enough there to put off very much more kindly disposed and less sensitive foreign observers than Rilke would have been—and they often are put off. It would have been a risky thing to get Rilke over the English Channel—especially if he had been coerced into the journey by well-meaning friends and had entered into it with the same kind of tacit, preconceived resolution not to be deeply impressed as he did upon his reading of Shakespeare. Nor can one be fully confident that even the finest things Great Britain has to show would have evoked more than a perfunctory response from Rilke. He knew most parts of Germany very well, and yet how little the finest buildings and landscapes there, buildings and landscapes it is worth travelling half way round the world to see, really ever meant to him, after 1902! He pays his due tribute to the 'pretty German Gothic' of St Elizabeth's Church in Marburg[1] in 1905 and 1906, and to the stained-glass windows and statues at Naumburg in 1911,[2] but the cathedral as it really moves him and assumes symbolical significance in the *New Poems* and the seventh *Duinese Elegy*, is still for him always and only the French cathedral, Rodin's cathedral, and Gothic is for him pre-eminently, even exclusively French Gothic. The most magnificent German buildings could not evoke so deep a response from him as a typical dingy Paris street corner. It is quite conceivable that he could have seen the Cambridge Backs from Clare Bridge or strolled through the Close of York Minster with comparative indifference.

When Rilke has in mind those industrial and technical aspects of the English-speaking world which play so great a part, perhaps the principal part in rousing and maintaining his antipathy, he nearly always refers to America, the culmination, rather than to England, the cradle of these developments. It is because of these things that America means for him 'an absolute void' (see above p. 6) and that the American 'appears monstrous to him' (see above p. 39). It is not to be supposed, however, that in not referring expressly to England in this connexion Rilke was leaving us out, or making a distinction in our favour. It seems more probable that we are, so far as culture and the mind are concerned, regarded by him as part and parcel of America, since we are not in his eyes a part of Europe, and he apparently nowhere envisages the possibility of a third, commensurable cultural entity poised between America and the European continent and distinguished in character from them both. His judgment that England does not belong to Europe clearly enough implies that it really belongs to America, that morally speaking the Atlantic Ocean is narrower than the Straits of Dover.

'American' is Rilke's favourite word for those tendencies in modern civilization which he is most afraid of and repelled by—but he means it for Britain too. It is directed not so much against the people themselves as against the mechanizing processes which have originated amongst them and gained the upper hand of them, and which they find themselves compelled to accept and to serve, some of them reluctantly, but most of them uncritically and with jubilation:

> Alles Erworbne bedroht die Maschine, solange
> sie sich erdreistet, im Geist, statt im Gehorchen, zu sein.
> Dass nicht der herrlichen Hand schöneres Zögern mehr prange,
> zu dem entschlossenern Bau schneidet sie steifer den Stein.

Translated:

> Machines will destroy all our gains, if we let them usurp us,
> lording it still, as they do, in minds they were made to obey;
> relentless they grind out the free-stones for buildings all plumbline and purpose,
> ousting the chiselling hand, its wayward and delicate play.[1]

In this sense, of course, Rilke sees 'Americanism' all around him on the European continent too, dominating more and more influential groups of the continental peoples, and destined in the end to subdue them all. Of Germany's large contribution to modern mass-producing industrialism, once it had been fairly launched, he does not often expressly speak, just as he does not even expressly speak of England's ultimate responsibility for it. But he is aware of it, and it certainly counts for much in his hostility to Germany, especially as he assigns the chief blame for the 1914 war to Germany and at the same time regards that war as essentially a result and manifestation of modern industrialism and mechanization, and as having, for that reason, a more appalling character than earlier wars. All this is implied in his description of Germany as 'a vaguely *Americanized parvenu*'.

Rilke's aversion to the machine is not merely that of the Romantic or sentimentalist. In 1901, indeed, in two passages in the second part of the *Book of Hours* ('Die Könige der Welt sind alt' and 'Alles wird wieder groß sein und gewaltig') he does prophesy an idyllic future with no more machines, much in the manner of the *Dream of John Ball* and *News from Nowhere*, but it is only at this still early and immature stage in his development that he appears as a throw-back to Ruskin and William Morris. Later he is as a rule enough of a realist to regard the machine as something inescapable and irresistible; as something that must be put up with and even, in a certain sense (which many of his readers misunderstand) 'praised':

Hörst du das Neue, Herr,
dröhnen und beben?
Kommen Verkündiger,
die es erheben.

Zwar ist kein Hören heil
in dem Durchtobtsein,
doch der Maschinenteil
will jetzt gelobt sein.

Sieh, die Maschine:
wie sie sich wälzt und rächt
und uns entstellt und schwächt.

Hat sie aus uns auch Kraft,
sie, ohne Leidenschaft,
treibe und diene.

Translated:

Lord, do you hear it there,
throbbing and humming?
Prophets with zeal declare
new things are coming.

What though no ear be hale,
clangours so daze it?
Let the machine prevail;
ours but to praise it.

Machine, pound away,
blemish and slacken us,
get your own back on us.

Though you partake our strength,
you shall be tamed at length,
drive and obey.[1]

Rilke praises the machine here only because he at this point regards it as the supreme mission of the poet to praise *everything*, without discrimination, that is to say, above all, to praise what is most terrifying, suspect and odious to him, since praising what he in any case likes and approves of is easy. *That* 'does not need to be learnt first';[1] no special merit attaches to it. Only when the poet even 'extols that which tortures him' ('da er selbst noch feiert, was ihn peinigt')[2] does he show the full range of his commission and of his power. So in the *Sonnets to Orpheus* Rilke 'praises' not only the machine, but also cruelty, loathsome diseases, treachery, beggary, capital punishment, the putrescence of corpses and all other abominations. It is almost conceivable that at such a moment he might even have brought himself to bestow his blessing upon the English language. He 'praises' all these things not in themselves or for their own sake, but for the sake of 'the Whole' ('das Ganze, die Vollzähligkeit') of which they, too, form a part, and his praise does not imply moral approval or a real jettisoning of all discriminative judgment. Rilke is here in a large measure inspired by and reproducing in very much secularized and de-transcendentalized form such Old Testament utterances as Job's 'Though he slay me, yet will I trust him' (xiii.15) or the Psalmist's 'If I go down to hell, thou art there also' (cxxxix.7). Rilke's great act of faith in 'Life' no more obliterates his code of values than that of the Old Testament seers in Jehovah does the general tenet: 'I will ascribe righteousness to my Maker' (Job xxxvi.3). Even Job, immediately after he has declared: 'Though he slay me, yet will I trust him,' goes on to say: '*but I will maintain my own ways before him.*' So Rilke too 'maintains his own ways', especially about the machine, even within the very sonnet specially dedicated to its praise, and still more in the companion sonnets on the same theme.

The feeling of Rilke about America as the land of the machine is, after all, by no means peculiar to him. It is a feeling that many other continental Europeans have had about America since long before Rilke was born; it is a feeling that very many inhabitants of Great Britain have had about America; it is a feeling that many

Americans themselves have had about America. What is interesting is the particular way in which Rilke intensifies and formulates this wide-spread feeling and relates it to his other apprehensions and aspirations, so that it comes to play a central part in his greatest work, the *Duinese Elegies*.

On 28 October 1893 the seventeen-year old Rilke records naively in a still unpublished diary that he has just become a member of the 'ICA' (? International Correspondence Association) and looks forward to indulging in extensive literary 'correspondence both of a learned and of a practical and entertaining character with all parts of the world... with Egypt, *America*, even with the Faroe Islands'. Nothing seems to have come of these aspirations, and it is not long before we find Rilke referring to America in that hostile tone which he seldom departs from to the end of his life.

On 16 October 1832 the Austrian poet Lenau (Nikolaus Franz, Edler von Strehlenau), who had shortly before landed in the United States, full of the most sanguine hopes and enthusiasms, wrote in a letter:

> The American has no wine, no nightingale. Let him listen to his mocking-bird over a glass of cider, with his pocket full of dollars, I would rather sit with the German and listen, over his wine, to the beloved nightingale, even though he has less in his pocket. Brother, these Americans have the souls of shopkeepers, they are dead to all life of the mind, as dead as mutton. The nightingale is in the right, not to visit these fellows. It seems to me seriously and profoundly significant that America has no nightingale. It seems to me like a poetic curse.

At the age of twenty Rilke read these words of Lenau's and they made a considerable, perhaps also an abiding impression on him. In June 1896 he wrote to a friend from Budapest:

> I don't know how it is, but things are going with me on my journey to Hungary as they did with Lenau on his to America. I too miss the *nightingale*—my lyrical mood.[1]

America appears to Rilke throughout his life a region unfavourable for poetry, for the 'lyrical mood'. To have to emigrate to

America seems to him the most fearful thing that could happen to one, especially when he imagines that he himself might be reduced to it. Thus on 13 February 1903 he writes to Ellen Key:

And how about Frau Ljunggren, who now, on top of everything else, has got to go to that dreadful America? Was there no avoiding it? ... She has probably by now begun her wearisome voyage to the foreign land (which I have always thought of as the most foreign of all!) ... But what is the object of it? Is it really possible, in the American country, to earn lots and lots of money with the work of one's hands, so that one can save and put something on one side for the future? Perhaps we ought to have done something of the kind.... But even if one can do that in America, make a pile of money by going into service, and save it, we still don't feel that we have enough youth and blindly trusting courage for such an undertaking.

Four years later, in a curious imaginary letter written, to please a child, as a kind of little sequel to the *Stories of God* (*Geschichten vom Lieben Gott*), Edwald the cripple, an important figure in that early work, speculates as to what has become of Rilke in all these years:

Even before I heard people talking about your unexpected departure I told the children that you were far away again, and the children asked where, and guessed at America. Then I said I didn't believe that. No, I didn't believe that. Let us leave that open, I begged the children. When he returns, then I shall know all about it.[1]

Here again Rilke evokes the extreme foreignness to his nature of America, the unthinkableness of his ever going there. As the most incomprehensible point of all in the adventures of a certain Swiss woman, Regula Engel, of the Napoleon period, whose memoirs had fascinated him in 1920, Rilke records: 'She is driven as far as America!'[2] What particularly horrifies Rilke about the death of Eleanora Duse, whom he had known personally, is that it should have occurred in America—'in an alien land—one might almost say in an alien world';[3] or again: 'in one of the countries which were not mirrors of her soul':[4] 'How she must have suffered when she died in an indifferent town of that continent which she loathed. Baltimore, Washington, Pittsburg were horrible names to her.' This feeling that the soul cannot really live outside the

Old World shows itself also on the single occasion when Rilke mentions Australia. He told Katharina Kippenberg after the war that it had quite shattered him, in looking up the history of one of the oldest noble families of the Grisons, to find against the name of the last descendant: 'Became an artisan in Australia, lost trace of.'[1] When Lisa Heise wrote to him in 1924 that there was nothing left for her but to emigrate to Canada, he was shocked: 'And such a new beginning on new soil—must it really be in the New World? Has it been impossible to find a patch of earth anywhere so that you could continue in Germany?'[2] In *Malte Laurids Brigge* the pathos of exile from Europe is evoked in the passage about Graf Christian Brahe, the hero's uncle, who has disappeared and of whom nobody knows whether he is alive or dead:

> Perhaps he is still travelling about, as was his habit; perhaps the news of his death is on its way from some remotest corner of the earth, written by the hand of his foreign servant in bad English or some unknown language.[3]

This, by the way, is the only allusion to the English language in the whole of Rilke's creative work—as the *lingua franca* of persons of dubious nationality who move about in the most godforsaken parts of the earth.

Repeatedly one sees how the word 'America' had become for Rilke a designation rather for a code of values and a mental attitude which were repugnant to him than for a country or a people. In one of his most impatient outbursts against Christianity he speaks contemptuously of

> Protestants and American Christians who still will go on brewing an infusion from these old tea-leaves which have been drawing for two thousand years.[4]

The following year he says:

> I no longer love Paris, partly because it is disfiguring and Americanizing itself, partly because I need it less.[5]

What Rilke means by Paris 'Americanizing itself' appears in part from a letter written to André Gide two months later, when he is looking for suitable accommodation for Magda von Hattingberg:

'None of the *pensions* that I knew here are suitable, and what is more they are so English and American and God knows what....'[1]

In 1918 Rilke was much irritated by a new publication of the Insel-Verlag entitled *The Gothic Spirit*, in which the author Karl Scheffler, had claimed that there is something essentially Gothic about lofty, many-storied industrial buildings. Rilke protested against this view:

> The upward elongation of factory-buildings is just out-and-out American and therefore the absolute opposite of the spirit of anything to which we could concede the name of Gothic, even in the most comprehensive sense.[2]

It is, one perceives, a revolting profanation of the word 'Gothic' in Rilke's eyes, to approximate it in any way to the kind of modern technical developments that flourish most in America. The Swiss intimates of Rilke's last years sum up their recollections of his utterances on America as follows:

> As for America, it was for him the quintessence of everything abominable, because, as he thought, there were no tradition, no fixity of abode, and therefore also no familiar landmarks there, either amongst the human beings or amongst the plants and inanimate things.[3]

Rilke's loathing of mechanization and mass-production, which led him to regard America as representing, so to speak, the diabolic principle in his world, belonged to a special sphere of mental vision, in which he by no means habitually lived. He owed something, as we have seen, to Emerson, Poe, William James and Breasted, he was on cordial terms with the young Americans Sulzberger and Lüdeke, as also with Miss Jessie Lemont and Mrs Edith Wharton, and he recognized a temperament closely akin to his own in Natalie Clifford Barney. He even surprises us by recommending the American Dewey system of cataloguing libraries to Princess Marie Taxis as 'quite practical' ('ganz praktisch')[4]—one of the very rare occasions on which he is found attaching value to that eminently American virtue of practicalness. Nor are these the only indications that Rilke's hostility towards America was not absolutely intransigent. In 1920 he wrote to his friend Elisabeth von Schmidt-Pauli, who had been living for some time in the United States and was on the point of returning there after a long stay in Germany in connexion with American war relief work. 'Manage my American capital well for me,' Rilke exhorts her, 'it would not be the only thing of mine to increase in your dear and faithful keeping.'[1] It is a puzzling passage. Possibly the phrase 'my American capital' ('mein amerikanisches Vermögen') is only figurative or playful and has nothing to do with money, at least not with any appreciable sum of money. It would be strange if it should turn out that Rilke really had money invested in America, the land which was for him 'an absolute void' and 'the quintessence of everything abominable'.

How integral the conception of America as the mass-producing land with 'no tradition, no fixity of abode and no familiar landmarks' was to Rilke's interpretation of the modern world and of life altogether, and also to his poetry, emerges from his famous letter to Witold Hulewicz of November 1925, the most important formulation of his credo—or one should perhaps rather say, the formulation of his most important credo, since Rilke was not the man to restrict himself to one credo alone. In explaining the central doctrine of the *Duinese Elegies* he speaks in this letter of the 'Laric' value (derived from *Lares et Penates*) which the things of daily use still had in the times before mass-production, when they were lovingly designed and made by hand according to local traditions, and handed down from generation to generation,—

> hardly a thing that was not a vessel in which our grandparents found human sentiment inhering, or in which they did not, in their turn, store up an additional hoard of human sentiment. But now empty, indifferent things come surging down upon us, across from America, mere semblances of things, mere dummies of life. . . . A house in the American sense, an American apple[2] or one of their vines, have nothing whatsoever in common with the house, the fruit, the grapes, into which the hopes and the pensiveness of our forefathers have been transfused.[3]

Rilke's attitude towards America is thus the opposite of that to which Goethe, impatient with our complex European cultural heritage, committed himself by implication in *Wilhelm Meisters Wanderjahre* and more explicitly in the doggerel verses of 1827:

> Amerika, du hast es besser
> Als unser Kontinent, das alte,
> Hast keine verfallene Schlösser
> Und keine Basalte.
>
> Dich stört nicht im Innern
> Zu lebendiger Zeit
> Unnützes Erinnern
> Und vergeblicher Streit.

Translated:

> America, your continent
> Is better off by far than ours—
> No basalt in your whole extent,
> No crumbling castle towers.
>
> Your soul lives at one with
> The present, unblighted
> By mem'ries long done with
> Or wranglings benighted.[1]

Without the comparatively lucid prose exposition of his ideas which Rilke gives in the letter to Hulewicz one might not recognize how much he is concerned in the difficult 7th and 9th Duinese Elegies (which mattered to him far more than the other eight) with protesting against and, so far as possible, circumventing that Americanization of the world in which so many, from Walt Whitman onwards, have seen the only true gospel for modern man. The machine has made it increasingly difficult, so Rilke thinks, for the sensitive, imaginative temperament to live on good terms with the external, physical world as in its appropriate element or as in a projection or prolongation of its own identity, to find itself mirrored by memory-hallowed, time-hallowed things all around it, and in its turn to mirror them.

In the present age, he writes, when everything seems to be volatilized and rarified, when the events that are of the greatest moment to us decline to become visible, when almost everywhere material catastrophes have taken the place of events permeated with spirit, it is the indefatigable, indifferent *machine* that represents what survives of the visible world; it is what one *sees*, it and its nasty products and super-products, born, without love, of an invention which takes nothing into account except profit, so much so that it succeeds in ignoring the vital and human meaning of a thing.[1]

(*To Duchess Aurelia Gallarati-Scotti, January 17th, 1926*)

The man of extensive cultural sympathies and comprehensive imaginative power will no longer find himself surrounded on every hand by heirlooms, as it were, from a more recent or remoter, closer or more distant common European ancestry. Even nature will no longer be what it was, now that it is being exploited and harnessed so systematically and effectively in numerable ways. What is to happen to our delicate, pensive moods, our subtle shades of emotion, in a noisy, glaring, strenuous world, a world without heirlooms or patina? Rilke's answer to this question is, to put it simply, that the soul (and for him 'soul' is just this capacity for subtle, exquisite feeling) that the soul will have, until further notice, like the camel in the desert, to live on her hump. The ancient European *Lares et Penates*, comprehensive symbols for Rilke's own particular apprehension of beauty, must be snatched away from the machine-beleaguered visible and external world, and transplanted to new temples in an unseen inner world of memory, imagination and nostalgic longing.

In setting forth this vision Rilke, in the 7th Duinese Elegy, evokes the forces of Americanization, by which all that he most cherishes is being threatened and driven into exile, under two images: that of the sky-scraper and of ferro-concrete buildings in general for the threat to our specifically human and cultural heritage, that of the electric generating station for the threat to nature and to the old comparative symbiosis between human civilization and the natural world. The *Duinese Elegies* are written with such stenographic condensation of phrase that it would be impossible to bring out the meaning of the passage that concerns us simply by translating it, either literally or freely. It runs in the original:

Wo einmal ein dauerndes Haus war,
schlägt sich erdachtes Gebild vor, quer, zu Erdenklichem
völlig gehörig, als ständ es noch ganz im Gehirne.
Weite Speicher der Kraft schafft sich der Zeitgeist, gestaltlos
wie der spannende Drang, den er aus allem gewinnt.
Tempel kennt er nicht mehr.

This may be paraphrased, with explanatory amplifications, as follows:

We no longer have any use for the old house that once stood there, so at one with its surroundings, outlasting generations. Instead, what commends itself now to our craving for practicalness is a purely abstract construction, no matter how obliquely and ruthlessly it may intrude upon and mar the former peace and harmony of the spot; a construction so abstract and soulless with its geometrical lines and its nondescript material that, even when it has been erected, it might, so far as any appeal it can make to the feelings and imagination is concerned, just as well have remained unbuilt, a mere blue-print inside the calculating-machine of a brain that devised it. Then too the spirit of the age constructs for itself vast store-houses in which to accumulate sheer bodiless power; and these storehouses, these power-stations are just as amorphous as the restless striving and tension which that same spirit of the age is for ever wringing out of all things at the expense of contemplation and repose—be it as electric current won from harnessed water-falls and sent along high-tension cables, be it as a mania for record-breaking and a worship of efficiency and success amongst human beings. As for temples, of course the spirit of the age no longer sees any sense in them.

The mechanizing process which Rilke here inveighs against on the historical plane as the 'spirit of the age', the *Zeitgeist*, bears, however, on that other, quite as important or even more important plane of his experience and thought, the geographical, another name, the name of America—or England. From the remote outskirts and obscure byways of Rilke research we have after all arrived at the very centre.[1]

XI

TRIBUTES

I've a Friend, over the sea;
I like him, but he loves me.
It all grew out of the books I write . . .

BROWNING

SOON after the 1914 war Rilke is found rejoicing—prematurely, alas!—over the revival of friendly relationships between the belligerent nations, not excluding Great Britain. On 18 January 1920 he writes to Princess Marie Taxis:

Do you get any news from England? Countess Mary Dobržensky,[1] my hostess in Nyon, came back from there three weeks ago; she writes to me: '. . . It was so beautiful and good to find in England again the things one believes in. And the many compassionate hearts for the sufferings in Vienna, and how they are working to send food there! And how everybody is working to create a new era of happiness, and how the barriers of social distinctions have fallen away in this one great effort: those are all things that give one courage to live once more.'—Nor is it as though Countess Dobržensky had only been staying with close friends and at one spot all the time; she travelled around a good deal in England and Scotland from her headquarters, which were with Theresa Hulton (now Lady Berwick, if I manage to spell it correctly).

It is noteworthy that Rilke was sufficiently interested in such matters to transcribe this long passage from Countess Dobržensky's letter. He was less indifferent to the world situation, less indifferent even to politics, than is usually supposed. No parts of Rilke's correspondence have so far been more rigorously withheld from publication than those in which he expresses himself on the more practical questions of international relationships, especially during and immediately after the 1914 war;[2] not till 1956 did his important letters to Duchess Aurelia Gallarati-Scotti appear, in which he declares himself, like D. H. Lawrence and W. B. Yeats, an enthusiastic admirer of Mussolini. There can hardly fail to be various references to Great Britain and the United States, possibly some of them quite friendly references, in this still inaccessible material.

The countries to which Rilke stubbornly refused his interest, sympathy and affection were themselves unremitting in their devotion to him, paying him a full tribute of homage during his lifetime and since his death. Whereas in France, in spite of all Rilke's close personal connexions there, hardly any translations[1] from his work were published till 1923, with the one important exception of André Gide's version of some passages from *Malte Laurids Brigge* in the *Nouvelle Revue Française* in July 1911, the English-speaking lands were here earlier in the field, only the Czechs, who began publishing translations of Rilke as early as 1896, outstripping them. The *Rodin* monograph had not been out for more than four or five weeks before, in March 1903, an English publisher began negotiations, (of which at this time nothing came) for an English version.[2] In September 1909 Jethro Bithell[3] submitted his translations of nine of Rilke's poems (five of them from the *Neue Gedichte* of 1907/8), which appeared in his anthology, *Contemporary German Poetry* in the same year. In August 1913 a certain Miss A. E. Grantham,[4] (apparently a great-granddaughter of Herder's) submitted to the Insel-Verlag an English translation of *The Lay of Love and Death of Cornet Christoph Rilke* (1899), which, however, remained unpublished.

The outbreak of war in 1914 inevitably interrupted for a considerable period all activities in England for the translating of Rilke's work and for making it known. The lead passed, however, to the United States,[5] which only became involved in hostilities with Germany much later, for a far shorter period and with less far-reaching cultural repercussions, and it was natural that, to begin with, Americans of German extraction here played the dominant part. In 1914 and 1916 Margarete Münsterberg published in two anthologies translations of eleven of Rilke's earlier poems, some of these translations appearing also separately in the *Bookman, Poetry* and *Poet Lore* in 1916. In 1915 Sasha Best published three translations of Rilke's earlier poetry in *Poet Lore*. In

1918 there appeared in New York *Poems* by R. M. Rilke, translated by Jessie Lemont,[1] with an introduction by her husband, Hans Trausil, dedicated 'To the memory of Auguste Rodin through whom I came to know Rainer Maria Rilke'. This publication with its fifty-three systematically arranged poems and its well-informed, discerning introduction, is the most comprehensive presentation of Rilke's work to appear in English within his lifetime, and takes into account his development down to 1908. Between 1919 and 1923 Jessie Lemont followed it up with translations of about ten further poems in *Poetry* and *Poet Lore*. In 1919 there also appeared in New York her translation of the Rodin monograph, in which Hans Trausil collaborated. In 1920 Ludwig Lewisohn printed translations of five of Rilke's earlier poems in the New York *Nation*. In 1921 the English translator R. G. L. Barrett[2] published in Würzburg his version of *The Life of the Virgin Mary*, specially recording that 'This translation was submitted to Herrn Rainer Maria Rilke'. In 1922 there was published simultaneously in New York and London an anthology of *Contemporary German Poetry* translated by the Americans Babette Deutsch and Avrahm Yarmolinsky, containing thirteen poems of Rilke, some of them belonging to the 1906–8 phase. In 1925 Mrs Anne Goodwin-Winslow[3] published in the *North American Review* a five-page article on Rilke's '*Book of Hours*' (*Stundenbuch*), embodying some hundred lines in her own verse translation. In May 1926 Freddie Döhle Lee published nine passages from *The Lay of Love and Death of Cornet Christoph Rilke* in the *Dial* under the title: *Nine Prose Poems*. In the previous year, 1925, B. J. Morse had begun his extremely valuable work as a Rilke translator with his anthology, *Songs in Transit*, containing four poems from the *Neue Gedichte* (1907–8). This he followed up in 1926 with *Ten Poems* (ranging from Rilke's beginnings to 1913) and with the *Second* and *Sixth Duinese Elegies*—all these translations being issued in private editions in Trieste. It is with Morse and with him alone that the extremely important *late* Rilke is given recognition during his lifetime in the form of English translation, the only other work of later date than 1908 so far translated, the *Life of the Virgin Mary* (1912), not being truly representative of his final phases.

Most of these people who were translating Rilke into English during his lifetime tried, as was only natural under the circumstances, to get into touch with him personally, but few of them succeeded, as he soon acquired the habit, where English translations were involved, of handing everything over to his publishers to attend to. Side by side with this translating activity there are about eleven reviews, articles and essays[1] on Rilke published in England and the United States during his lifetime to be recorded, in addition to the introductions written by Trausil and Babette Deutsch. This is perhaps a comparatively meagre harvest. The real discovery of Rilke in the English-speaking world does not begin till about 1930, manifesting itself from then onwards in a multitude of translations and critical studies which it is impossible to keep track of and which in any case do not concern us here. What is of importance to us is, however, that everything done for making Rilke known in the English speaking world during his lifetime was done without the least particle of encouragement from the poet himself. He enters into lively correspondence with his French, Danish, Italian and Polish translators, he sometimes allows himself to be interviewed, particularly for French papers, and if what at last begins to appear about him in France after 1923 is more voluminous and better informed than what is published in England or the United States before his death, the chief reason is that he himself is actively at the back of it, inspiring it and taking a lively interest in it. When it came to the point Rilke could act as his own literary agent, and do it very effectively too. Sometimes one has, however, the impression that the translations of his works, either in manuscript or in print, and the other tributes that came in an admittedly not very copious, but still quite steady flow from the English-speaking world did gratify him, and that he was even at times somewhat mollified by this recognition from a quarter whence he had so few grounds to expect it.[2] Thus he writes on 18 January 1920 to Princess Marie Taxis with reference to Jessie Lemont's translations:

A kind of friendship seems to be setting in between me and America. They have translated my *Rodin* and a selection from my poems quite decently, it would seem—at least the volumes look very respectable; and I am getting letters and even invitations to come to New York 'for a holiday'. Vous m'y voyez, n'est-ce pas?

These American relationships were not without their more substantial advantages. Thus we find Rilke on 21 March 1923 writing to Kippenberg:

Yesterday the enclosed letter from America was forwarded to me, by the Insel-Verlag, as it happens; there was a cheque with it for ten dollars. Unless you wish to make some other arrangements, I was thinking of keeping this here as a small, highly necessary reserve of pocket-money, but I would ask you to have the receipt of the payment kindly acknowledged in my name by the firm, since, so far as I can remember, I did not myself conduct the negotiations regarding these translations, and furthermore don't write English.[1]

Rilke was by no means so unpractical in business matters as is sometimes supposed.

The 1914 war was alone responsible for Rilke's fame not becoming quite definitely international a good deal earlier than it did. By the time that Europe had settled down again after the armistice, his international fame was there, as an indisputable fact, and this meant, amongst other things, that he was expected, as a matter of course, to fraternize with the outstanding Anglo-Saxon authors of the day. That he was invited by Galsworthy to represent Czecho-Slovakia at a banquet of the PEN Club in 1925 has already been mentioned. (See above p. 109.) Similarly he was invited in August 1922 to one of the famous *Entretiens de Pontigny* together with Lytton Strachey and Arnold Bennett.[2] Both of these invitations he refused, the latter reluctantly. If his health had been better in these last years of his life he would almost certainly have been brought together more or less officially with some of his outstanding British and American literary contemporaries.

When his fiftieth birthday came Rilke was a sick and almost broken man, too much occupied with anxiety on account of his health to care greatly about the tributes that day brought him.

Completely indifferent to his fame he was not, nor is it to be demanded of him that he should have been. 'Und ich brauche selbst ein wenig Ruhm'[1] ('And I even need a little fame') he had written in a draft of a poem of August 1907. But a small quantity of fame fully sufficed him, and what he wanted now above all things was neither fame nor admiration, but health. Such fantastic numbers of letters arrived for him on 4 December 1925 that they filled a large hamper, and it took him over three days to open and read them, a task which gave him little pleasure. But amongst them all one specially arrested his attention—it could hardly fail to do so, since it was of unusually large dimensions and written in the finest calligraphic script. From his reference to it when he wrote to Kippenberg on 7 December one can safely infer that it had specially pleased him.

This remarkable letter[2] was from the German Department of the University of Edinburgh. It was in German and bore the signatures of thirteen students, followed by those of the members of the staff, Edith Aulhorn, M. L. Barker, H. F. Eggeling and of the actual writer, Professor (then Dr) Otto Schlapp. In this letter, which is a penetrating summing up of Rilke's achievement down to his latest and most difficult works, couched with great tact and grace in the form of a congratulatory tribute, the following passage is of special interest:

> Since 1917 your works have been familiar to us. . . . We have followed the steep curve of your ascent, looking forward to each new work with eagerness and greeting it with joy. As teachers and learners we have devoted unforgettable hours to their interpretation.[3]

On 18 December 1925 Rilke replied with a letter which through the kindness of Dr Robert Schlapp is now preserved in Edinburgh University Library. It is no mere formal acknowledgment, such as Rilke in the bad state of his health, and with a whole hamperful of letters to answer, might have been tempted to write, and it fully confirms the impression created by the mention of Edinburgh's tribute in the letter to Kippenberg, that he had been moved and delighted by the words of Professor Schlapp and his colleagues and students as by very few of the innumerable congratulations that had reached him from most parts of the world. What Rilke writes runs, in translation:

To the German Department of the University of Edinburgh,
to be delivered to Dr Otto Schlapp:

Your painstaking and ample pronouncement has been for me a great and abundant present; valuable through the assent of each one participating in it, significant through the evidence it affords that so much activity, exertion and joy of the mind could be stimulated by my books at a far distant place; gratifying through the distribution of the accents, which bears witness to a thorough and altogether appreciative study of my works—especially of the most recent ones, which are the ones that matter most to me. And finally it is altogether a true present by virtue of the liveliness and generosity of the sympathy which it expresses.

That I should, in the face of such declarations, feel myself poor, seems to me only to contribute yet further to that pure understanding between us, in which chance plays no part: for who, where the essential character of art is concerned, could ever be more than one temporarily deputed to bring to a conclusion in a special kind of obedience things initiated he himself knows not how far away?

Yet in order not to stop short at the mere expression of gratitude with which I conclude, allow me to present you and your circle with my just published translations of some of Paul Valéry's poems, for your common use—and certainly you will already have given some attention to that great poet. It makes me happy, believe me, to go on contributing some stimulus to your fellowship and your studies. I remain gratefully at one with you all on the plane of our true realities.

Rainer Maria Rilke.

It was a compliment to Professor Schlapp and his associates that Rilke should have written to them as he could only write to people by whom he felt himself understood. It counts for something that, on such an occasion as his fiftieth birthday, when he was besieged from all sides with homage, the conviction that he had many understanding readers of the kind he most wished for in just those countries which he habitually dismissed as alien to his nature, was brought home to him so arrestingly by the German Department of the University of Edinburgh.

In conclusion it may be said that throughout Rilke's career he had much ampler and livelier, much more varied and cordial relationships to the English-speaking world than he was ever himself fully conscious of or ready to admit. As in the case of his personal encounters, so also in the field of literature and art we can point to a number of impressions coming to him from that world which, without bringing about any radical revolution within him, did nevertheless penetrate to the sensitive depths of his nature. There was his abortive but not altogether unfruitful attempt to make something of Shakespeare in the years 1911–13; there was English Romanticism, which moved him most powerfully in the person of Shelley during the last years of his life, but also in the legend, at least, of Keats (1914) and in the paintings of Blake; there was Emerson, who meant much to him about the turn of the century, and Elizabeth Barrett-Browning who, in 1907, was for him an experience of the first importance; there was Pre-Raphaelitism, with the aesthetic movement arising out of it, which counted for so much in his early development from 1896 to 1903, and profoundly stirred him in the figures of Walter Pater and Oscar Wilde; there were the Anglo-Irish writers, particularly Shaw, whom he bore in mind from 1906 to his final phase, and Synge, whose *Playboy* so much impressed him at the beginning of his Swiss years; and among the various Anglo-Saxon writers whom he read in translation in his final phase two at least quite carried him away: G. K. Chesterton and above all D. H. Lawrence whose *Rainbow,* as he himself declared, meant a turning-point in his life. Taking all things together, one can claim that the English-speaking world did after all play a considerable and a by no means unfavourable part in Rilke's life and work, little though he himself realized it. In this connexion it is interesting to note that Hans Egon Holthusen,[1] one of the most competent judges on such questions, arrives at the conclusion, in his investigation of the history of Rilke's influence and fame during the thirty years since his death, that few nations have proved themselves more devoted to Rilke or more faithful in their devotion than the Anglo-Saxon ones:

There are far more definite and personal signs of Rilke-discipleship to be found in foreign countries [than in Germany], particularly in Eng-

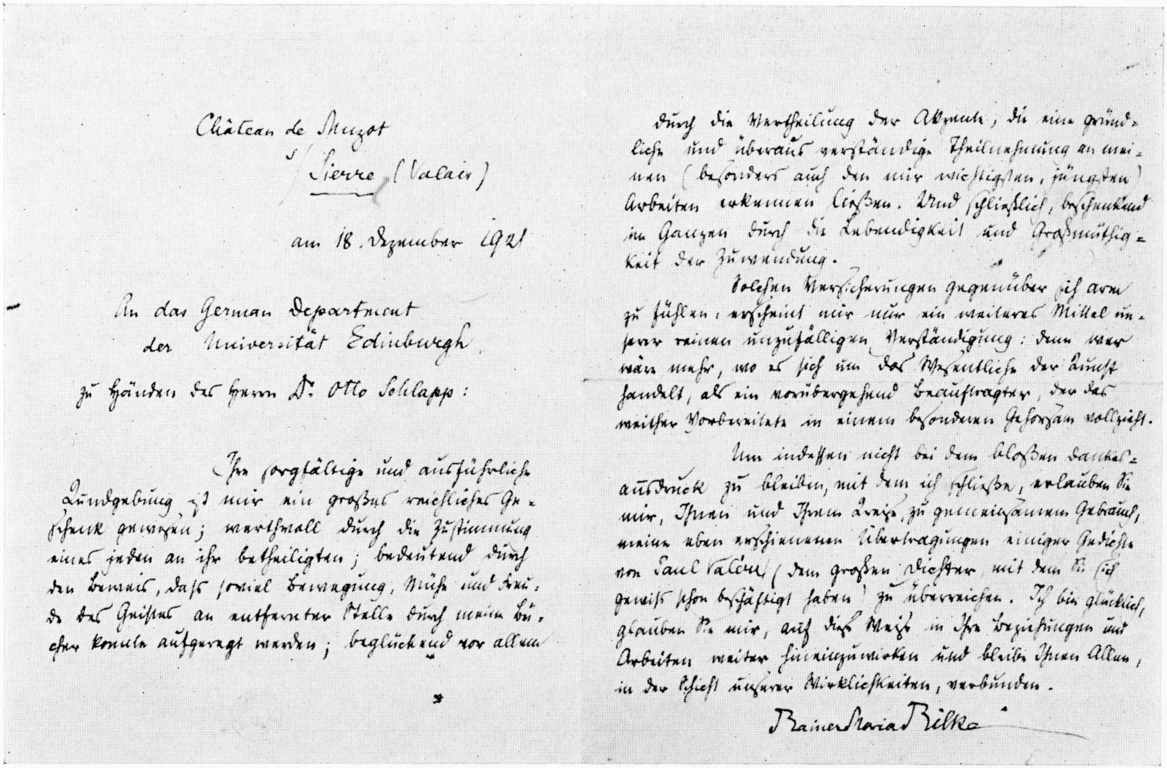

Château de Muzot
s/Sierre (Valais)

am 18. Dezember 1925

An das German Department
der Universität Edinburgh

zu Händen des Herrn Dr. Otto Schlapp:

Ihre sorgfältige und ausführliche Kundgebung ist mir ein großes wirkliches Geschenk gewesen; werthvoll durch die Zustimmung eines jeden an ihr betheiligten; bedeutend durch den Beweis, daß soviel Bewegung, Mühe und Treue des Geistes an entfernter Stelle durch meine Bücher konnte aufgeregt werden; beglückend vor allem durch die Vertheilung der Abschnitte, die eine gründliche und überaus verständige Theilnehmung an meinen (besonders auch den mir wichtigsten, jüngsten) Arbeiten erkennen ließen. Und schließlich, beschenkend im Ganzen durch die Lebendigkeit und Großmüthigkeit der Zuwendung.

Solchen Versicherungen gegenüber sich arm zu fühlen, erscheint mir nur ein weiteres Mittel unserer reinen unzufälligen Verständigung: denn wer wär mehr, wo es sich um das Wesentliche der Kunst handelt, als ein vorübergehend Beauftragter, der das meiste Vorbereitete in einem besonderen Gehorsam vollzieht.

Um indessen nicht bei dem bloßen Dankesausdruck zu bleiben, mit dem ich schließe, erlauben Sie mir, Ihnen und Ihrem Kreise, zu gemeinsamem Gebrauch, meine eben erschienenen Übertragungen einiger Gedichte von Paul Valéry (dem großen Dichter, mit dem Sie sich gewiss schon beschäftigt haben) zu überreichen. Ich bin glücklich, glauben Sie mir, auf diese Weise in Ihre Beziehungen und Arbeiten weiter hineinzuwirken und bleibe Ihnen Allen, in der [illegible] unserer Wirklichkeiten, verbunden.

Rainer Maria Rilke

Rilke's letter to the German Department of the University of Edinburgh of 18 December 1925.
(See text p. 173.)

land and America. . . . The distinctive feature in the most recent phase of the history of Rilke's influence, that is to say, the situation in the 'fifties, is that his exceptional status remains unchallenged and his fame unquestioned in all the other countries of the free world, whereas in the German-speaking territories it has to contend with a powerful current of partly serious, partly cheap and platitudinous antagonism. . . .

These are developments that Rilke himself, of course, could not foresee, but to which he would by no means have been indifferent. If he could have foreseen them, he might have taken a kindlier view of us.

Ernst Robert Curtius, criticizing in 1948 the Good-Europeanism of Mr T. S. Eliot, writes: 'Seen from Anglo-America the Latin Spirit was in fact Europe. . . . In this kind of Europe there was no place for Germany.'[1] This acute criticism could be applied also in considerable measure to the later Rilke who, in his enthusiasm for the Latin Spirit, was ready to exclude not only England, but also Germany from his Europe. But the Latin Spirit itself, as he discovered, and as Mr T. S. Eliot—who has long since made amends for the one-sidedness of which Curtius would convict him—also has discovered, recognizes, at its best, that it needs to be supplemented both by Germany and by England. Even Rilke's own experiences throughout his lifetime with people and with books refute his impatient, disparaging declarations to Betz of 1925 and testify, when one examines them dispassionately, that, whether he was conscious of it or not, England after all did, no less than Germany, belong to Europe as he knew it.

EXCURSUS I

RILKE AND THE GESTURE OF WITHDRAWAL

PARTICULARLY characteristic of Rilke is what may be called the gesture of withdrawal. It appears not only in his relationship to the English-speaking world, but again and again, under innumerable different guises, in his dealings with all things, both in his life and in his work, and presents one of the chief difficulties in all attempts to tie him down to any one set of convictions or beliefs, because he always withdraws himself from his own professions of faith—which is something different from simply repudiating them. Indeed, this gesture of withdrawal tends itself to assume for him a quasi-doctrinal character, especially when he pronounces on love and on God. What really interests him most in all human relationships, particularly in those between man and woman and between children and parents is the question, 'why people who love one another separate before there is any need for them to do so.'[1] The many women he loved, or tried to love, all of them had sooner or later in one way or another to see him withdraw himself from them, and to find it expected of them that they should accept this withdrawal as the natural, necessary and highest culmination of his love. One might even say of him that, in dismissing marriage as a mere conventional bourgeois contract, he assigns to divorce something of the sacramental sanctity usually associated with matrimony—and on at least two occasions his friends are found exerting themselves to keep him out of the divorce court.[2] With a curious fervour he congratulates Paula Modersohn[3] in 1906 on leaving her husband and R. H. Junghanns[4] in 1921 on leaving his wife, and he specially urges the latter not to relent out of pity in his step. Similarly in 1896 he is found urging Siegfried Trebitsch[5] to break away from his parents and in 1898 he presses advice of the same kind on a Russian girl, Helene Woronin in Viareggio:[1] 'Go away from your home.... Go away and don't think of returning.' What attracts him so much in one of his favourite figures, the Prodigal Son, is not his return, but his departure: 'Und dann doch fortzugehen, Hand aus Hand' ('And yet to go away, hand out of hand'), he says in the poem 'Der Auszug des verlorenen Sohnes' in the *Neue Gedichte*. So it is that he can re-interpret the Prodigal Son in *Malte Laurids Brigge* as 'the one who did not want to be loved' and who resolved 'never to love, so as not to bring anybody into the awful position of being loved'. In speaking of the return of the Prodigal Son on this occasion Rilke transforms the 'unheard of gesture' with which, according to tradition, he asks his father's forgiveness, into a gesture of withdrawal, 'the beseeching gesture with which he cast himself at their feet, *imploring them not to love him*.'[2] Herbert Steiner, who knew Rilke personally, speaks of his way of 'giving and withdrawing himself at one and the same moment with the most tender politeness',[3] and many other of his acquaintances have recorded the same impression. He himself confirms it in his words to Magda von Hattingberg in 1914: 'But wherever I was under an obligation to life, I have withdrawn myself.'[4] He appeals, however, to the highest precedent to justify this procedure—he is only behaving, he says, as the gods themselves behave: 'There is nothing I understand better in the life of the gods than the moment when they withdraw themselves. What would a god be without the cloud that screens him? What would be the good of a used-up god? Duino is the cloud of my being; away from everything and everybody, to live in withdrawal! You feel, don't you, how much that is what I need?'[5] It is not, however, as often used to be supposed, the actual *state* of being withdrawn ('Abgeschiedenheit', 'Entrückung') that Rilke really desires—he can never endure that for more than a few months at most; what he has to experience again and again is the *process* of withdrawing himself, and for this he has constantly also first to go forward, to return, to offer himself. On one occasion he describes himself as 'a place where giving and taking back have often been almost one and the same thing, so swiftly would the most genuine impulse swing round to its opposite.'[1] The moment of withdrawal is for him the creative moment.

EXCURSUS II

PROBLEMS OF THE DUINESE CREDO

THE interpretations of the 18th of the Sonnets to Orpheus (Part I) and of the passage on the *Zeitgeist* in the seventh Duinese Elegy given above on pages 158 and 165-6 differ sharply, it may be noted, from those commonly accepted. It is taken for granted by most critics and translators that Rilke identifies himself with the 'prophets' of the new mechanized order of things in the sonnet, and with the *Zeitgeist* in the elegy, instead of polemically dissociating himself from both alike. What misleads the critics here, and in many similar cases, is the fallacious belief from which they set out, and for which Rilke himself must indeed largely be held responsible, that he is never in the opposition, that it is incompatible with his nature ever to resist or revolt against anything. It would be truer to say of him that he is *always* in the opposition, though as a rule it remains a curiously disguised and therefore easily overlooked kind of underground opposition. Thus his concern in the sonnet and elegy before us is, how to circumvent modern technical developments by apparently capitulating to them. Some light is thrown on the way in which his mind works in such matters by what he writes to A. de V. on 25 August 1915:

> What is called upholding 'ideals' at bottom only means not allowing one's faith in one's own inner world, the world one inwardly aims at, to waver, even though the most alien, nay hostile realities confront one and are in the right against one.

The machine was just such an 'alien, nay hostile reality' for Rilke, against which he felt he had to defend the 'world he inwardly aimed at'. The paradox of his peculiar mode of resistance and revolt by apparent submissive and passive self-surrender is the central secret of his nature and his art—so long as one fails to understand it, one goes wrong about him at every turn. One of his most illuminating expositions of this idea—for to the last it remains only an idea, and a never fully realizable one—is in a letter to General-Major von Sedlakowitz of 9 December 1920:

There is, at least for the Slavonic soul, a degree of submissiveness so perfect, one might well term it, that it establishes for that soul, even under the harshest and most crushing oppression, something in the nature of a secret breathing space, a fourth dimension to its existence, in which, however irksome circumstances may become, a new, infinite and truly independent freedom begins for it.

Similarly Rilke on another occasion, in writing to one of the angry young men of those days, advocates, instead of the open revolt which he had himself to begin with indulged in, a subtler policy of what he calls 'escaping into the depths' ('Ausweichen ins Tiefere'):

—that they [i.e. his youthful readers], instead of revolting against the pressure of circumstances, should rather make it serve as an agency to install them in a denser, profounder and more personal stratum of their own natures.[1]

Rilke's apparent submission to the machine in the 18th Sonnet to Orpheus is just such a submission with mental reservations and ulterior motives as is indicated in these two letters, that is to say, it is only a veil concealing a peculiar form of revolt. Rilke is very far here from making common cause with the 'Verkündiger', with the latter-day prophets who enthusiastically welcome modern technical developments, believing in them and looking forward to the solution of all human problems from them. On the contrary, he dissociates himself from these machine-worshippers; his own 'praising' ('Loben') is fundamentally different from such naive, uncritical enthusiasm, and takes place on quite a different plane. He praises the machine *in spite of* what it is and does, not *because of* what it is and does. Three months before writing this sonnet Rilke had expounded the ideas embodied in it in a letter to Countess Mariette Mirbach:

If in the old days, when the Flood was trying to subside, there had been newspapers, as there are now, I am sure that the waters would *not* have subsided, or at most would only have done so artificially, through the invention of some enormous pumping machine which, as is always the way with machines, would in some other radical manner have *got its own back* on mankind, making them pay dearly for the service it had rendered them.[1]

Here is exactly the same expression—'sich rächen'—applied to the machine as in the sonnet; in both cases the machine is only personified in order that some treacherous, vindictive and malevolent instincts may be attributed to it. The most striking passage, after the sonnet here discussed, in which Rilke 'praises' the machine is in the *Letter from a Young Artisan* (see above p. 115), also written in February 1922:

The machine, for example, is something I can't explain to Christ; he doesn't take it in. . . . God, on the other hand—I have the feeling that I could bring my machine and its firstborn to Him, or the whole of my work, indeed, there is easily room for it all in Him.

That Rilke here seems ready to speak comparatively favourably of the machine is probably to be accounted for by the circumstance that he is for the time being concerned in the first place with something against which he has an even more deepseated aversion, namely Christianity. Of all the innumerable poetic masks variously assumed by Rilke in his work, from that of the pious Russian monk onwards, none is more remarkable than that of the young artisan, about whom much more might be said.

In his Sonnets Rilke personifies the machine as a daemonic being, distinct both from humanity and from nature, though deriving powers from each. As against this view it might be contended that the machine is simply the objective manifestation and affranchisement of something within human nature, within *all* human nature, not only that of its inventor; a materialization of what Nietzsche calls the 'Will to Power'. If this is so, the responsibility for the machine rests inalienably and solely *with man himself*. Whether one worships and trusts the machine or not, would, on these assumptions, simply be a matter of whether one approves of and has confidence in those elements in human nature which it embodies and exalts above the rest. To say, then, with Rilke and with so many others, that the machine should serve man, instead of dominating him, is, in this view, only another way of saying that man should control *himself*, should revise his 'code of values' or 'change his heart'. The 'new' problems presented by the machine are only the oldest of all human problems recurring under another guise and in far acuter form.

Most of what has been said here about Rilke's machine sonnets applies also to the passage on the *Zeitgeist* in the seventh Duinese Elegy. Many examples could be cited of this passage being misinterpreted, as though Rilke here regarded himself as being in partnership with and speaking in the name of the *Zeitgeist*, and as though that 'tense urgency' ('spannender Drang') which he describes as being generated from all things by that *Zeitgeist* were to be equated with his own poetic aspiration to transmute the external, visible world into something timeless, inward and invisible. It is interesting to see what Countess Nora Purtscher-Wydenbruck makes of this passage in her version which, she claims (see above pp. 52–3), had the benefit of being posthumously censured, revised and approved by Rilke himself:

In the place of a durable house
A phantom *we build* intervenes, standing athwart it, *so clearly*
Imagined that it seems *preserved entire in our brain.*
The spirit of the age creates vast stores of power,
Formless as is the urge it draws from all things....

The bitter, denunciatory terms which Rilke had devised to express his dislike for the modern ferro-concrete structure that ousts the mellowed old house have, without any warrant, been twisted round here into something innocuous and reassuring that could apply to, and is meant to apply to, the poet's own invisible perpetuation of the same old house within his inner world: 'erdachtes Gebild' becomes 'a phantom we build'; 'zu Erdenklichem völlig gehörig' becomes 'so clearly imagined'; and 'als ständ es noch ganz im Gehirne' becomes 'preserved entire in our brain'—

as though the brain ('Gehirn') could ever symbolize Rilke's invisible world, which he always closely associates or identifies with his favourite image of the *heart.* The word-constellation 'erdacht-erdenklich-Gehirn' can, in accordance with Rilke's linguistic values, only have a polemical, pejorative sense in this context. Two other words with similar pejorative meaning, which sufficiently indicate the polemical, satirical purport of the whole passage, 'quer' and 'gestaltlos', are, indeed, perforce accurately enough translated as 'athwart' and 'formless', but the clue they provide to the interpretation of the passage as a whole has not been recognized, so that their negative meaning intrudes unaccountably in an apparently affirmative context, just as there is also no sign of awareness that the 'vast stores of power' here referred to are the electric power-stations which Rilke abominates, and can therefore have nothing in common with his own transmuting powers of poetic inwardness.

The account given here and in Chapter X of the doctrines underlying the Duinese Elegies and more or less systematically expounded in the letter to Hulewicz of November 1925 might easily produce a misleading effect, if it is not clearly realized that it is concerned only with that particular aspect of them which has a bearing on Rilke's attitude towards the English-speaking world. It is therefore desirable to indicate the ways in which this account would need to be supplemented and modified, if it were a matter of presenting Rilke's Duinese gospel comprehensively, and not just of pointing out one particular aspect of it.

Above all it should be understood that Rilke's outlook is nowhere, either in the Duinese Elegies or in the rest of his work, anything like so conservative as his detestation of industrialism and the machine and his devotion to the old *Lares et Penates* might lead one to suppose. These circumstances, taken by themselves, do indeed suggest that there must have been something almost reactionary, or at least strongly traditional about him—and so within certain limits there was, though only in a not easily comprehended, paradoxical sense. The *Lares et Penates* were the *only* traditional gods for whom he had any veneration or tenderness—nor did they mean for him, as they would for most people, belief in the sanctity of the family. Fundamentally Rilke is an extreme, consistent individualist, impatient of all disciplinary restraints exercised upon the individual's liberty by established religion, by society, by accepted ethical codes or by the family, be it in the relationship of husband and wife, or of parent and child. All these institutions, and all obligations to respect, loyalty and obedience regarded as unquestionably arising from them, he dismisses as mere convention and conventionality. No one could be on principle more revolutionary in these respects than he is. Nevertheless there is much that appeals powerfully to his solitary imagination and sensibility not, indeed, in these traditional institutions themselves, or in the beliefs and principles which they embody and without which they cannot exist, but in their trimmings and appurtenances, their regalia and ritual, their incrustations of usage and gesture, the atmosphere of solemnity, mystery, joy, sorrow or whatever else it may be that attends them. All this sensuous and emotional appanage of tradition Rilke treasures for its own sake and wishes to see conserved, but the underlying structure, tradition itself, as an ethically and intellectually binding system of convictions and loyalties, he violently rejects. Only in this sense can he be called an adherent of traditionalism. This is particularly clear in his attitude towards the Church, which is for him, characteristically, always only the Catholic or the Eastern Orthodox Church—for Protestantism he has no use at all, since Protestantism must necessarily appear to him as an attempt to preserve just those things in Christian tradition which he himself rejects, and to reject those things which he would preserve. He visited churches a great deal, often attending services too, but his attitude in doing so was almost as distinct from that of the unambiguously freethinking art-enthusiast, who is interested in the building only as a work of art or as the repository of works of art, or who is there for the sake of the music, as it was from that of the genuine believer, who is fulfilling a duty, and for whom no 'higher' motive for his attendance than that of simply fulfilling a duty is conceivable. Rilke's attitude in these matters is nearer to that of the thousands who, without belonging to any church, flock to midnight Mass on Christmas Eve in a vague sentimental urge; only he differs again from them in being not lukewarmly indifferent, but fiercely hostile to the Christian creed, and in being at the same time animated not by a vague sentimental urge, but by the keenest and most discriminating appetite for emotional stimuli which only the concrete manifestations of that creed can supply. He is like a man who whole-heartedly approves of the Mass, while whole-heartedly abhorring the Incarnation and the Atonement, which alone give to the Mass point and significance; like one who could adore the Real Presence and at the same time abominate Christ. He contrives, when the mood is upon him, to attend Christian worship, to go through the motions of it, without ceasing for a moment to hate Christianity in every form and to ponder means for eradicating it. Nor is this his attitude towards established religion alone; it is also his attitude to everything traditional, especially towards the family and marriage. The peculiar possibilities of subtle and intense emotional experience and of moving situations provided by the traditional order are precious to him almost to the point of sacredness, while that order itself fills him only with impatience.

Rilke's real problem is, how the subtlety and depth of human feeling, as they have developed under the traditional order, are to be maintained in a future where this traditional order will no longer continue to operate, and where he himself is anxious to see that it does not operate. The life of the emotions, as an end in itself, is what matters most to him. Tradition is valuable to him not for its own sake, but as having, in spite of all the faults he has to find with it, so far provided a basis and framework for the emotional life. But now it is a matter of finding another basis for this emotional life, and it must not be inferior to the old one. That the specifically modern machine-dominated mentality does not provide such a satisfactory basis for the life of the emotions appears to him self-evident. He would like to believe in the possibility of the emotional life finding its basis solely *within itself*, becoming self-poised, autonomous, independent of the external world, of human ties and of all doctrines, beliefs, ideas or principles—that is the aspiration embodied in the symbolical figure of the angel of the Duinese Elegies. But transferred to the human plane this aspiration resolves itself into Narcissism, into the impossibility of Narcissus' existence. To say that art should take the place of traditional beliefs and sanctities is, he has come to realize, only to restate the problem in a new form—or rather to revert to its original form—not to solve it. For art, at least as Rilke experiences it, arises from the impossibility either of accepting traditional spiritual values or of getting on without them, and never transcends this dilemma. Life is only problematic for him in the particular way here under discussion because art is problematic. But as the artist is incomparably better qualified than other men by his sensitivity to perceive and by his creative power to conserve those 'Laric' qualities which in Rilke's eyes constitute the sole truly valuable element in the traditional order, the doctrine of the Duinese Elegies does after all amount to a glorification in new terms of art as a substitute for religion.

APPENDIX

THE EDINBURGH GERMAN DEPARTMENT AND RILKE

PROFESSOR SCHLAPP'S LETTER (ORIGINAL)

The University of Edinburgh,
German Department.
29. November 1925.

Sehr verehrter Herr Rilke,

Vor nun mehr als hundert Jahren sandten acht Edinburgher Freunde der deutschen Literatur dem siebzigjährigen Goethe einen Geburtstagsglückwunsch. Der Krieg hat die alten von Thomas Carlyle geknüpften geistigen Bande zwischen Schottland und Deutschland nicht ganz zerrissen. Auch heute vereint sich eine Gruppe von schottischen Verehrern deutschen Schrifttums, um ihrem erwählten Meister und deutschen Lieblingsdichter am festlichen Tage seines fünfzigsten Geburtstags ihre Huldigung und den Ausdruck ihrer Dankbarkeit darzubringen.

Seit dem Jahre 1917 sind Ihre Dichtungen uns vertraut. Wir besitzen Ihre Schriften in z.T. zerlesenen und von unsern commentierenden Randbemerkungen umrankten Exemplaren. Wir haben die steile Kurve Ihres Aufstiegs verfolgt, jedem Ihrer neuen Werke mit Spannung entgegengesehen und es mit Freude begrüßt. Unvergessliche Stunden haben wir als Lehrende und Lernende dem Studium und der Interpretation derselben gewidmet. Zwei unserer begabtesten Studenten arbeiten seit einem Jahr an längeren Untersuchungen über den Stil und den Ideengehalt Ihrer Dichtung.

Dürfen wir hoffen, daß Sie unserem Bemühen, wissenschaftliche Forschungsmethoden auf Ihre Kunst anzuwenden, nicht allzu skeptisch und kaltlächelnd gegenüberstehen oder gar in solchen 'Vivisektionsversuchen' 'the last indignity of noble souls' beklagen? Wir können Ihnen versichern, daß bei unserm kritischen Bestreben, das Wesen Ihres Geistes und Ihrer Kunst durch Analyse zu erfassen, unser menschliches Interesse nicht gelitten hat, und unsere Verehrung für Ihr Werk und für Ihre Dichterpersönlichkeit, sowie unsere Dankbarkeit für Alles, was Sie uns geschenkt haben, nur vertieft worden ist. Vor drei Jahren hatten wir eine für die Kunst des Vortrags glänzend ausgestattete Studentin, die gelernt hatte, Ihre Gedichte in unserm Kreise ergreifend vorzulesen. Wir haben mehrfach in unserer Deutschen Gesellschaft Rilke-Abende veranstaltet, und wir beabsichtigen, auch in der Woche des 4ten Dezember Ihrer feiernd zu gedenken.

Wir sind uns bewußt, wenn wir Ihre Form betrachten,

> Der weiche Gang geschmeidig starker Schritte,
> der sich im allerkleinsten Kreise dreht,
> ist wie ein Tanz von Kraft um eine Mitte,
> in der BEWUSST ein großer Wille steht,—

der Wille zur Vollendung. Zugleich erkennen wir in Ihrem Werk jene polare Ergänzung des Formvollendeten, die Goethe von aller wahrhaft großen Kunst fordert: die Tiefe, die mystische Tiefe des Gehalts.

Sie schufen uns, ein neuer Orpheus, 'Tempel im Gehör'. Ihr 'Gesang ist Dasein', 'in allen Adern Dasein'. Sie sind uns 'einer der bleibenden Boten', der sein 'Leiden und Gelingen zusammenfaßt zu dauerndem Durchdringen'.

Ob wir nun Ihre Gedichte und Ihre Prosa studieren, 'um unserer Jugend den schönen echten Bruch der massiven Schmucksprache zu zeigen, die in so starken Flammen gebogen ward,' und ihr ein Gefühl davon zu geben, wie Sie mit jedem neuen Werke sich wandelnd reiften,

> den unerschöpflichen Erlös
> Königlicher Größe noch vermehrend,
> aus sich steigend, in sich wiederkehrend,
> huldvoll, prunkend, purpurn und pompös,

oder ob wir erkennen:

> Alles wird Weinberg, alles wird Traube
> in seinem fühlenden Süden gereift

für den, dessen

> Herz die vergängliche Kelter
> eines den Menschen unendlichen Weins

ist, wir möchten Sie in diesen Tagen erinnern an die auserwählte Schar Ihrer dankbaren Freunde, mit denen auch wir uns glückwünschend vereinigen, um Sie 'nur ein Lächeln lang' die tiefe Einsamkeit des Dichters vergessen zu lassen:

> Ich trete die Kelter allein, und ist niemand unter den
> Völkern mit mir.

Sie dürfen die wundervollen Worte Ihres 'Magnificat' auf sich selbst anwenden:

> Daß Er mich fand. Bedenk nur; und Befehle
> um meinetwillen gab von Stern zu Stern—
> Verherrliche und hebe, meine Seele,
> so hoch du kannst: den Herrn.

Möge die Wiederkehr des festlichen Tages Ihnen noch oft die Zeugnisse der Verehrung und Dankbarkeit Ihrer Freunde erneuern und ins Gedächtnis rufen.

Mit diesem aufrichtigen Wunsche
zeichnen wir
Ihre sehr ergebenen

(Then follow the signatures of thirteen students and of the four members of the German staff at that time.)

TRANSLATION

The University of Edinburgh
German Department.
November 29th 1925.

Dear Herr Rilke,

Over a hundred years ago eight Edinburgh friends of German literature wrote to congratulate Goethe on his seventieth birthday.

The war has not completely sundered the old cultural ties knit by Thomas Carlyle between Scotland and Germany. To-day also a group of Scottish admirers of German letters have united to offer to their chosen master and favourite German poet on the festive occasion of his fiftieth birthday their homage and an expression of their gratitude.

Since the year 1917 your works have been familiar to us. We own your writings in copies that are in part tattered from much reading and interlaced with our marginal commentaries. We have followed the steep curve of your ascent, looking forward to each new work with eagerness and greeting it with joy. As teachers and learners we have devoted unforgettable hours to their interpretation. Two of our most gifted students have been engaged for a year on ampler research into the style of your poetry and into the ideas contained in it.

May we hope that you will not regard our attempts to apply systematic methods of research to your art too sceptically or disdainfully, or even deplore in such 'experiments in vivisection' 'the last indignity of noble souls'? We can assure you that, in all our critical endeavours to grasp the character of your mind and your art through analysis, our human interest has not suffered, and that our veneration for your work and for your personality as a poet, together with our gratitude for everything you have bestowed upon us, has only been deepened. Three years ago we had a girl-student here brilliantly endowed for the art of elocution, who had learnt to recite your poems most movingly in our circle. We have often arranged Rilke Evenings in our German Society, and we intend also to celebrate you in the week of December 4th.

What we are conscious of in contemplating your poetic form is:

> Lithe sinewy tread in smallest circle wheeling
> round upon round, all soundless, never still,
> is as a magic dance whose dizzy reeling
> enrings a mighty and a CONSCIOUS will.[1]

It is the will to perfection. At the same time we recognize in your work that complementary opposite pole to perfection of form that

Goethe demands of all truly great art: the profundity, the mystical profundity of the contents.

A new Orpheus, you have created for us 'temples in hearing'.[1] Your 'song is existence',[2] 'existence in every vein'.[3] You are for us 'one of the abiding envoys',[4] who 'gathers together his suffering and his success to permanent penetration'.[5]

Whether it be your poetry and your prose that we are studying, 'to show to our youth the beautiful, genuine flexure of the massive, ornate language, as it was twisted in such mighty flames,'[6] and to give them a feeling of how you have, with each new work, ripened by transforming yourself,

> Swelling further yet the royal state
> in its inexhaustible providing,
> now soaring high, now in itself subsiding,
> pompous, purple, gracious and ornate—[7]

or whether we recognize that

> all things turn to vineyard at touch of his feeling,
> to grapes sweetly swollen with gathering must—

for him whose heart is

> a wine-press, ah! destined to perish,
> while its infinite vintage remains to mankind—[8]

—we would wish in these days to call to your mind the chosen throng of your grateful friends, with whom we associate ourselves in congratulating you, so that you may, 'only for the duration of a smile',[9] forget the deep loneliness of the poet:

I have trodden the wine-press alone, and of the people there was none with me.[10]

You may apply to yourself the wonderful words of your *Magnificat:*

> That He should find me. Think. For my sake shifting
> stars in their courses, hither-thitherward—.
> Then magnify, my soul, as high uplifting
> as in you lies: the Lord.[11]

May the return of this festive day often renew for you and recall to your memory the testimonies of your friends' homage and gratitude.

With this sincere wish
we remain
Your . . . .

RILKE'S REPLY IN THE ORIGINAL

CHATEAU DE MUZOT,
s/ SIERRE (VALAIS).
am 18 Dezember 1925.

An das German Department
der Universität Edinburgh.
zu Händen des Herrn Dr. Otto Schlapp:

Ihre sorgfältige und ausführliche Kundgebung ist mir ein großes reichliches Geschenk gewesen; werthvoll durch die Zustimmung eines jeden an ihr betheiligten; bedeutend durch den Beweis, daß soviel Bewegung, Mühe und Freude des Geistes an entfernter Stelle durch meine Bücher konnte aufgeregt werden; beglückend vor allem durch die Verteilung der Akzente, die eine gründliche und überaus verständige Theilnehmung an meinen (besonders auch den mir wichtigsten, jüngsten) Arbeiten erkennen ließen. Und schließlich, beschenkend im Ganzen durch die Lebendigkeit und Großmüthigkeit der Zuwendung.

Solchen Versicherungen gegenüber sich arm zu fühlen, erscheint mir nur ein weiteres Mittel unserer reinen unzufälligen Verständigung: denn wer wäre mehr, wo es sich um das Wesentliche der Kunst handelt, als ein vorübergehend Beauftragter, der das weither Vorbereitete in einem besonderen Gehorsam vollzieht.

Um indessen nicht bei dem bloßen Dankesausdruck zu bleiben, mit dem ich schließe, erlauben Sie mir, Ihnen und Ihrem Kreise, zu gemeinsamem Gebrauch, meine eben erschienenen Übertragungen einiger Gedichte von Paul Valéry (dem großen Dichter, mit dem Sie sich gewiß schon beschäftigt haben) zu überreichen.

Ich bin glücklich, glauben Sie mir, auf diese Weise in Ihre Beziehungen und Arbeiten weiter hineinzuwirken und bleibe Ihnen Allen, in der Schicht unserer Wirklichkeiten, verbunden.

Rainer Maria Rilke

[for translation see above p. 173]

NOTES

Where no reference is given for quotations from letters, beyond the date and the name of the receiver, the letter in question is to be found in one or other of the Insel-Verlag's chronologically arranged collected editions of Rilke's letters:

A. The 6-volume edition (1929–37), edited by Ruth Sieber-Rilke and Carl Sieber, in which 896 different letters are represented, many of them only in short extracts. (Four letters are given twice.)

B. The 5-volume edition (1939–40), also edited by Ruth Sieber-Rilke and Carl Sieber, in which 785 different letters are represented, nearly of them substantially complete; the volume for 1914–21 is taken over quite unchanged from edition A.

C. The 2-volume edition (1950), edited by the 'Rilke-Archiv' in conjunction with Ruth Sieber-Rilke and Karl Altheim, in which 435 different letters are represented, many of them only in short extracts.

Textually and in the annotations edition B shows a great advance on A, and C on B. But in contents neither of the earlier editions have been superseded by C. For serious purposes all three editions have to be used side by side, and the following facts show how difficult and pointless it would be to try to indicate with page- and volume-numbers exactly where each of the many quotations here involved is to be found:

(i) Of the 1,119 different letters represented in all three editions together, 391 occur in one of them only (188 in edition A, 65 in B, 138 in C);

(ii) 459 occur in two editions only (431 in A and B; 8 in A and C; 20 in B and C);

(iii) 269 occur in all three editions;

(iv) Letters given more or less completely in one edition (especially in B) are often represented only by short extracts in others (especially in A and C).

(v) Edition C of 1950, in giving us 138 letters not contained in A or B, is not really enriching us with new material anything like so much as at first appears. Of these 138 additional letters, no fewer than 69 (exactly half) are simply taken over from the *Briefe an einen jungen Dichter* (1929), *Briefe an eine junge Frau* (1930) and *Briefe an seinen Verleger* (1934), publications which have been much reprinted in very large numbers and can by no means be regarded as superseded. Of the remaining 69 additional letters in edition C, 40 had appeared in print previously, but were not easily accessible. Only 29 are really new, but they are extremely important.

A very large number of Rilke's letters have been published outside the three great collected editions, either in volume form (often privately) or in periodicals or as quotations in critical or uncritical studies. At the highest estimate it is, however, improbable that the total number of his letters which have up to the present in one way or another been printed, even in brief extracts, exceeds 2,500. The present writer was informed by the late Dr Carl Sieber about 1938 that Rilke wrote approximately 10,000 letters during the course of his life, and of these the great majority are certainly still in existence. There are therefore probably at least three times as many of his letters still unprinted as have so far (1958) been published. The most important and numerous groups still being withheld from publication are probably intimate love-letters and letters concerned with politics and international relationships. Enough specimens of both type of letter have, however, already begun to appear, for us to be able to form an idea of what to expect, and of how the established conception of Rilke's personality may have to be modified. For the rest, he repeats himself a great deal in his letters, especially on religious questions, and many of the still unpublished ones probably represent only slight variations on others already long since known.

The following publications of Rilke's correspondence with individuals are referred to in the notes by the abbreviations indicated:

A.G.S. *Lettres Milanaises 1921–1926* (Paris, 1956). Letters to Duchess Aurelia Gallarati Scotti, edited by Renée Lang.

A.K. *Briefe an seinen Verleger* (Insel-Verlag, 1949). Letters to Anton Kippenberg, in two volumes, replacing the less ample earlier edition in one volume of 1934.

B.K. *Rainer Maria Rilke et Merline—Correspondance* (Zürich, 1954). Rilke's correspondence with Baladine Klossowska, superseding the selections published under the title *Lettres françaises à Merline* published in Paris in 1950.

G.N. *Die Briefe an Gudi Nölke* (Insel-Verlag, 1953).

Gr.S. *Die Briefe an Gräfin Sizzo* (Insel-Verlag, 1950).

K.K. *R. M. Rilke/Katharina Kippenberg: Briefwechsel* (Insel-Verlag, 1954).

L.A.S. *R. M. Rilke/Lou Andreas-Salomé: Briefwechsel* (Zürich and Insel-Verlag, 1952).

M.H. *Briefwechsel mit Benvenuta* (Esslingen, 1954). Rilke's letters of February 1914 to Magda von Hattingberg.

T.T.H. *R. M. Rilke und Marie von Thurn und Taxis-Hohenlohe: Briefwechsel* (Zürich and Insel-Verlag, 1951, in two volumes).

Where references are given from these publications, the date of the letter has usually been regarded as sufficient, without addition of the page-number.

In the case of letters not printed in any of the major publications here described, the necessary bibliographical information is given at the first time of occurrence and referred back to with the number of the note in question, whenever occasion demands. (Here again page-numbers are as a rule not given, if the publication involved is a straightforward series of letters in chronological order.)

The same practice regarding bibliographical information is adopted in the case of references to books and articles about Rilke. No more than the necessary minimum of bibliographical detail is given. For what goes beyond this Walter Ritzer's great standard *Rilke-Bibliographie* (Vienna, 1951) should be consulted.

Titles alone have been regarded as sufficient references for all quotations from such of Rilke's own works as appear in the 6-volume *Gesammelte Werke* (Leipzig, 1930), which still remains the only complete collected edition. A supplementary volume, *Erzählungen und Skizzen aus der Frühzeit*, appeared also in 1930, and is referred to in n. 3 to p. 15, nn. 2 and 3 to p. 62, n. 1 to p. 93. Very little use could be made of the new, complete edition of Rilke's works (*Sämtliche Werke*) which began to appear in 1955, because up to winter 1958–9 only the first two of the five volumes had appeared.

* * *

PAGE xii

1 Cp. above p. 8 and n. 1 to p. 8.

2 This is shown by the still unpublished portions of Rilke's correspondence with Hulewicz.

3 C. J. Burckhardt, *op. cit.* p. 24.

PAGE xiii

1 Von Schlözer, *op. cit.* p. 33. The phrase 'our (my) country, right or wrong' appears to have been a drinking toast about 1815. I am anxious to trace the process by which it came to be adopted in the very garbled form 'Right or wrong, my country' or even 'Wrong or right, my country' as a catch-phrase by extremer German nationalists, both to expose British unscrupulousness and to condone and foster unscrupulousness in the cause of Teutonic self-aggrandisement. Imperfect knowledge of the English language leads to the phrase always being misunderstood in Germany as meaning: 'I don't care whether what I am doing is right or wrong, so long as it benefits my country.' This is something very

different from the still not unexceptionable, but comparatively innocuous true meaning: 'Even when my country puts herself in the wrong I will stick to her.' The earliest recorded form of the toast is attributed to Stephen Decatur (1816): 'Our country! In her intercourse with foreign nations may she always be in the right; but our country, right or wrong.' (See Gurney Benham's *Book of Quotations* (1907), p. 106.)

2 Leopold von Schlözer himself records that he showed the manuscript of his compilation to Rilke, who in response described it as 'something very intimate and circumstantial' ('etwas sehr Intimes und Ausführliches')—a phrase with which he committed himself to nothing. The tone of these *Gespräche auf Capri* is throughout one of consistent banality. In 1937, in the *Deutsche Rundschau*, von Schlözer contrived to print a letter of 1920 which he had received from Rilke, chiefly in glorification of Russia and France, with such omissions and underlinings of words that Rilke appears in it as an enthusiastic prophet of the Nazi system. The decisive passage, after von Schlözer had judiciously doctored it, ran: 'Who is there to help when all are perplexed and at their wits' end? Nowhere a helper, nowhere a *Führer*, nowhere some great man superior to the rest!' ('Wer hilft im ratlosen Verlorensein Aller? Nirgends ein Helfer, nirgends ein *Führer*, nirgends ein großer Ueberlegener!') The word 'Führer' had not been given any special emphasis in Rilke's original letter. One can judge from this how reliable von Schlözer's reproduction of Rilke's conversations is likely to be.

PAGE 1

1 See Stephen Spender, *Der Einfluß Rilkes auf die englische Dichtung, aus einer B.B.C. Sendung für den Fernen Osten*, trans. by Erich Fried, *Ausblick* (Pen Press, London, October 1946), pp. 21–5; W. H. Auden, 'Rilke in English' (*New Republic*, New York, 6 September 1939), p. 135; B. J. Morse, 'Contemporary English Poets and Rilke' (*German Life and Letters*, Oxford, July 1948), pp. 272–85; Hans Galinsky, *Deutsches Schrifttum der Gegenwart in der englischen Kritik der Nachkriegszeit* (Munich, 1938), pp. 216–307; Werner Milch, 'Rilke und England' (*Universitas*, Stuttgart, December 1947), pp. 1463–74.

PAGE 2

1 Rilke does, however, on two recorded occasions, just touch on Scotland and Scottish people as something distinctive; see text pp. 118 and 167.

PAGE 3

1 The attacks on Rilke seem to have appeared chiefly in the German nationalistic press in Bohemia. The *Prager Tageblatt* published on

28 November 1924 an article: 'Rainer Maria Rilke—kein Deutscher?' A similar article, 'Ein "deutscher" Dichter', appeared on 1 December 1924 in the *Reichenberger Zeitung*. For about two years these attacks would appear to have continued intermittently in this quarter. More weighty was the article in the Berlin monthly, *Der Türmer*, in August 1925, 'Rilke in Paris'. Of this alone is any record to be found in the Rilke-Bibliography of Ritzer or elsewhere. The best indication of how frequent and wide-spread these attacks must have been is the number of articles which were written in Rilke's defence; the most important ones are: 'Der Fall Rilke', Walter Mehring, in *Das Tagebuch*, Berlin, 15 August 1925; 'Rilke in Paris', Friedrich Märker, in *Berliner Tageblatt*, 19 August 1925; 'Rainer Maria Rilke', Arthur Fischer-Colbrie, in *Tages-Post*, Linz, 4 December 1925; 'Der Fall Rilke', Otto Pick, in *Literarische Welt*, Berlin, 4 December 1925; 'Der französische Dichter Rilke', E. Korrodi, in *Neue Zürcher Zeitung*, 4 July 1926.

The particular occasions of the nationalistic attacks on Rilke were: his utterances in interviews with Witold Hulewicz (October 1924) and with Maurice Martin du Gard (March 1925); his telegram of homage to President Masaryk in 1925; and the first publications of his French poems in Valéry's *Commerce* (autumn 1924) and in the *Nouvelle Revue Française* (July 1925). Further light is thrown on the whole question by Rilke's letters to Arthur Fischer-Colbrie of 18 December 1925 and to Eduard Korrodi of 20 March 1926. Mehring, Pick and Korrodi were all three acting at Rilke's request and with material provided by him, in their defensive articles. Rilke's publisher did not, of course, look on unconcerned at these happenings, or allow Rilke himself to look on at them without doing anything about them; and Rilke for his own part, indignant though he always was with all those, '(die) eine Kunst von mir erwarten, die von Lesern weiß,' (19 August 1909 to Baron Uexküll), still did, when it came to the point, most decidedly want his books to be read, and widely read too. In Germany the tendency has been, since Rilke's death, to make as little as possible of this episode. In France it has been more freely discussed, especially by Maurice Betz.

PAGE 4

1 Rilke on the receptivity of the younger generation in post-war France for foreign culture: 'Nie ist vielleicht Ausländisches, vom französischen Geiste aus, gerade indem er sich auf sich besinnt, . . . besser und verhältnismäßiger erkannt worden' ('Never before perhaps has what is foreign been better or more aptly appreciated from the standpoint of the

French mind, just in the very process of its striving after fuller awareness of itself') (20 December 1923 to Nora Purtscher-Wydenbruck). 'Dort [in Frankreich] sind nun wirklich die Grenzen gefallen; auf sich selber in einer neuen vitalen Weise besonnen, fürchtet der französische Geist nicht mehr, Fremdes und Entlegenes in sich aufzunehmen; auf einmal wird, wie es von dort aus nie geschah, italienische oder spanische, russische oder skandinavische Art, aber auch englische und sogar deutsche—, erkannt und eigentümlich gewertet...' ('There the barriers have now really fallen; aware of itself in a new, vital manner, the French mind is no longer afraid to assimilate what is foreign and remote; all at once, in a way in which it has never happened before from those quarters, what is characteristically Italian or Spanish, Russian or Scandinavian, also English and even German is appreciated and estimated at its own peculiar value') (13 February 1924 to Gertrud Oukama Knoop). 'Viénot... gehört zu den, in seiner Generation nicht seltenen, jüngeren Leuten, die eine Orientierung über deutsches Wesen sehr tief und ernst meinen' ('Viénot... is one of those younger people, not rare in his generation, who are very profoundly and earnestly bent upon understanding the German character') (5 May 1925 to Helene von Nostitz). Rilke seems to be unaware of the considerable influence exercised by the German Romantics in France in the first half of the nineteenth century.

2 Valéry on Rilke's Good-Europeanism: *Rilke et la France* (Paris, 1942), p. 199; Helmut Wocke, *Rilke und Italien* (Gießen, 1940), p. 167 (quoted without reference to source); *Stimmen der Freunde* (Freiburg im Brg., 1931), p. 175 (I have not traced the French original of Valéry's *Gedenken und Abschied*, given here in German translation).

3 Maurice Betz, *Rilke vivant* (Paris, 1935), p. 202; and in the amplified German edition of the same work, *Rilke in Frankreich* (Wien, 1938), pp. 195–6. (In the notes that follow references will usually be given from the German version only.)

4 'meiner ganzen weltisch-offenen unnationalen Anlage nach'—to Paul Zech, 24 December 1920; in Zech, *R. M. Rilke, Der Mensch und das Werk* (Dresden, 1930), p. 240.

PAGE 5

1 A. G. S. pp. 94–7, original in French. The receiver of these letters was a Countess by birth, but had—a circumstance that Rilke was ignorant of—become a Duchess by marriage. Therefore he always erroneously addressed her as 'Contessa'.

2 For a playful allusion to the United States of Europe see B.K., p. 562.

3 A. G. S., p. 98.

4 28 November 1925 to Supervielle, in the special Rilke number of *Les Lettres* (1952), p. 49.

PAGE 6

1 Betz, as above in n. 3 to p. 4.

2 Jules Romains' *Europe*, bearing the inscription 'à Genève en Juin 1919', is amongst the books in Rilke's Muzot library.

PAGE 7

1 Perhaps one can recognize one first faint trace of Rilke's Good-Europeanism in the conversation he had with Romain Rolland, Stefan Zweig, Verhaeren and de Bazalgette in Paris on 17 March 1913; Romain Rolland records: 'Ce qui nous paraissait un devoir essentiel, ce qui me tenait particulièrement au cœur, c'était de travailler à la fondation morale et intellectuelle de l'unité européenne' (What seemed to us an essential duty and what I in particular had set my heart upon was to work at the moral and intellectual foundation of European unity') (*Souvenir de son voisin*, quoted in *Rilke et la France*, p. 201). Rilke, however, during his Swiss years, often expressly dissociated himself from Romain Rolland, especially from *his* idea of European cultural unity, which he found too humanitarian and too German.

2 Russia as Rilke's true fatherland: 18 January 1902 he writes to Friedrich Huch: 'Dort ist meine Heimat... so will ich wenigstens so leben, daß mein tiefstes Wesen jenem Lande ähnlich werde' ('That is where my fatherland is.... At least I am resolved to live in such a way that my deepest nature may become like that country') (unpubl.). / 'In Rußland nur, auf meinen beiden weiten Reisen durch dieses Land, habe ich Heimat gefühlt; dort war ich irgendwie zu Hause...' ('Only in Russia, during my two extensive journeys through that country, did I have the feeling of being in my fatherland; somehow or other I was at home there') (3 April 1903 to Ellen Key). / 'Daß Rußland meine Heimat ist, gehört zu jenen großen und geheimnisvollen Sicherheiten, aus denen ich lebe,—aber meine Versuche hinzugehen... sind wie ein Nichts...' ('That Russia is my fatherland is one of the strange, mysterious certainties out of which I live—but my attempts to go there have come to nothing' (15 August 1903 to Lou Andreas-Salomé). / 'Was verdankt ich Rußland—, es hat mich zu dem gemacht, was ich bin, von dort ging ich innerlich aus, alle Heimat meines Instinkts, all mein innerer Ursprung ist dort!' ('How much I owed to Russia—it has made me what I am, inwardly it was the point from which I set out, all the fatherland of my

instinct, all my inner origins are there') (21 January 1920 to Leopold von Schlözer). / 'jenes mir wahlheimatliche Land . . .' ('that country which is my elective fatherland') (9 December 1920 to von Sedlakowitz).

PAGE 8

1 In his letters to Hulewicz Rilke always addresses him with 'von'. This has led to his being referred to in most books on Rilke as 'von Hulewicz', sometimes as 'Baron von Hulewicz'. In reality he had no such title. In the third collected edition of Rilke's letters this is corrected. Hulewicz was Rilke's guest in Sierre from 23 or 24 to 26 October 1924, and his long article 'Rozmowa z Rainerem Maria Rilke' appeared in Warsaw in the *Wiadomosci Literackie* for 16 November 1924. (See above, n. 1 to p. 3.) The quotations from this article in the present study are from an unpublished English translation made by Miss Anna Gasowska, to whom I owe much gratitude.

PAGE 10

1 21 January 1920 to Leopold von Schlözer.

2 21 May 1896 to Laska van Oesteren; in *Briefe an Baronesse von Oe* (Johannespresse, New York, 1945), p. 40. Hans-Egon Holthusen points out in his *Rilke in Selbstzeugnissen und Bilddokumenten* (Rowohlt, 1958), p. 22, that the title of Baroness was conferred on this young lady by Rilke's exuberant imagination, just as Hulewicz (see above, n. 1 to p. 8) was given the title of Baron.

3 10 January 1912 to Lou Andreas-Salomé; cp. letter to Katharina Kippenberg of 13 January 1912, K.K., p. 35.

4 To Ilse Erdmann, 11 September 1915.

5 Lou Andreas-Salomé: *Lebensrückblick* (Zürich and Insel-Verlag, 1951), p. 185.

6 A.G.S., pp. 27–8.

PAGE 11

1 8 August 1911 to Anton Kippenberg.

2 'Thiel entwickelt seine streng deutsche-patriotische Meinung im Gegensatz zu meinem Weltgedusel . . .' ('Thiel expounds his austerely patriotic German views in opposition to my cosmopolitan gushings') (7 March 1896 to Bodo Wildberg).

3 The few scraps of evidence which might be appealed to to invalidate what is here said of Rilke's hostile attitude towards Prague, Bohemia and Austria weigh too light to prove anything. They are (*a*) the youthful publications *Larenopfer* (1896) and *Zwei Prager Geschichten* (1899)—for which see n. 1 to p. 14; (*b*) his acceptance in 1899 of a subsidy from the

'Gesellschaft zur Förderung deutscher Wissenschaft, Kunst und Literatur in Böhmen' towards the printing of his volume *Mir zur Feier*; in 1902 of a substantial grant from the Prague 'Concordia'; and in May 1910 of an 'Ehrengabe' of '600 Kronen' from the Austrian 'Kultusministerium'. He always thought that he was worthy of his hire, and for the rest believed in taking from Caesar what is Caesar's and from God what is God's. (*c*) His contribution of a poem to the Austrian *Kriegs-Almanach 1914–16*; this was done unwillingly, however, under pressure, and as something he could not with decency refuse. (See T.T.H., 9 July 1915.) (*d*) The permission he gave in 1919 for three of his old poems to be reprinted in the anthology *Deutsche Dichter aus Prag*. He had refused when the project was first mooted before the war (see A.K., 16 April 1912); the concession, when at last made, was certainly not made willingly.

4 A.G.S., p. 28.

PAGE 12

1 'rätselhafte Diktate'—this and similar phrases are frequently used by Rilke after 1921 of his own experience of poetic inspiration, and occasionally also earlier. See letter to Xaver von Moos of 20 April 1922.

2 2 Feb 1923 to Lisa Heise.

3 15 February 1924 to Hulewicz.

PAGE 13

1 A.G.S., p. 97.

2 For the supposed Czech element in Rilke's blood, cp. Simenauer, *R. M. Rilke, Legende und Mythos* (Bern, 1953), pp. 104–5.

3 2 April 1904 to Ellen Key.

PAGE 14

1 Both in *Larenopfer* (1896) and in *Zwei Prager Geschichten* (1899) Rilke takes sides with the Czech nationalists. This was, however, only a brief passing phase. It was already over when the *Zwei Prager Geschichten*, which had been written in winter 1896–7, were actually published. The subject of one of these stories, 'König Bohusch', is the unsuccessful Omladina rising of the Czechs, of 1893. Where Rilke's sympathies lay at the time of that rising is shown from an unpublished diary-letter of October 1893, in which he speaks of the offence given to him by a young Czech smoking opposite him in a crowded train: 'Ich saß still da und hielt es bei den obwaltenden Verhältnissen für das beste, ihm dieses

unschuldige Vergnügen zu gönnen, um nicht die unverschuldete Ursache des aufflammenden Zornes *der großen Nation* zu werden' ('I sat tight deeming it best, under the prevailing circumstances, to indulge him in this harmless pleasure, rather than become the innocent occasion for the blazing wrath of *the great nation*'). This is evidence that Rilke still uncritically adhered to that contempt for the Czechs in which he had been brought up, at least till the end of his eighteenth year. On this whole question see Peter Demetz in his 'Czech Themes of R. M. Rilke', *German Life and Letters*, October 1952, pp. 35–49, and in his *René Rilkes Prager Jahre* (Düsseldorf, 1953), pp. 136–63; see also Clara Mágr's article 'Sprach Rilke tschechisch?' in *Das Antiquariat* (Vienna, 1957), pp. 83–5.

2 As n. 3 to p. 13.

3 K.K., p. 419.

PAGE 15

1 The relevant passage in the letter to Ellen Key of 2 April 1904 runs: 'Es ist nicht unmöglich, daß in den Frauen meines Geschlechtes auch solche slawischen Blutes waren; wenn gleich nicht in jüngerer Zeit. Seit die Familie in Böhmen angesiedelt ist, war sie betont deutsch, wie es dort die Verhältnisse, die zu klaren Entscheidungen zwingen, mit sich brachten. Aber früher könnte (ich weiß davon noch nicht genug) immerhin manche Verschwägerung mit böhmischen Geschlechtern stattgefunden haben. Die Tschechen freilich sind mir nicht nahe, auch die Polen nicht (die Verbindung von Slawentum mit dem katholischen Element hat etwas Unerträgliches für mich—). Aber Sie wissen ja, was Rußland mir ist; was war das für ein Ereignis, es zu finden! Und als ich zuerst nach Moskau kam, da war alles bekannt und altvertraut; um Ostern wars. Da rührte es mich an wie *mein* Ostern, mein Frühling, meine Glocken. Es war die Stadt meiner ältesten und tiefsten Erinnerungen, es war ein fortwährendes Wiedersehen und Winken: es war Heimat' ('It is not impossible that amongst the women folk of my line there may also have been some of Slavonic blood, though not in more recent times. Since the family settled in Bohemia it has been emphatically German, as was entailed by the circumstances there, which force one to clearcut decisions. But earlier (I don't as yet know enough about it) various intermarriages with Bohemian houses might after all have occurred. The Czechs, admittedly, are not congenial to me, nor are the Poles (there is something I cannot endure about the combination of the Slavonic with the Catholic element). But you know what Russia means to me; what an event it was for me to discover it! And when I first came to Moscow everything was well

known to me and familiar as from of old; it was Easter. It affected me as being *my* Easter, my spring, my bells. It was the city of my oldest and profoundest memories: it was a continuous recognition and beckoning: it was home'). The point of all this, in its context, is, of course, that it must have been some Russian element in Rilke's own blood, transmitted to him from the remote aristocratic 'Frauen meines Geschlechtes', that had thus responded to the appeal of Moscow as to a familiar memory. The same conceptions find expression also much later, at the height of Rilke's maturity, when he writes to his future son-in-law, Carl Sieber, on 10 November 1921 of 'unserer, seit dem 13 Jahrhundert groß und zu Zeiten weitläufig angesessenen Familie ...' ('Our family which from the 13th century onwards was of established eminence and at times widely diffused').

2 From a letter of 25 March 1922 to his mother, Phia Rilke, quoted by Carl Sieber in *René Rilke* (Leipzig, 1932), p. 21.

3 There was the strongest physical resemblance between Rilke and his mother, as is testified by many who knew them both. Nor was this resemblance only physical; her imagination and emotions were lively and restless and worked themselves out largely in religion. There can be little doubt that, so far as heredity is concerned, Rilke had much more in common with her and owed much more of his genius to her than to any of his paternal forebears. He was unable to like or respect her, and this was one of the most important factors in his development. He seems to have recognized in her with horror a kind of travesty of himself. In 1932 Nadler, in the fourth volume of his *Literaturgeschichte der deutschen Stämme und Landschaften* refers to her more than once as 'Rilke's jüdische Mutter'. In a footnote to an article in the special Rilke number of *Dichtung und Volkstum* of 1936, p. 76, Pongs says, with reference to Nadler: 'Die Legende von der jüdischen Mutter ist durch das Rilke-Archiv widerlegt' ('The legend of his Jewish mother is refuted by the Archives'). So far as the present writer knows, nothing more has been made known about Rilke's descent on the maternal side, and there certainly appears to have been no more official pronouncement on the question from the Rilke-Archiv than Pongs' footnote of 1936. Under the Nazi régime such genealogical research could not be undertaken dispassionately. If sufficient evidence had been available to refute Nadler's statement circumstantially and conclusively, it is hard to understand why this was never done. Most probably no conclusive evidence exists one way or the other. The possibility is, however, not to be ruled out, that Rilke may have inherited through his mother a slight strain of Jewish blood, as has been sup-

posed also of Browning and Cardinal Newman. He had many Jewish friends, was sometimes taken for a Jew, but regarded himself as very distinct from the Jews, as appears particularly from his letter of 22 October 1913 to Hofmannsthal on Franz Werfel, and from the vehemence with which he insists that there is 'nichts Jüdisches an und in' Kassner (7 February 1912 to Lou Andreas-Salomé). See also the early short story *Teufelsspuk* (Simplicissimus 1899, now *Erzählungen und Skizzen aus der Frühzeit*, pp. 389–97), where the destiny of the Jewish race is referred to as 'das Schicksal jener, die ohne Heimat sind' ('the fate of those who are without any fatherland'). In view of the importance which Rilke himself attached to these questions of 'blood' in general and his own blood in particular, criticism cannot afford to leave them completely out of account. It is his great-grandmother on the maternal side, Theresia Entz, née Mayerhof, of Brünn, about whom more would need to be known.

4 See Sieber, *René Rilke*, pp. 9–20. It has been suggested that the account there given of Rilke's ancestry on the paternal side is untrustworthy and betrays a readiness to conform to Nazi ideology. (See Nora Purtscher-Wydenbruck, *Rilke, Man and Poet* (London, 1949), p. 16.) There is no true foundation for these suspicions. Much information was withheld as long as possible by those responsible for looking after Rilke's papers, much is perhaps still being withheld; and thence misleading impressions have flourished. But this happens inevitably after the death of any eminent person, in some degree, and is by no means indefensible. That any facts have, however, been actively and deliberately falsified I regard as completely out of the question.

PAGE 16

1 For Freud's 'Familienroman' and Rilke, see the chapter dedicated to this theme in Simenauer's *R. M. Rilke, Legende und Mythos*, pp. 383–414.

2 A.G.S. p. 28.

PAGE 18

1 Some idea of the extent to which the German-speaking minority in Bohemia regarded Germany as their spiritual fatherland can be gained by glancing through any number of the Prague periodical *Deutsche Arbeit*, to which Rilke contributed regularly from 1901 to 1907, and in which his famous 'Cornet' first appeared. On this point consult P. Demetz, *loc. cit.* (see n. 1 to p. 14).

2 Almost the only occasion on which Rilke shows signs of recognizing a positive and distinctive value in old Austrian cultural tradition is when he

discovers Stifter, shortly before the 1914 war: '—und so kam er, naiv dahin, sich aus Angestammtem und Erfahrenem ein Deutsch bereit zu machen, das ich, wenn irgend eines, als Oesterreichisch ansprechen möchte, so weit es nicht eben eine Eigenschaft und Eigenheit Stifters ist und nichts anderes als das' ('And so he came naively to fashion for himself out of what he had inherited and what he had experienced a German to which I should be inclined to assign, if to anything, the designation "Austrian", so far as it is not just a peculiarity and idiosyncrasy of Stifter's, and nothing more than that') (11 January 1913 to August Sauer). In praising the poems of Lernet-Holenia in 1921 Rilke says 'es überlebt viel altes Oesterreich in ihnen' ('much of ancient Austria survives in them') (25 March 1921 to Anton Kippenberg). [See also p. 257.]

3 Of Rilke's innumerable vehement outbursts from every stage of his development on the irreparable harm the military academies had done to him, the letter to von Sedlakowitz of 9 December 1920 is the most striking. It is, indeed, one of the chief contentions of Peter Demetz in his *René Rilkes Prager Jahre* that Rilke was in reality quite happy at these military academies and that his sufferings there were only a subsequent invention. The present writer gives his reasons for rejecting this opinion in his review of Demetz' book in *Wort und Wahrheit* (1953), pp. 854–9.

4 15 April 1904 to Lou Andreas-Salomé.

PAGE 19

1 13 December 1906 to Lou Andreas-Salomé and 14 December 1906 to Hedwig Fischer; the latter in Rilke: *Briefe an das Ehepaar S. Fischer* (Zürich, 1947).

2 13 May 1904 to Lou Andreas-Salomé.

3 Thus Rilke said to Charles du Bos in January 1925: 'Et pourtant il y a eu une période de ma vie où je me suis demandé si je n'écrirais pas en russe plutôt qu'en allemande . . .' ('And yet there was a period in my life when I asked myself whether I should not write in Russian rather than in German') (*Rilke et la France,* p. 211). Many other such declarations could be quoted.

4 Reported by Korfiz Holm in Sophie Brutzer's *Rilkes russische Reisen* (Königsberg, 1934).

5 17 March 1922 to Gräfin Sizzo—Gr. S. pp. 20–1.

PAGE 20

1 *Ibid.*

2 From Walter Mehring's article in defence of Rilke in *Das Tagebuch,* 15 August 1925. (See above, n. 1 to p. 3.)

3 *Rilke/Gide: Correspondance* (Paris, 1952), p. 87; published in *Incidences* (1924).

4 J. R. von Salis, *Rilkes Schweizer Jahre*, Third Edition (Frauenfeld, 1952), p. 145.

5 F. W. Wodtke: 'Das Problem der Sprache beim späten Rilke', *Orbis Litterarum*, vol. XI, pp. 1–2, 1956. (A valuable article.)

PAGE 21

1 T. S. Eliot, *Burnt Norton*.

2 For 'paume / palma' see above, n. 3 to p. 20; for 'verger', etc., see letter to Frau Nanny Wunderly-Volkart in J. R. von Salis, *Rilkes Schweizer Jahre*, p. 125. For 'offrande' see the French poem quoted on p. 139: 'Les offrandes usent l'autel....'

PAGE 22

1 Rilke and German culture: cp. E. C. Mason, *Rilke and Goethe*, Publs. of English Goethe Society, vol. XVII, pp. 131–5.

2 In speaking of the desert as having nurtured his heart, Rilke is referring to his journeys to Algiers and Egypt in winter 1910–11.

3 From about 1902 to about 1915 Rilke was given to reading the Bible a good deal (chiefly the Old Testament), for his own private poetic and speculative purposes.

4 11 September 1915 to Ilse Erdmann. (Edition C only.)

5 15 March 1921 to Tora Holmström, unpublished.

PAGE 23

1 A. G. S., p. 96.

2 24 May 1926 to Baladine Klossowska; B.K., p. 579.

3 'daß er 1925 ein Huldigungstelegramm an den tschechischen Präsidenten Masaryk, der die Deutschen entrechtet und verfolgt, als "den großen Humanisten" richtete...' ('that he in 1925 addressed a telegram of homage to the Czech President Masaryk who deprives the Germans of their rights and persecutes them, calling him "the great humanist"') (Adolf Bartels, *Deutsche Literaturgeschichte*, Bd III (1928), p. 559). The exact circumstances are unknown.

4 18 December 1925 to Arthur Fischer-Colbrie.

5 19 August 1920 to Princess Marie Taxis. Clara Mágr, *loc. cit.* (see above, n. 1 to p. 14) appeals to this letter in support of her quite sound contention that Rilke knew Czech much better than Sieber, Demetz and others admit, but she fails to mention the disgust which Rilke here shows.

6 As above, n. 5 to p. 22.

PAGE 24

1 A.G.S., p. 95.

2 *Ibid.*

3 Rilke and the German Youth Movement: Fräulein Marga Wertheimer told me that Rilke spoke enthusiastically to her about the German Youth Movement in September 1924; he was an admirer of Hans Blüher, a leading figure in this movement—see letters of February 1919 to Lou Andreas-Salomé and to Katharina Kippenberg.

PAGE 25

1 15 January 1918 to Frau von Mutius; Betz, *Rilke in Frankreich*, p. 53.

2 'Ist es denn, nach allem, was ich in deutscher Sprache gab, nötig, meine Zugehörigkeit zur deutschen Dichtung zu betonen?' Quoted by Walter Mehring in 'Einige Reminiszenzen an Rainer Maria Rilke', *Die literarische Welt*, 14 January 1927. Mehring does not give the date of this letter, but internal evidence shows that it must be some time in summer 1925.

PAGE 26

1 J. R. von Salis, *Rilkes Schweizer Jahre*, 1st edition, pp. 201–2. For the PEN Club invitation see letter to Anton Kippenberg of 26 May 1925.

2 In spite of Rilke's determined hatred of German nationalism, many attempts were made after 1932 to interpret him in a Nazi sense; Georg E. Blokesch, Erwin Cleff, Martin Kaubisch and Fritz Klatt may be mentioned as examples of this tendency. (See Ritzer's *Bibliography*.) The main line of argument in these Nazi interpretations of Rilke is his belief in 'blood' and his attachment to the irrational and the earthy. The circumstance, not made known till 1956, that he was a believer in Fascism and an admirer of Mussolini, shows that the Nazi interpretations of his work were not altogether without foundations.

PAGE 27

1 French was, however, the only foreign language that Rilke ever acquired well enough to use it accurately, and that not till about 1920. (See von Salis, *Rilkes Schweizer Jahre*, 1st edition, p. 45.) To the last his French was still that of a foreigner, both in pronunciation and in syntax. Léon-Paul Fargue says: 'Il aimait d'amour notre langue, et, durant les dernières années de sa vie, la parlait et l'écrivait avec une gaucherie subtile' ('He loved our language devotedly and during the last years of his life spoke and wrote it with a subtle awkwardness') (*Rilke et la France*, p. 221).

Paul Valéry once remarked in conversation on the great superiority of Hofmannsthal to Rilke in the use of spoken French. J. R. von Salis writes: 'Seiner Sprachenbegabung waren grundsätzlich keine Grenzen gesetzt' ('There were, on principle, no limits to his gift for languages') (*Rilke's Schweizer Jahre*, 3rd edition, p. 171).

2 15 January 1918 to Frau von Mutius: in Betz, *Rilke in Frankreich*, p. 53.

PAGE 28

1 Kindly communicated by Frau Baladine Klossowska.

2 Kindly communicated by Rilke's daughter, Frau Ruth Fritzsche.

PAGE 30

1 'Diese englischen Liebessonette sind von einer Vollkommenheit und Präzision des Ausdrucks ...' (15 April 1907 to Gudrun Baronin Uexküll).

2 18 April 1907 to Ellen Key.

3 Kindly communicated by Professor William McC. Stewart (see text pp. 140–1).

4 Rudolf Kassner, *Die Mystik, die Künstler und das Leben* (Leipzig, 1900), p. 244.

PAGE 31

1 Rilke's letter to Ellen Key of 18 August 1903 is still unpublished. The passage quoted runs in the original: 'Wenig belesen—dem Englischen fremd, kannte ich von den Brownings fast nichts und wußte nur aus ihres Lebens Gedicht die und jene glückliche Strophe—nun aber—bin ich des Wunsches voll, von diesen beiden Zeichen einer leidenschaftlicheren und tieferen Menschlichkeit viel zu erfahren.' (Rilke-Archiv.) The phrase drawn attention to by italics in my translation of this passage is not underlined in the original.

2 Frau Katharina Kippenberg writes in her *Rainer Maria Rilke, ein Beitrag* (2nd ed. Leipzig 1938): 'Frau Fähndrich ... übersetzte ihm die *Sonnets from the Portuguese* in die deutsche Sprache, und er übertrug sie wieder in die Dichtung' ('Frau Fähndrich translated the *Sonnets from the Portuguese* for him into German, and then he turned them into poetry') (p. 167). This is, however, quite certainly only a hypothesis devised by Frau Kippenberg to account for the facts, not a report of information given to her by Rilke himself. It is, indeed the hypothesis everybody must naturally arrive at, so long as Rilke's declarations about his total ignorance of the English language are accepted literally. I arrived at it

and adhered to it for some time, so long as there was no more serious objection to it than that, if correct, it convicted Rilke of drawing the long bow when he wrote to Baroness Uexküll and Ellen Key about the tone and diction of the English original. But a detailed comparison of translation and original convinced me that Rilke must have been able to understand the English text fairly well. Only in cases of special difficulty can he have needed a literal German rendering from Frau Faehndrich to guide him.

3 'Sprachinspirationen'—a phrase used by Rilke of himself in a letter of 24 February 1912 to Tora Holmström.

4 Rilke's use of English publications for his Russian studies of 1899: the evidence for this is given by Sophie Brutzer in her *Rilkes russische Reisen* (Königsberg, 1934), p. 71.

5 29 April 1902 to W. Schölermann, quoted by Helmut Wocke in his *Rilke und Italien* (Gießen, 1940), p. 160, from a sale-catalogue of autographs.

PAGE 32

1 Frau Alice Faehndrich (1857–1908) and her sister Gräfin Luise Schwerin (1849–1906) were born *Freiinnen von Nordeck zur Rabenau.* Their English mother was, before her marriage, a Clara Philips. It was through Gräfin Schwerin, whom he first met at the 'Weisser Hirsch' near Dresden in spring 1905, that Rilke's footing in German aristocratic circles was properly established. Her death inspired three of Rilke's poems, amongst them the outstanding 'Todes-Erfahrung' in *Neue Gedichte I.* The letter to Frau Alice Faehndrich of 14 February 1908 quoted in the text is unpublished; the passage runs in the original: 'Ich lese the Korrekturbogen unserer vorjährigen gemeinsamen Arbeit; sie kommt mir sehr schön und vollendet vor...' (Rilke-Archiv).

PAGE 33

1 Cp. Ingeborg Schnack in *Rilkes Leben und Werk im Bild* (Insel-Verlag, 1956), text to plates 147–9. I am grateful to Dr Ingeborg Schnack for the information that the process of translating was regularly initiated by Alice Faehndrich's reading the sonnet in question out loud to Rilke.

2 Cp. B. J. Morse: 'R. M. Rilke and English Literature' in *German Life and Letters* (New Series) I, 3, April 1948, pp. 215–28. I owe a great debt of gratitude to B. J. Morse for letting me have further information about Dora Heidrich-Herxheimer and for the patience and readiness with which he has answered my questions and helped me with useful suggestions.

PAGE 34

1 Rilke's letter to Dora Heidrich-Herxheimer of 14 July 1907 was first pub-

lished by B. J. Morse in the *Welsh Review*, 1944, III, 2, pp. 127 foll. It has since been reprinted by Dieter Bassermann in *Der späte Rilke* (München, 1947), p. 415, and amongst the notes to the second volume of Rilke's collected letters (1950), p. 575.

PAGE 36

1 From a letter of Dr Ingeborg Schnack's to the present writer.

PAGE 37

1 Rilke's letter to Jessie Lemont of 15 January 1909—see text pp. 77 and 124.

2 5 September 1909, A.K., p. 64.

3 The phrase is from Emerson's *Considerations by the way*. For Rilke's reading of Emerson in winter 1897–8, see text p. 44.

PAGE 38

1 31 May 1901 to Verlag S. Fischer.

2 12 May 1904 to Lou Andreas-Salomé.

3 'Die Flucht'—*Erz. und Skizzen*, p. 53.

4 (πτερόεσσα κόρα). See *Gedichte 1906–26* (Insel-Verlag, 1953), p. 493. From Ernst Zinn's study *R. M. Rilke und die Antike* ('Antike und Abendland', Band III, 1948, pp. 201–50) it emerges that Greek was one of the subjects in which Rilke received private lessons in the years 1893–95, but that he never advanced far enough in it to be able to read a Greek text, and let it drop after 1895.

5 Rilke's letter of 8 June 1912 to Jessie Lemont is given in facsimile in the 1946 edition of the English translation of Rilke's *Rodin* by Jessie Lemont and Hans Trausil.

6 A.G.S., p. 83.

PAGE 39

1 Katharina Kippenberg, *Rainer Maria Rilke, ein Beitrag*, 2nd edition p. 314.

2 Rudolf Kassner: *Buch der Erinnerung* (Insel-Verlag, 1938), p. 297; originally in the Rilke memorial number of the Inselschiff, April 1927.

PAGE 40

1 J. R. von Salis, *Rilkes Schweizer Jahre*, 1st edition, p. 136. The 3rd edition has here an interesting addition: 'Englische Bücher konnte sich Rilke nur in Uebersetzungen aneignen, da er dieser Sprache nicht genug mächtig war' ('Rilke could only read English books in translation, because he did not know this language well enough').

2 J. R. von Salis gives a substantially similar account of Rilke's relationship to the English language on p. 18 of his biographical essay prefixed to Ingeborg Schnack's *Rilkes Leben und Werk im Bild* (Insel-Verlag 1956).

The same not quite reliable version of the facts is given by Hansres Jacobi in 'Rilke als Europäer' (*Zürcher Woche*, 30 December 1955).

3 Frédéric Lefèvre: 'Une heure avec R. M. Rilke', in *Nouvelles littéraires*, 24 juillet 1926.

PAGE 41

1 'Eine Stunde mit R. M. Rilke', in *Neue Leipziger Zeitung*, 13 August 1926.

2 'Une année s'est passée depuis ma première entrevue avec Rilke' ('A year has elapsed since my first interview with Rilke'), Lefèvre writes, without mentioning that this first interview was also the last, as it quite certainly was. He is a journalist.

3 Lefèvre's inaccuracies: that Rilke knew Hofmannsthal personally as early as 1897 / that he had read all the French classical authors / that he had stayed in Norway / that the letters of the Portuguese Nun, Marianna Alcoforado, were translated by Rilke from the Portuguese, whereas the originals are in French / that Proust was a personal friend of Rilke's / that *Malte Laurids Brigge* was begun in Paris.

PAGE 42

1 Betz, *Rilke vivant*, pp. 56–7.

2 On this question of whether it could possibly have been Elizabeth Barrett-Browning after all, to whom Rilke was referring in 1925 as having disappointed him, see below, n. 1 to p. 106.

PAGE 43

1 Ingeborg Schnack, in *Rilke's Leben und Werk im Bild*, states in her comment on Plate 239 that Rilke had seen Severn's drawing at the Keats museum in Rome. This is not so. He never visited the Keats museum in Rome, and never saw the original of Severn's drawing. Rilke assumed mistakenly that Severn's drawing shows Keats *after* death. It was made some time before Keats actually died.

PAGE 44

1 The possibility may be taken into consideration that Rilke's more formal study of the English language, such as it was, took place in winter 1901–2, soon after his reading of Rudolf Kassner's *Die Mystik, die Künstler und das Leben* (see text p. 66), which contains essays on both Keats and Browning. This was a time when Rilke was interested in English poetry and art (see p. 71). But the new difficulties created by such a hypothesis would be so great that it can be ruled out.

2 The thought that all poets are really one, their individual identities being merged in the timeless mythical figure of the 'Urdichter', is of great

importance for Rilke. It occurs as early as 1900 in the drama *Das tägliche Leben* (pp. 35–6): 'und trotzdem das ganz verschiedene Dichter sind, Romantiker und Dekadenten, Franzosen, Italiener, Deutsche, Russen, oft scheinen mir meine Lieblingsgedichte alle von einem Dichter zu sein—so ähnlich sind sie einander' ('and although they are entirely different poets, Romantics and Decadents, French, Italian, German and Russian, my favourite poems often seem to me to be all by one and the same poet—so similar are they to one another'). Then it occurs again in the lecture on Rodin of 1905–6: 'Und ich fühle schon, wie mir der Name im Munde zerfließt, wie das alles nur mehr der Dichter ist, derselbe Dichter, der Orpheus heißt usw' ('and I feel how the name dissolves in my mouth, how that is all nothing but *the poet*, the same poet who is called Orpheus etc.'). This is taken up in February 1922 in the *Sonnets to Orpheus*:

> Denn Orpheus ists. Seine Metamorphose
> In dem und dem. Wir sollen uns nicht mühn
> um andre Namen. Ein für alle Male
> ists Orpheus, wenn es singt. Er kommt und geht. (I. v.)

'For it is Orpheus. His metamorphosis now in one, now in another. We ought not to trouble about any other names. Once and for all, it is Orpheus, when there is singing. He comes and goes.' In 1925 the same conception turns up in a letter to Natalie Clifford Barney: 'D'ailleurs, vous devez le savoir que là où la cupidité de l'art (comme celle de l'amour) disparaît, il ne reste qu'une seule voix qui infiniment varie sons et silences' ('Besides, you should know that where the cupidity of art (like that of love) vanishes, nothing remains but one sole voice infinitely varying sounds and silences') (Natalie Clifford Barney, *Adventures de l'esprit* (Paris, 1929), pp. 78–9).

PAGE 45

1 See Lou Albert-Lasard, *Wege mit Rilke* (S. Fischer Verlag, Frankfurt, 1952), p. 31.

PAGE 46

1 See Chapter IX, pp. 134–6.

2 Rilke's letter to Mrs Goodwin-Winslow is unpublished; the excerpt here given was kindly supplied to me by Frau Fritzsche from the Rilke-Archiv.

3 Gr. S., p. 12.

4 21 October 1924 to Professor Hermann Pongs.

PAGE 47

1 Fürstin Marie von Thurn und Taxis-Hohenlohe (1855–1934) was one of Rilke's best friends from December 1909 onwards. The *Duinese Elegies* are dedicated to her, because it was at her castle of Duino that they were begun. She is usually referred to in the present publication as 'Princess Marie Taxis' in accordance with the way in which she regularly signed her letters to Rilke.

2 Claire Studer, later by marriage Claire Goll, was on intimate terms with Rilke from 1918 onwards; his letters to her were published in New York in 1944 under the title: *Briefe an eine Freundin.*

3 B.K., pp. 60 and 534.

PAGE 48

1 See letter to Lou Andreas-Salomé of 17 July 1897.

2 See T.T.H., p. 396.

3 *Anmerkung zum Kentauer*, vol. VI, p. 68.

4 The analysis of Rilke's use of English loan-words is based only on comparatively casual observations; a systematic scrutiny would probably reveal further evidence.

5 'Essay'—introduced into German by H. Grimm, under the influence of Macaulay, ridiculed by Gottfried Keller. Used by Rilke 13 May 1897 in a letter to Lou Andreas-Salomé, 6 March 1898 in a letter to Dehmel; 4 July 1904 in a letter to Ellen Key; 27 June 1907 also to Ellen Key; 22 December 1911 to Anton Kippenberg, etc. The Germans are conscious of the English derivation of 'Essay', as opposed to French 'essai'.

6 'Lift': 9 March 1915 to Lou Andreas-Salomé; 'Banksafe': 21 January 1919 to the same; 'Eisenschrank': to Anton Kippenberg 9 February 1910; 'Generalstreik': to Lou Andreas-Salomé 19 March 1919; 'bridge-Tisch': 7 September 1923 to Princess Marie Taxis; 'Hall': to Baladine Klossowska 21 June 1923.

PAGE 49

1 'Shawl': *Gedichte 1906–26*, pp. 604/605/614; and letters to Claire Studer-Goll of 9 and 22 March 1919.

PAGE 50

1 'lunchen': Magda von Hattingberg's anonymously published *Rilke und Benvenuta* (Vienna 1943), p. 108.

2 Letter to Junghanns—*Briefe* [*an Junghanns und Zimmermann*] (Olten, 1945), p. 8.

3 Letter to Elisabeth von Schmidt-Pauli in the *Neue Deutsche Rundschau*, September 1927.

4 On 14 January 1892 Stefan George wrote to the not quite 18-year-old Hofmannsthal threatening him with a duel: 'Also auf etwas hin und gott weiß welches etwas "das Sie verstanden zu haben glauben" schleudern Sie einem *gentleman* der dazu im begriff war Ihr Freund zu werden eine blutige kränkung zu' ('So on the strength of something—and God knows what something—"that you believed you had understood" you hurl a cutting insult at a *gentleman* who, on top of everything else, was on the point of becoming your friend').

5 Cp. J. R. von Salis, *Rilkes Schweizer Jahre*, 3rd edition, p. 142.

6 Cp. Betz, *Rilke vivant*, p. 240.

7 See Rilke, *Sämtliche Werke* (ed. Zinn), vol. II, p. 612.

PAGE 51

1 Paula Becker's criticism of Rilke's spellings with 'y'; this emerges from an unpublished letter of Rilke's to Paula Becker kindly lent to the present writer by the late Otto Modersohn.

2 Letter to Mme. Contat-Mercanton, original French, quoted here from von Salis' German rendering in his first edition, p. 141.

3 Rilke's minutes of the spiritualistic séance of October 1912 are given as an appendix to T.T.H., pp. 913–14.

PAGE 52

1 For the Duino séances of April 1915 see T.T.H., p. 419.

2 See Nora Purtscher-Wydenbruck: *The Paranormal* (London, 1939), pp. 67–75.

PAGE 54

1 See Gabriel Marcel: 'Rilke et l'occulte' in the special Rilke number of *Les Lettres*, p. 145.

PAGE 55

1 Amongst the innumerable examples that could be cited here, the following two may be selected as typical: 'Rodin ist gestern nach London gefahren'—21 February 1906 to Lou Andreas-Salomé; 'Der Präsident, Dr Bodmer, ist bis gegen Ende Oktober in Amerika'—20 September 1919 to Elya Nevar—in her *Freundschaft mit R. M. Rilke* (Bern, 1946), p. 130.

2 13 August 1912, T.T.H., p. 194. B. J. Morse, *loc. cit.* (see n. 2 to p. 33) writes of Rilke's having 'mentioned the possibility of his paying a visit to London in a letter to Julie von Nordeck zur Rabenau in January 1912',

but the place mentioned in the letters of 2 January and 9 April 1912 to this lady would appear to have been not *London,* but *Londorf* near Giessen.

PAGE 56

1 'Rilke and the Gesture of Withdrawal'—see Excursus I, p. 176.

2 12 September 1905 to Clara Rilke.

3 Reception in Dotation Carnegie—see Betz, *Rilke in Frankreich*, p. 206, 1925.

4 Rilke and the teddy bear: on 13 January 1912 he writes to Katharina Kippenberg of his unsuccessful attempts to find a suitable Christmas present for her little daughter in a toyshop in Trieste: '—ich sah nur noch alberne Pelüche-Bären, kindische Nachkommen jener ersten, die vor ein paar Jahren die Welt eroberten' ('I only saw some silly plush bears, childish descendants of those first ones that took the world by storm a few years ago'). It had been in 1906 that the toy bears invented some three years earlier by the firm of Steiff had been used in great quantities to decorate the tables at the wedding-breakfast of Theodore Roosevelt's daughter and that, as a humorous compliment to him, somebody called them 'Teddy Bears', a name under which they at once became popular far and wide.

Lesley Gordon gives in *Peepshow into Paradise* (Harrap, 1953, pp. 151–2) a slightly different account of the origins of the Teddy Bear.

5 L.A.S., p. 460.

6 B.K., p. 83.

PAGE 57

1 One of the first to formulate challengingly in English that new evaluation of the pursuit of the arts and liberal sciences which Schiller so felicitously designated as 'ästhetische Erziehung' and which by common consent soon came to be known simply as 'culture', was, it is surprising to find, Blake with his 'The Whole Business of Man Is the Arts' (*Laokoon* sheet) and his 'Men are admitted into Heaven . . . because they have cultivated their Understandings . . .' (*Vision of Last Judgment*).

PAGE 60

1 It may be noted that Rilke only spent five months in all in Russia, five and a half months in Denmark and Sweden, and under four months in Spain. Professor E. M. Butler says that Rilke only saw Russia 'in a dream' (*Rilke,* Cambridge, 1941, p. 60.) Similarly Professor Steffensen says of Rilke's conception of Scandinavia that it was 'von literarischen Fiktionen, von Traum und Sehnsucht gestaltet' ('moulded by literary

fictions, by dreams and yearnings') (*Rilke und Skandinavien*, Munksgaard, 1957, p. 37).

PAGE 61

1 See F. W. Wodtke, *Rilke und Klopstock* (Kiel, 1948), p. 9.

2 Heine: *Shakespeares Mädchen und Frauen*; cp. also his *Englische Fragmente* passim. I have dealt at length with the disparagement of English culture by the German Romantics in my *Deutsche und englische Romantik*, Göttingen 1959, especially on pp. 11–19.

3 Nietzsche, *Jenseits von Gut und Böse*, §252.

PAGE 62

1 Writers of appreciable talent who frequently abuse their own fellow-countrymen in their books usually stand a fair chance of becoming popular with foreign readers. This factor is chiefly responsible for the over-estimation of Byron and Heine outside the lands of their origin, and very much complicates the task of assessing them justly for all concerned.

2 *Erzählungen und Skizzen aus der Frühzeit*, p. 164. In the same story, p. 155, there is mention of an English valet who speaks the 'correct High German of the foreigner'.

3 *Erzählungen und Skizzen aus der Frühzeit*, p. 241.

PAGE 63

1 See Rilke's review of Ellen Key's *Jahrhundert des Kindes* of 8 June 1902; *Bücher—Theater—Kunst* (Vienna, 1934), pp. 20/5.

2 14 August 1919 to Lotte Tronier-Funder (*Briefe an eine Reisegefährtin*, Vienna, 1947, p. 84).

PAGE 64

1 Lou Andreas-Salomé: *Lebensrückblick*, pp. 76, 121, 226.

PAGE 65

1 See Nietzsche: *Jenseits von Gut und Böse*, Nachlass § 12: 'Europa (hat) wahrscheinlich nötig, sich ernsthaft mit England zu verständigen' ('Europe will probably need to come seriously to some arrangement with England').

2 For Rilke's relationship to Nietzsche see Fritz Dehn: 'Rilke und Nietzsche', in *Dichtung und Volkstum* (1936), vol. XXXVII, no. 1,

pp. 1–22: and Erich Heller: *The Disinherited Mind* (Cambridge, 1952), pp. 99–140.

3 Rudolf Kassner, born in 1873 in Moravia, died 1 April 1959 at Sierre Switzerland. Some of the information utilized in the present work was kindly supplied by him in letters or in conversation.

4 Cp. E. C. Mason: 'Kassner und England', *Neue Zürcher Zeitung*, 6 September 1953 and 'For Rudolf Kassner's 80th birthday', in *German Life and Letters*, January 1954.

PAGE 66

1 Rudolf Kassner: *Die Mystik, die Künstler und das Leben* (Leipzig, 1900), re-issued in a revised form under the title *Englische Dichter* in 1920 by the Insel-Verlag.

2 From Kassner's 'Geleitwort' to T.T.H., p. XXIII.

PAGE 67

1 *Jetzt und in der Stunde unseres Absterbens*, performed with disastrous reception on 6 August 1896, in Prague. It had been printed on 1 April 1896 as *Wegwarten II*; only reprint so far in Hünich's *Aus der Frühzeit R. M. Rilkes*, Leipziger Bibliophilen-Abend 1921.

PAGE 69

1 Hugo Steiner-Prag records this in his *Fröhliche Erinnerung*, published under the title *Aus einer Kneipzeitung* in Prague in 1933, p. 7.

2 See Ernst von Wolzogen: *Wie ich mich ums Leben brachte* (Braunschweig, 1922), p. 183.

3 Cp. 'I am sure it was Mrs James who put Carrie up to writing on dark slate-coloured paper with white ink' (*Diary of a Nobody*, George and Weedon Grossmith, Everyman Library, p. 227).

4 Cp. Sedlmayr, *Verlust der Mitte* (Salzburg, 1948), p. 101: 'Aus einer englischen Gegenbewegung gegen Historismus und Maschinen-Architektur . . . war in der Spätphase am Kontinent der "Jugendstil" hervorgewachsen' ('Out of an English re-action against historicism and machine-architecture there had developed, in a later phase, the Jugendstil').

PAGE 71

1 Hofmannsthal's early essays on English life and literature are reprinted in *Loris—Die Prosa des jungen Hugo von Hofmannsthal* (Berlin, 1930), pp. 131–73. Swinburne and Pre-Raphaelite painting are amongst his themes, besides Pater. See also his letters 1891–1900 passim.

PAGE 72

1 *Tagebücher aus der Frühzeit* (Leipzig, 1942), p. 33: 'Präraffaeliten: einfach eine Laune. usw.'

2 *Ibid.*, p. 72.

3 *Ibid.*, p. 99.

4 References to Ruskin in 'Heinrich Vogeler' (*Deutsche Kunst und Dekoration*, Darmstadt, April 1902, not reprinted), p. 301; and in a review of Pater's *Renaissance*, *Bremer Tageblatt*, 27 July 1902, reprinted by R. von Mises in *Bücher—Theater—Kunst* (Vienna, 1934), p. 36.

5 *Bücher—Theater—Kunst*, p. 224.

6 *Bücher—Theater—Kunst*, p. 36. B. J. Morse, *loc. cit.* (see n. 2, to p. 33), deduces from the phrase 'der Dichter unsterblicher Sonette' here applied to Rossetti that Rilke must have 'read him either in translation or in the original'. I see no *necessity* for assuming this, though it *may*, of course, be right enough. He had certainly read Kassner's essay of 1901 on 'Dante Gabriel Rossetti: Sonette und Frauenköpfe', which contains many quotations from Rossetti in the original. Rilke's chief source of knowledge about Rossetti and his contemporaries will have been articles in reviews.

7 *Worpswede* (Bielefeld und Leipzig, 1903), pp. 56 and 121.

PAGE 73

1 *Bücher—Theater—Kunst*, p. 78.

2 22 January 1901 to Otto Modersohn (unpublished).

3 *Worpswede*, p. 14.

4 *Bücher—Theater—Kunst*, p. 241.

5 The connexion between Rilke's poem and John Pettie's painting is taken for granted by Hellmut Rosenfeld in his *Das deutsche Bildgedicht* (Leipzig, 1935) and by Kurt Wais in his 'D. H. Lawrence, Valéry, Rilke in ihrer Auseinandersetzung mit den bildenden Künsten' (*Germanisch-Romanische Monatsschrift*, October 1952). I have not been able to ascertain who first pointed it out.

6 *Bücher—Theater—Kunst*, p. 9.

PAGE 74

1 'Mag, was den Inhalt dieser merkwürdigen Blätter betrifft, die dekadente Linienphantastik Aubrey Beardsleys anregend auf Vogeler gewirkt haben, das Wesentliche an ihnen wuchs aus ihm heraus...' ('However much the decadent arabesques of Beardsley may have acted as a stimulus on

Vogeler so far as the contents of these remarkable drawings is concerned, what is essential about them developed out of his own nature') (*Worpswede*, p. 114).

2 'Zeichnungen von Beardsly (sic), die für Vogeler eine Offenbarung waren ...' ('Drawings of Beardsley's which were a revelation for Vogeler') ('Heinrich Vogeler', p. 320).

3 Our dictionary definitions of decadence (e.g. 'a period of decline in art or literature'—Shorter Oxford) give no idea of what the word really means for the French or Germans. A deterioration of mere animal robustness and vitality is regarded as fostering unprecedented subtlety of perception and expression, and therefore also an art far superior in depth and fineness to that of healthier ages. See Thomas Mann passim. The phenomenon of decadence is frequent enough in our *fin de siècle* art and poetry, though we still refuse to accord the word a positive interpretation.

PAGE 75

1 The myth of decadence presented with a certain obviousness in such earlier poems of Rilke's as 'Der Sänger singt vor einem Fürstenkind (*Buch der Bilder*) re-appears in a subtler and intenser form in the 17th Sonnet to Orpheus (I. Part): 'Zu unterst der Alte, verworrn ....'

2 Letter of 4 January 1911 to Katharina Kippenberg.

3 Letter of 26 April 1911 to Anton Kippenberg.

4 Liberty's (founded as East India House in 1875 by Arthur L. Liberty and instrumental, together with the enterprises of William Morris, in bringing about decisive reforms in domestic furnishings, etc.)—see *Bücher—Theater—Kunst*, p. 226.

5 Fragments of two letters from Rilke to Schölermann of 29 April and 5 July 1902 are reprinted by Helmut Wocke from a sale catalogue in his *Rilke und Italien* on pages 154 and 160. From these it emerges that Rilke had read Pater's book as early as April 1902, three months before his review of it was printed. It also appears possible that he may have seen the English original as well as Schölermann's translation.

6 *Bücher—Theater—Kunst*, p. 36.

PAGE 76

1 Wocke, *Rilke und Italien*, p. 154.

2 25 April 1903 to Arthur Holitscher.

3 *Worpswede*, p. 3.

4 Rilke: *Ausgewählte Werke* (Insel-Verlag, 1938), vol. II, p. 218.

5 In an unpublished 'Arbeitsliste für Malte Laurids Brigge' ('List of possible themes for my work on Malte Laurids Brigge'), probably of 1909, Rilke notes down: 'Monna Lisa: (Wie in Greisen das Leben ist und die Erinnerung, ins Innerste verlegt, so ist in ihr die Malerei)' ['Mona Lisa: (As in old men life and memory are transferred to the inmost point, so also is painting in her)'].

PAGE 77

1 For Rilke's interest in and translation of Michelangelo's poems see Wocke, *Rilke und Italien*, pp. 80–94; Rilke worked intermittently on his translations of Michelangelo from about 1912 to about 1921. See letters to Lou Andreas-Salomé of 7 February 1921 and to Gide of 23 December 1921.

2 From an unpublished letter of Rilke's to Jessie Lemont, in French, now in the Library of Columbia University. Cp. p. 128.

3 *Gesammelte Werke*, vol. IV, pp. 398–9. The *Rodin-Vortrag* was first published in October 1907 in the periodical *Kunst und Künstler*, then in December of the same year in book-form (together with the monograph of 1903) as 'Zweiter Teil'. The passage on Oscar Wilde was not in the lecture as Rilke first wrote it in October 1905, but was added when he prepared the manuscript for the press in July 1907. The point is not without interest for us, as it makes a difference whether Rilke introduced Wilde into his presentation of Rodin before or after reading Hofmannsthal's essay on Wilde, which appeared under the title *Sebastian Melmoth* about December 1906 in the Insel-Almanach for 1907. One would like to know whether Rilke's passage on Wilde was in some measure inspired by Hofmannsthal's essay or not.

PAGE 78

1 See *After Berneval: Letters of Oscar Wilde to Robert Ross* (1922).

2 Kassner: *Umgang der Jahre* (Erlenbach-Zürich, 1949), p. 326.

3 That the imaginary conversation between Rodin and Wilde is really only a reproduction of Rilke's own conversations with Rodin is proved by the following passage in a letter to Heygrodt of 12 January 1922: '*Rodin*, da ich ... ihn nach seiner Kindheit und Jugend fragte, verwies auf eben dieses sein Werk und sagte kurzhin: "moi—? j'étais quelqu'un; ce n'est que plus tard que l'on commence à comprendre"' ('When I asked Rodin about his childhood and youth, it was just this work of his that he referred me to, saying curtly: "Me?—I was just anybody; it is not till later that one begins to understand"').

4 Hofmannsthal on Wilde—see above, n. 3. to p. 77.
5 26 April 1906 to Elisabeth von der Heydt.

PAGE 79

1 29 February 1908 to S. Fischer; R. M. Rilke, *Briefe an das Ehepaar S. Fischer*, p. 26.
2 Rilke's 'Arbeitsliste für Malte Laurids Brigge'; the present writer would like to express his gratitude here to the late Georg Reinhart of Winterthur, owner of this manuscript, who kindly supplied him with a photocopy of the relevant sheet.
3 Rilke visited Normandy and Brittany in winter 1902–3 and again in 1911. That was the nearest he ever came to England.

PAGE 80

1 Rilke's 'Randbemerkungen zu Bichat' were printed in the *Botteghe oscure*, vol. XVII, pp. 347–51. The passage on Wilde and Verlaine is on p. 350. Probably the names of Wilde and Verlaine were transferred direct from these Notes on Bichat to the Malte list.
2 The earliest definite evidence we have as to Rilke's friendship with Gide is of the year 1910. But there is good reason to suppose that they met before this. See Renée Lang on this question in her edition of the *Correspondance* of the two poets (see n. 3 to p. 20), pp. 12–14.

PAGE 81

1 An early indication of Rilke's reaction against the 'Jugendstil' occurs in a letter of 26 June 1904 to his wife, in which he criticizes the furniture of his Swedish hosts as having 'etwas Altertümelndes und zugleich *Jugendstilhaftes*, so daß man ihrer nicht froh werden kann' ('There is a hankering after the antiquated about it, and at the same time something of the *Jugendstil*, so that one cannot take any pleasure in it').
2 In all Rilke's journalistic writings of the years 1896–1903 there is only one that shows any awareness of the phenomena of newer French art which were soon to become all-important to him. This is an account of an exhibition of 'Neo-Impressionisten' in Berlin, published in the *Wiener Rundschau* in November 1898 and reprinted in *Bücher—Theater—Kunst* on pp. 227–30. The only artist mentioned by name in this immature effusion, which anticipates nothing of Rilke's later insight, is Seurat. Of the newer trends in French literature Rilke had up to 1903 discovered only the two Flemish writers Georges Rodenbach and Maurice Maeterlinck, both of whom he was to drop on entering the new phase of his development that began with his first stay in Paris in 1902–3.

3 Charles Vildrac: see special Rilke number of *Les Lettres*, pp. 38–9; also letter to Hans Reinhart of 19 November 1920.

4 Valéry Larbaud: a copy of *Barnabooth* which belonged to Rilke and is still in Muzot contains the inscription: 'Fini, pour relire tantôt, un Dimanche, celui avant Noël 1922.'

5 Maurois: *Les Silences du Colonel Bramble* and *Les Discours du Docteur O'Grady* are both in Rilke's library in Muzot and are mentioned also in his correspondence with Baladine Klossowska.

6 Paul Morand: his *Lewis et Irène* is enthusiastically discussed in a letter of Rilke's to Princess Marie Taxis of 7 March 1924.

PAGE 82

1 St. Jean Perse: see Rilke's poem, 'Robinson nach der Heimkehr', in *Gedichte 1906–26*, p. 628.

2 Mallarmé—see von Salis, *Rilkes Schweizer Jahre*, 3rd edition, p. 134.

3 Whistler—see n. 5 to p. 78.

4 27 March 1903 Rilke writes to Rodin: 'Un éditeur anglais a l'intention de publier dans quelques semaines une traduction anglaise . . .' ('An English publisher intends to publish an English translation in a few weeks').

PAGE 83

1 See postcard to Clara Rilke of 17 September 1905.

2 Sir John Lavery: 9 January 1906 to Clara Rilke and as above, n. 2 to p. 73. Lavery had in 1904 officially tendered to Rodin the invitation to become President of the International Society of Sculptors, Painters and Engravers, which Whistler had founded. (See Judith Cladel: *Rodin, sa vie glorieuse et inconnue*, Paris, 1936, p. 250.)

3 24 July 1904 to Clara Rilke.

4 Kassner on Poe—see *Die Mystik, die Künstler und das Leben*, pp. 152–3.

5 26 November 1925 to Sophy Giauque; *Rilke en Valais*, numéro spécial de la revue *Suisse Romande* (Sept. 1939), p. 198.

6 Musil, in his *Rede zur Rilke-Feier* (16 January 1927) writes: 'Die Deutschen lernten, was ein Gedicht sei, erst wieder durch das Ausland, durch Verlaine und Baudelaire, durch *Poe* und *Whitman* kennen . . .' ('It was only through foreign literatures that the Germans once more found out what a poem really is, through Verlaine and Baudelaire, through Poe and Whitman . . .'). Musil does not actually name Rilke here; he speaks of the generation of German poets to which Rilke belonged. Cp. von Salis in *Rilkes Leben und Werk im Bild*, p. 18.

PAGE 84

1 19 April 1906 to S. Fischer.

PAGE 85

1 11 March 1907 to Ellen Key.

2 'Es hat kürzlich hier, in München, eine Versammlung von Gelehrten und geistig-lebendigen Menschen stattgefunden, die die Gründung einer internationalen Zeitschrift beschlossen haben; R. Rolland, Shaw, van Eeden und mehrere andere "feindliche" Ausländer sind bereits für die Teilnahme gewonnen worden . . .' ('Recently here in Munich there was an assembly of scholars and of people with some intellectual vitality who have resolved to start an international periodical; Romain Rolland, Shaw, van Eeden and several other "enemy" aliens have already been secured as contributors') (18 January 1915 to Marianne von Goldschmidt-Rothschild, unpublished).

3 See n. 1 to p. 8.

4 14 February 1926 to Duchess Aurelia Gallarati-Scotti.

PAGE 87

1 See T.T.H., pp. 131–315 (March 1912 to August 1913), passim.

PAGE 88

1 T.T.H., 29 March 1912. In 1950 B. J. Morse wrote to the 81-year-old Algernon Blackwood, asking him about his recollections of Rilke, and transcribing for his benefit, amongst other passages, this one where Rilke speaks of his having been attired like an Arctic explorer or a lion-hunter. In his reply of 7 March 1950, of which Morse has kindly given me a copy, Algernon Blackwood shows himself extremely nettled by Rilke's sallies of thirty-eight years earlier, and asserts that, while his own clothing had been perfectly normal, he distinctly recollects Rilke incongruously wearing a black tail-coat and a billycock hat in a Venetian gondola. And that was *all* that Algernon Blackwood could remember about Rilke in 1950. He felt much inclined to deny that there had been any earlier meeting between himself and Rilke in Cairo or Heluan, and in general he obviously felt sore on the entire subject, chiefly, it would seem, on account of those lion-hunters and Arctic explorers. The phrasing of Rilke's letter of 29 March 1912, however, leaves no room for doubt that he had met Blackwood before—and that can only have been in Egypt in the previous year, whether Blackwood himself could remember it still in 1950 or not. Blackwood is certainly right when he says in his letter to Morse that the meeting in Egypt was far more likely to have taken place at Heluan than at Cairo, the place assigned to it in Rilke's letter to Baltusz Klossowski of February 1921. Rilke stayed at Baron Knoop's palatial Hotel 'al Hayat' at Heluan from 24 February to 24 March 1911, and this was a favourite

haunt of Blackwood's just at that time of year. But from the perspective of Switzerland it would have been impossible to convey any meaning to a thirteen-year-old boy by naming Heluan without adding 'near Cairo' or 'in Egypt', and it was legitimate enough for Rilke here to simplify his narrative by using the place-name that everybody has heard of and that therefore calls for no further explanations. So far as Algernon Blackwood's letter of 1950 conflicts with the contemporary evidence of Rilke's correspondence one must regard it sceptically. The one new piece of information it contains is that regarding Rilke's 'billycock hat'. This is an article of headgear to which his father was much addicted, but which I have nowhere else found attributed to Rilke himself, who always went in for Homburgs, except when solemn occasions demanded a topper. All my attempts to visualize Rilke in a billycock hat have had to be abandoned.

2 A. Blackwood, *The Education of Uncle Paul* (London, 1909), p. 182.

PAGE 89

1 'Vers la fin de février 1921', to Baltusz Klossowski. (Only in Edition C.)

PAGE 90

1 *Bücher—Theater—Kunst*, p. 187.

2 *Tagebücher*, p. 13. We regard 'All the world loves a lover' as proverbial, but it appears to have been originated by Emerson, and there is no corresponding proverbial phrase in German.

3 Lefèvre—see n. 3 to p. 40.

4 Rilke and older literature. One of the prices that the average cultured German has to pay for the great efflorescence of his country's literature in the later eighteenth century is that all the ages anterior to it, particularly the sixteenth and seventeenth centuries, to which the educated French or English reader, thanks to the greater continuity of French and English literary tradition, has comparatively easy access, are in a large measure cut off from him and left to the specialist, who tends to make them remoter and more alien still. This defect, if one may so term it, of the German mind's qualities, which works itself out in a tendency to read the spirit of the age of Goethe into such older foreign writers as, for example, Dante, Cervantes and Shakespeare, is fundamentally different, however, from Rilke's bewilderment when confronted with the literature of the past. What hampered Rilke here was the sketchiness of his formal education and the circumstance that, unlike Hofmannsthal, he had very little of the scholar in his composition.

PAGE 91

1 At the military academies which he attended from the age of ten to fifteen Rilke was too wretched and too much out of his element to learn a great deal. From the Commercial College at Linz, which he attended for rather less than a year after leaving the military academy of Mährisch-Weißkirchen he certainly profited little. His entire effective education was concentrated in the three years 1892 to 1895, when he received intensive private tuition in Prague to enable him to pass the standard Austrian school-leaving examination. After this he was matriculated as a student first at the university of Prague (for a year), then at that of Munich (for a year) and subsequently at Berlin. But he never so much as made a serious beginning with university study, which was uncongenial to him and of which he was, indeed, temperamentally almost incapable. Down to his fortieth year he still had not completely given up the hope of taking up university work seriously and qualifying for the doctorate. He wrote revealingly on these questions to Lou Andreas-Salomé, especially on 10th August 1903 and on 12th and 13th May 1904.

2 Rilke and history. Underlying the *Duinese Elegies* from their first conception in 1912 to their belated completion in 1922 there is a curious quasi-historical theory of the kind beloved by German philosophers of history and historians of culture: the theory of 'das Zurückschlagen einer im Aeußeren überfüllten Welt ins Innere' ('the inward recoil of a world outwardly overcharged') (5 March 1912 to Ilse Sadée) since the end of the Middle Ages. This idea, which Rilke tries to put on some sort of a historical basis about 1912, can be traced back to his earlier phases, certainly as far back as 1898, and accompanies him throughout his entire development. It is really only a very arbitrary and unhistorical projection into the historical sphere of what Rilke feels to be the distinguishing peculiarity of his own poetic soul. What is chiefly to be noted about it, so far as its claim to be taken seriously as an interpretation of history is concerned, is that it flies completely in the face of everything that responsible historical thinkers have to say about the difference between mediaeval and modern mentality.

PAGE 92

1 23 December 1917 to Princess Marie Taxis (T.T.H., p. 527).

2 Sieber, *René Rilke* (Leipzig, 1932), p. 116. (It is not clear from Sieber's account whether Rilke's seventeenth, eighteenth or nineteenth birthday is intended.)

PAGE 93

1 *Erzählungen und Skizzen aus der Frühzeit*, p. 123. According to P. Demetz, *loc. cit.* (see n. 1 to p. 14), this passage alludes to Sladek's Czech translation of *Hamlet*. I can see no evidence for this. That *Hamlet* may be performed in Czech translation is taken for granted by all the speakers —that is not the subject under dispute; it is only a question of whether the play should be interpreted in the German way or not.

2 *Tagebücher*, p. 44.

3 *Worpswede*, p. 45. B. J. Morse, *loc. cit.* (see n. 2 to p. 33) sees in the cyclic poem 'Aus einer Sturmnacht' of 21 January 1901, each of whose eight sections commences 'In solchen Nächten—' clear evidence that Rilke must have known and been influenced by the dialogue between Lorenzo and Jessica at the beginning of Act V of the *Merchant of Venice* with its eightfold 'In such a night as this—' (rendered by Schlegel: 'In solcher Nacht—'). This is a case on which it is difficult to make up one's mind. The sinister naturalism of this particular cycle of poems is utterly different from the airy sweetness of Shakespeare's reverie.

4 Kassner, *Buch der Erinnerung*, p. 300.

PAGE 96

1 Katharina Kippenberg gives the date of this visit wrongly as July 1913, instead of August–September 1911, in her *Rainer Maria Rilke, ein Beitrag*.

2 *Ibid*, p. 188.

3 17 September 1911 to Princess Marie Taxis.

PAGE 98

1 28 November 1912 to Elsa Bruckmann.

2 12 July 1912 to Princess Marie Taxis.

3 6 February 1913 to Princess Marie Taxis.

4 9 August 1912 to Anton Kippenberg.

5 Kassner, 'R. M. Rilke zu seinem 60. Geburtstag am 4. Dez. 1935', in the *Frankfurter Zeitung*. The phrase in question, 'So wurde er zu Shakespeare durch den Hamlet Moissis gebracht', is omitted from the reprint of this essay in *Buch der Erinnerung*, p. 318.

PAGE 99

1 Katharina Kippenberg, *op. cit.* p. 231, from conversations probably of 191

PAGE 100

1 24 July 1914 to Norbert von Hellingrath.

PAGE 101

1 25 August 1915 to A. de V.

2 Undated note to Princess Marie Taxis of the Viennese months (1916)—T.T.H., p. 482.

3 Moissi's *Hamlet*—see text p. 98 and n. 5 to p. 98.

4 Letters to Hans Reinhart of 19 November 1920; of 6 December 1920 to Baladine Klossowska; and of 13 December 1920 to Charles Vildrac. (This last in the special Rilke edition of *Les Lettres*, p. 39.)

5 See p. 679 of the *Briefwechsel* with Katharina Kippenberg.

6 Carl J. Burckhardt—see the Preface to the present publication, pp. xii–xiii.

PAGE 102

1 Rilke's admiration of Klopstock's *Ode to Young* is vouched for by Wodtke, *Rilke und Klopstock*, pp. 8–9.

2 M.H., p. 98. Sterne was one of the great favourites of Kassner, who made an admirable translation of *Tristram Shandy* into German.

3 Kassner, *Buch der Erinnerung*, pp. 311–12.

PAGE 103

1 The view that Keats may have been too sensuous and fleshy for Rilke seems to underlie Mr J. B. Leishman's discussion of this question in his *Later Poems* (Hogarth Press, 1938), p. 199. Many examples could be cited of Rilke's unreservedly relishing the fleshiest kinds of poetry and art.

2 4 September 1908 to Clara Rilke.

3 16 July 1903 to F. X. Kappus. In the second volume of Rilke's *Sämtliche Werke* (dated 1956) a curious series of phallic poems of Rilke's was published for the first time—pp. 435–8.

4 Kassner, *Buch der Erinnerung*, p. 315.

5 See above, n. 1 to p. 103.

6 This jotting belongs to Rilke's still unpublished notes. The publication concerned is: *John Keats: Lettres à Fanny Brawne, traduites par M. L. Des Garet* (Paris, editions de la Nouvelle Revue Française, 1912). Whether Rilke actually procured a copy of this book or not is uncertain.

PAGE 104

1 From a letter in French to his bookseller, Mme Paul Morisse, quoted by Renée Lang in A.G.S., pp. 49–50.

2 René was Rilke's true baptismal name. He changed it to Rainer in May

1897, giving, perhaps somewhat disingenuously, as a reason to his mother, that Rainer is 'schön, einfach und deutsch'. (See Angelloz, *R. M. Rilke, évolution spirituelle,* Paris, 1936, p. 55). In his relationship with Baladine Klossowska (Merline), which began in 1919, Rilke once more adopted the name René, in spite of its associations with the humiliations of his youth.

3 B.K., p. 477—the letter is dated 'mi-décembre 1923'.

4 A.G.S., p. 46.

5 A.G.S., p. 49.

PAGE 105

1 A.G.S., p. 51.

2 A.G.S., p. 45.

3 At Christmas 1920 Rilke gave Baladine Klossowska a copy of his translation of the Sonnets from the Portuguese with the inscription: 'Einer der großen Vogelrufe in den Landschaften der Liebe' (unpublished).

PAGE 106

1 These verses, to which the title 'Sonett auf Elisabeth Barrett-Browning' was added by an editor in 1933, were inscribed by Rilke in a copy of his translation of the *Sonnets from the Portuguese* dedicated to Frau Wunderly-Volkart on 3 November 1919, and it has thence been assumed both by Ernst Zinn and Friedrich Wilhelm Wodtke, the chief authorities on the chronology of Rilke's works, that this was the actual date of composition. In all probability this assumption is correct. But Lou Albert-Lasard, *Wege mit Rilke* (see n. 1 to p. 45), pp. 31–2, quotes this sonnet in a way which implies that she had known it in manuscript as early as 1914. B. J. Morse, *loc. cit.* (see n. 2 to p. 33), it may be noted, postulates that Rilke was disappointed in Elizabeth Barrett-Browning and took little satisfaction in his own translation of her sonnets: 'But even she ... did not engage more than his partial interest. The truth is that Rilke was probably attracted to her poetry because the subject-matter of her sonnet-sequence seemed to provide a confirmation of his personal ideas about love ... ; and that when he found that his theories did not hold good in her case, he just obliterated her from his intellectual world. There are no subsequent references to any other poems from her pen; she is never included in the gallery of his famous women-lovers, and appears nowhere in his creative work as a character or as a personage in her own right.... Mrs Browning did not suffer as one whose love was unfulfilled, and consequently, in his opinion, could not be regarded as being of the elect who claimed his admiration and sympathy.' This interpretation is evidently in part determined by Betz' report (see above, p. 41) that Rilke

had spoken of being 'disappointed by Keats and Browning', of which Morse says: 'the reference to Browning should evidently be emended to read Mrs Browning.' I see no evidence, however, that Rilke was at any stage disappointed in Mrs Browning. He must have known from the very outset and without any shadow of uncertainty that she did not fit into that particular category of women whose love is unfulfilled, to whom he was specially devoted. He was, however, not so exclusive or pedantic in these matters that he could not occasionally also admire and sympathize with women who are in the more ordinary sense happy in their love. He could never have had illusions on this score about Elizabeth Barrett-Browning, nor can one fairly say that he 'obliterated her from his intellectual world'. Admittedly he does not refer to any other poems from her pen—but how many British readers since 1890 or so have ever looked at anything she wrote except the *Sonnets from the Portuguese*? That those Sonnets were far more valuable than everything else she wrote Rilke had learnt from Kassner in 1901, and everybody else must have confirmed it. She *does* appear as 'a character in her own right' in Rilke's creative work, for example in the dedicatory verses 'O Wenn ein Herz, längst wohnend im Entwöhnen' of 3 November 1919 to Frau Wunderly; and also in the similar dedicatory verses to Frau Gudi Nölke of 21 September 1919 ('Und Dürer zeichnete das große Glück...'); to Pfarrer Becker of 5 March 1921 ('Daß Demut je in Stolzsein überschlüge...'); to René d'Harnoncourt of March 1921 ('Wenn es ein Herz zu jener Stille bringt ...'); and to Marga Wertheimer of 5 October 1924 ('Was unser Geist der Wirrnis abgewinnt...'). Four of these five dedicatory poems of Rilke's last years invoking the figure of Elizabeth Barrett-Browning stand high in rank within his most characteristic creative work, and in particular the phrase of Christmas 1920, 'Einer der großen Vogelrufe in den Landschaften der Liebe' is quite incompatible with the kind of disappointment in the English poetess that Morse would attribute to Rilke. I fully agree with Morse that Rilke's translation of these sonnets is, *as a translation*, not good, but it is *in its own way* as good as any of his other verse translations and quite the same in character as the rest. As late as 29 December 1918 Rilke could still speak of it in a letter to Katharina Kippenberg as 'meine doch wohl beste Uebertragung' ('after all probably my best translation').

In fact, neither so far as his own version nor so far as the original is concerned can one find any trace of disappointment or misgiving on Rilke's part. Elizabeth Barrett-Browning is, indeed, never cited by name in those lists of love-intoxicated women that Rilke likes to compile—but need we seek for any further reason for that, than that her name really cannot for a moment compete for mellifluousness with Héloise, Gaspara Stampa, Clara d'Anduze, Marceline Desbordes and the rest of them? Names like 'Barrett' and 'Browning' are admirable examples of just those purely phonetic qualities in the English language that Rilke found it hard to endure.

2 This quotation from Wordsworth is on the envelope of one of Baladine Klossowska's letters to Rilke; I am very grateful to Mme Klossowska for kindly lending me this envelope and giving me permission to reproduce it.

PAGE 107

1 14 May 1912 to Princess Marie Taxis.

2 I am grateful to M. Pierre Klossowski for this information about Rilke's interest in Blake in 1925.

3 *Aufzeichnungen des Malte Laurids Brigge, Gesammelte Werke*, p. 236.

PAGE 108

1 31 October 1913 to Princess Marie Taxis.

2 Allusions to Tagore: 5 December 1913 to Anton Kippenberg; 16 December 1913 to Princess Marie Taxis; 30 December 1913 to Contessa Pia di Valmarana. The earliest mention of Tagore is in two notes to Lou Andreas-Salomé of 19 and 20 September 1913.

3 A.G.S., p. 83—17 January 1926.

4 G.N., pp. 43, 45, 98—28 February and 9 March 1920 and 31 October 1922.

PAGE 109

1 6 February 1913 to Princess Marie Taxis.

2 George Henry Lewes: *Theil aus Leben und Werke,* autorisierte deutsche Ausgabe, übersetzt von J. von Sydow (Berlin, 1878), forming the first volume of an edition of Goethe's works. (This information was kindly supplied to me by Fräulein Frieda Baumgartner.)

3 Rilke's letter to Sophie Liebknecht of 2 July 1917 is unpublished; the excerpt here quoted was kindly supplied by Frau Fritzsche-Rilke.

PAGE 110

1 Rilke's enthusiasm for David Garnett's *Lady into Fox* was communicated to me in private conversation by Fräulein Wertheimer.

2 This information from Rilke's letters to his booksellers, M. et Mme Paul Morisse, has been kindly communicated to me by Professor Renée Lang,

whose edition of these letters may shortly be expected. The title of George Moore's book was translated into French as *Confessions d'un jeune anglais*.

3 Cp. Valéry Larbaud's review of Logan Pearsall Smith's *Trivia* in the *Nouvelle Revue Française*, May 1922.

4 Cp. von Salis, *Rilkes Schweizer Jahre*, 'Er . . . sprach mit teilnehmender Wärme von den Seemannsschicksalen Joseph Conrads, von dem ihm Valéry während seines Besuchs in Muzot erzählte' ('He spoke with sympathetic warmth of Joseph Conrad, about whom Valéry had told him during his visit to Muzot, and of his vicissitudes upon the high seas' (3rd edition, p. 134).

5 Rilke's prophecy regarding Julien Green was made in conversation to Frau Wunderly-Volkart, who records it in the fly-leaf of his copy of *Mont-Cinère*.

PAGE 111

1 Claire Goll—cp. n. 2 to p. 47.

2 As above, n. 2 to p. 110.

3 This fact was kindly communicated to me by Frau Wunderly-Volkart.

PAGE 113

1 Maurois' *Dr. O'Grady*—see letter to Baladine Klossowska of 6 December 1923.

2 Professor Rose's essay was published in *Rainer Maria Rilke, Aspects of his Mind and Poetry*, edited by William Rose and G. Craig Houston (London, 1938).

3 See J. Hone's *W. B. Yeats 1865–1939* (Macmillan, 1942), pp. 473–5.

4 Edmond Jaloux writes in the publication *La dernière amitié de Rainer Maria Rilke* (Laffont, 1949) on the subject of Muzot: 'Un album recueille les signatures des rares visiteurs. J'ai eu la surprise d'y découvrir celle de William Butler Yeats . . .' ('An album contains the signatures of the rare visitors. I was surprised to discover that of W. B. Yeats') (p. 24). Jaloux was here misled by an entry made by Dorothy Moulton in July or August 1931. After writing down a quotation from Yeats' *To the Rose upon the Rood of Time*:

> To find in all poor things that live a day
> Eternal beauty wandering on her way,

Dorothy Moulton wrote Yeats' name, then: 'Oxford-Sierre' and her own signature.

PAGE 114

1 See K.K., p. 685.

PAGE 115

1 K.K., 14 March 1923; p. 487.

2 K.K., 27 February 1924; p. 523.

3 5 December 1924 to Anton Kippenberg. The essay 'On being religious' is reprinted in *Phoenix, Posthumous Papers of D. H. Lawrence.* Rilke's phrase 'in meinen Anmerkungen' (here translated 'in my papers') is curious in its context, implying, as it does, annotations to some existing text. I find it unthinkable that Rilke should here be referring, as Frank Wood assumes in his 'Rilke and D. H. Lawrence' (*Germanic Review,* Columbia University Press, vol. XV, 1940, pp. 213–23), to his *Aufzeichnungen des Malte Laurids Brigge,* which had been in print since 1910. This would simply amount to a suspicion of plagiary on Lawrence's part. Rilke is surely struck by close parallels between Lawrence's essay and some still *unpublished* writing of his own—probably the *Brief des jungen Arbeiters* of 1922, which was first printed posthumously, under the title *Ueber Gott* in 1933. The resemblances here are remarkable enough. Compare Lawrence's 'Bei der großen Wanderung des Himmels hat auch der Fuß des Kreuzes sich fortbewegt' ('in the great wandering of the heavens, the foot of the Cross has shifted'), with Rilke's 'Ich kann mir nicht vorstellen, daß das *Kreuz bleiben* sollte, das doch nur ein Kreuzweg war' ('I cannot imagine that the cross, which after all was only a cross-way, was meant to persist').

4 Frank Wood, in his publication named in the preceding note, deals impressively with this problem in outline. I cannot, however, concur in Wood's view that Rilke 'still maintained transcendence' as against Lawrence who 'equated the deity with the life-force', and that therefore Rilke succeeded where Lawrence failed. In hardly any question is it more difficult to recognize any fundamental distinction between Rilke and Lawrence than in this of transcendence and immanence.

PAGE 116

1 Lawrence to Lady Cynthia Asquith on 30 April 1922, in *Letters of D. H. Lawrence* (Heinemann, 1932), p. 546.

PAGE 118

1 24 March 1903 to Clara Rilke.

2 1 April 1903 to Friedrich Huch.

3 7 April 1903 to Clara Rilke.

PAGE 119

1 1 May 1910 to Anton Kippenberg.
2 18 May 1914 to Princess Marie Taxis.
3 G.N., p. 194.
4 Baladine Klossowska to Rilke, 23 December 1923.
5 Betz, *Rilke in Frankreich*, p. 86.
6 Baladine Klossowska to Rilke, 12/15 September 1925.

PAGE 120

1 17 December 1912 to Princess Marie Taxis. Rilke was staying in the Hotel Reina Victoria at Ronda from the middle of December 1912 to the middle of February 1913—more than half of his entire time in Spain.
2 18 December 1912 to Anton Kippenberg.
3 Rilke and open fires: see letters to Ilse Blumenthal-Weiß of 28 December 1921 and to Baron von Ungern-Sternberg of 28 January 1922; and the lines in the *Sonnets to Orpheus*, II, 2:

> Was haben Augen einst ins umrußte
> lange Verglühn der Kamine geschaut:
> Blicke des Lebens, für immer verlorne.

('How eyes of old have gazed into the slow smouldering of fireplaces with soot surrounding it, gazes of life, lost for ever.')

4 Hotel Liverpool—see Marie Thurn und Taxis: *Souvenirs sur Rainer Maria Rilke* (Paris, 1936), p. 19. (A German translation by Blokesch of these important memoirs was published in Munich in 1933 under the title: *Erinnerungen an Rainer Maria Rilke*.)
5 See letter to Anton Kippenberg of 27 April 1911.
6 See letter to Anton Kippenberg of 10 February 1911.
7 Haus Amerika—see *Tagebücher*, p. 233—1 September 1900.

PAGE 121

1 18 May 1912 to Princess Marie Taxis.
2 The Johnstons in Venice: see letters to Princess Marie Taxis of 14 and 18 May and of 12 July 1912.
3 Magda von Hattingberg, *Rilke und Benvenuta* (see n. 1 to p. 50), p. 233—a quotation from her diary of May 1914.
4 26 June 1920 to Gräfin Mariette Mirbach.
5 *Ibid.* The passage in question will be found in R. F. C. Hull's translation, *Selected Letters of R. M. Rilke* (Macmillan, 1946), pp. 303–4.
6 See letter to Gräfin Sizzo of 12 April 1922.

7 Friedrich Graf Jenison-Wallworth—see *Briefe an Baronesse von Oe.*, pp. 39 and 68–9.

PAGE 122

1 Nathan Sulzberger: see R. M. Rilke, *Briefe, Verse und Prosa aus dem Jahre 1896* (New York, 1946), pp. 55–6 and 107. One of the poems in *Advent* (1898) is dedicated to Sulzberger. 26 June 1920 Rilke writes to Gräfin Mirbach: 'als ich es (Venedig) zuerst sah, im Jahre 1897, geschahs als Gast eines Amerikaners!'

2 Harry Louis von Dickinson collaborated with Rilke in the third *Wegwarten* publication in 1896, and there was a plan for the two young poets to start a 'Bund für moderne Fantasiekünstler' ('an Association of Modern Imaginative Artists'). His pen-name was Bodo Wildberg. See *Bücher—Theater—Kunst*, pp. 86–9 and 277; also *Briefe an Baronesse von Oe.* (New York, 1945), pp. 30–2.

3 The Gibsons of Jonsered: the poem 'Zeiten giebt es, in denen wie hinter Türen . . .' printed in the *Insel-Almanach* for 1959, p. 44, is dedicated to a Johnny Gibson who must have belonged to this family.

4 Nyström-Hamilton—see letter to Lou Andreas-Salomé of 6 January 1905.

5 Montgomery—see letter to Tora Holmström of 24 February 1912: 'So tun Sie mir also einen lieben Gefallen, wenn Sie mir den Titel des Montgomeryschen Buches genau angeben . . .' ('You would be doing me a kindness if you gave me the exact title of the book by Montgomery'). Fräulein Holmström informs me that the book she had recommended Rilke was the Memoirs of a certain Frau Malla Montgomery who travelled from Sweden to Germany in the Romantic period.

6 See Augustus John, *Chiaroscuro* (Cape, 1952), p. 251. The Rilke Archives were unable to supply any further information about Gwen John's acquaintance with Rilke.

PAGE 123

1 *Ibid.*, p. 255.

PAGE 124

1 Conversation of May/June 1911, recorded by Katharina Kippenberg in her *Beitrag*, p. 151. Cp. letter to Lou Andreas-Salomé of 28 December, 1911. In an important earlier letter to Clara Rilke of 3 November 1909 Rilke still struggles to find excuses for Rodin's infatuation, suggesting that he only needs the Marquise de Choiseul as a kind of shock-absorber to ease the strain of descending from the heights to the plains of everyday

life. Rilke soon, however, realised that all such reassuring explanations were untenable.

2 Marquise de Choiseul—see letters of 30 December 1911, 27 October 1912 and 21 March 1913 to Princess Marie Taxis—T.T.H., pp. 87, 212 and 281.

3 See Judith Cladel: *Rodin—sa vie glorieuse et inconnue* (Paris, 1936), p. 267: 'elle vint me parler avec . . . le plus anglo-saxon des accents' ('she came and spoke to me in the most Anglo-Saxon of accents').

4 The three letters from Rilke to Jessie Lemont here quoted are now in the possession of the Library of Columbia University, to whom I would express much gratitude for providing me with copies of them and permitting me to make use of them. The only one so far published is that of 8 June 1912, of which a facsimile appears in the 1946 edition of Jessie Lemont's and Hans Trausil's translation of the Rodin monograph. I would also express my gratitude to Professor Henry W. Wells of Columbia University for patiently and kindly answering my questions about Jessie Lemont.

PAGE 125

1 Edith Wharton—see *Rilke Gide Correspondance*, pp. 131–2, and 215.

2 Isadora Duncan—see Betz, *Rilke vivant*, pp. 168–9.

PAGE 126

1 Miss Greenham and Rilke—see the *Souvenirs* of Princess Marie Taxis, pp. 85–6, and letters of Princess of 18 May 1912 and of Rilke in reply of 22 May 1912.

2 The reading 'Pincent' in the letter in question (T.T.H., pp. 148 and 1003) is unquestionably a mistake for 'Vincent'. Rilke's capital 'V' can easily be taken for a 'P', when he uses German writing.

PAGE 127

1 See *Souvenirs* of Princess Marie Taxis, p. 65.

2 Letter to Princess Marie Taxis of 26 June 1912.

3 This book presented to Horatio Brown by Rilke used to be in the possession of the late Mr. E. K. Bennett of Gonville and Caius College, Cambridge, to whom I am very grateful for letting me have a copy of the dedication.

PAGE 128

1 Rilke to Princess Marie Taxis, 16 December 1913.

2 Kassner, 'Geleitwort' to T.T.H., p. XXIX.

3 See letters of Princess Marie Taxis to Rilke of 27 May 1914 and 31 May 1920—T.T.H., pp. 381 and 600.

PAGE 129

1 *Rilke und Benvenuta*, pp. 195–7. The phrase translated 'to credit only one particular class of mankind with culture' is: 'nur einer bestimmten Klasse Menschen *Bildung* zuzutrauen'. Whatever language Brown expressed himself in on this occasion, it was certainly not German; very likely it was English. Obviously he could not have said or meant 'education'.

2 *Rilke und Benvenuta*, p. 184.

PAGE 130

1 The supposition of B. J. Morse, *loc. cit.* (see n. 2 to p. 33), that Horatio Brown probably 'guided Rilke's reading on Carlo Zeno, the Venetian admiral about whom he longed to write a book' is very acute and convincing. It is just in the year 1912 that Rilke's Zeno studies fall. Somewhat less cogent is Morse's suggestion that Brown may have introduced Rilke to John Addington Symonds' edition of the works of Michelangelo, since there is no evidence of Rilke's having used any other editions than those of Guasti and Frey.

2 See Horatio Brown's delightful essay 'The Carlops' in the *Cornhill Magazine*, November 1915: 'Returning home after a prolonged stay in Italy, the writer found he had come perilously near a *semiplena probatio* of papistry; nor was it long before the inquisition was applied by the leading spirit of the place in this point-blank remark—"Well, Mr. Broon, I canna abide the Virgin Mary," and a close scrutiny of my countenance under the proof. . . . / There was a pious fiction abroad to account for my long absences, and it reached me thus—"Ye'll be about through with your schooling, Mr. Broon?"' (The suspicion that Brown had turned Catholic seems not to have been ill-founded.)

3 Kassner, 'Geleitwort' to T.T.H., pp. XXIX–XXX. The rest of what Kassner said to Horatio Brown on this occasion was much more kindly, but does not concern us here.

PAGE 131

1 *Souvenirs*, p. 46.

2 For Captain and Mrs Barton see Princess Marie Taxis' letter to Rilke of 8 August 1912 (T.T.H., p. 191); for the young English architect and Miss Mary C——, see *Souvenirs*, pp. 48 and 64.

3 Kindly communicated to me by Professor Leonard Forster of University College, London.

PAGE 132

1 *Souvenirs*, p. 128.
2 Letter to Princess Marie Taxis of 21 October 1913.
3 Princess Marie Taxis writing to Rilke, 20 July 1912—T.T.H., p. 176.
4 Princess Marie Taxis to Rilke, 5 January 1913—T.T.H., pp. 252–3.
5 Rilke to Princess Marie Taxis, 25 May 1913—T.T.H., p. 282.
6 Kitchener—see Kassner, 'Geleitwort' to T.T.H., p. XXVIII. According to Kassner's account, however, Kitchener's visit to Duino in 1914 took place *before* Rilke's, i.e. in April. This proves incompatible with everything else that is known of Kitchener's movements at this time. Kitchener left Egypt on 18 June 1914, arriving at Dover on 23 June. It was presumably about 20 or 21 June that he interrupted his journey at Trieste for a flying visit to Duino. I am grateful to Sir Philip Magnus Allcroft for his kind help and advice in this matter.

PAGE 133

1 Marianne Mitford—see letter to Lou Andreas-Salomé of 31 January 1915—L.A.S., p. 382 and note on p. 608.
2 Sibyl Vane—see letter to Katharina Kippenberg of 11 December 1916.
3 22 September 1918 to Marie von Bunsen.
4 Count John von Salis: see letter to Edith von Schmidt-Pauli of 14 August 1919 (published in *Neue Rundschau,* September 1927). Cp. also letter to Katharina Kippenberg of 11 August 1919 (K.K., p. 361): 'Das Haus . . . gehört noch dem Gfn. John Salis, britischen Botschafter am Vatikan' ('The house still belongs to Count John Salis, the British Ambassador at the Vatican')
5 Professor Henry Lüdeke's 'Mit Rilke in Soglio, eine Reminiszenz' was first published in the *Basler Nationalzeitung*, 22 August 1937, and has since been reprinted as a supplement to the *Briefe an Frau Gudi Nölke* (Insel-Verlag, 1953), pp. 159–66. A friendly allusion to 'Dr Lüdecke' (sic) occurs in Rilke's letter to Frau Nölke of 3 November 1919.
6 Dorothea Parker: see *Briefe an Frau Nölke,* pp. 27 and 176.

PAGE 134

1 See Rilke's letter to Baladine Klossowska of 24 December 1921—the passage in question is only to be found in the earlier and very much shorter selection from this correspondence, *Lettres françaises à Merline* (*1919–22*) (Paris, Editions du Seuil, 1950), p. 176. The box with the old English colour-print is still to be seen at Muzot.
2 Alma Moodie—see letters of 7 April 1923 and 12 May 1924 to Princess Marie Taxis—T.T.H., pp. 751 and 801.

PAGE 136

1 *Sämtliche Werke,* vol. II, p. 655; all further information here given is from Ernst Zinn's note on p. 800 of the same volume.

2 Enthusiastic references to Elisabeth Bergner occur in Rilke's letters to Claire Goll (see n. 2 p. 47) of 29 December 1918, 5 August 1919 and 29 June 1925. Rilke met Elisabeth Bergner in Paris in June 1925.

3 Nimet Eloui Bey—Edmond Jaloux gives an account of Rilke's friendship with this beautiful Egyptian girl in his *La dernière amitié de R. M. Rilke.* See n. 4 to p. 113.

PAGE 137

1 *Souvenirs* of Princess Marie Taxis, pp. 192–3.

PAGE 138

1 From Edgar Taylor's translation of 1823.

2 This presentation of the relationship between Rilke and Natalie Clifford Barney is based on her own account of it in her *Aventures de l'esprit* (Paris 1929) under the heading *Reconnaissance tardive,* pp. 75–85. There are discrepancies between this account and the versions given by André Germain in *Chez nos voisins* (1927) and by Betz, *Rilke in Frankreich,* p. 285–9.

PAGE 139

1 This poem to Natalie Clifford Barney is now included in volume II of Rilke's *Sämtliche Werke,* p. 678.

PAGE 140

1 Professor Stewart's report here reproduced is from a letter written to me on 2 February 1958.

PAGE 141

1 Norbert von Hellingrath (1888–1916) belonged to the circle of Stefan George. He is chiefly remembered for his remarkable achievement in editing Hölderlin. He was killed in action on 14 December 1916 before Verdun.

PAGE 142

1 The two poems are to be found in *Sämtliche Werke,* II, pp. 270 and 271.

2 The information here given was kindly supplied to me by Miss Harriet Cohen herself in letters of 18 April and 17 May 1957 and 19 June 1958.

PAGE 148

1 See von Salis' essay in Ingeborg Schnack's *Rilkes Leben und Werk im Bild*, p. 13.

PAGE 149

1 See *Erzählungen und Skizzen*, pp. 224–5.

2 See Peter Demetz, *René Rilkes Prager Jahre* (Düsseldorf, 1953), p. 160.

3 See Kassner, *Buch der Erinnerung*, p. 295 ff.

4 Letter to Princess Marie Taxis of 6 September 1913—T.T.H., p. 440—original in French.

PAGE 150

1 *Tagebücher*, 29 September 1900—p. 331.

2 Letter to Friedrich Huch, 16 December 1902.

3 Friedrich Märker, 'Rilke in Paris', in *Berliner Tageblatt*, 19 August 1925; reprinted by Betz, *Rilke in Frankreich*, p. 211.

PAGE 152

1 Letter to Duchess Aurelia Gallarati-Scotti of 14 February 1926—A.G.S., p. 95.

PAGE 154

1 One of the novels Rilke was most moved by, Annette Kolb's *Das Exemplar* (1913) is chiefly concerned with presenting vividly, authentically and most attractively a house-party in an English country mansion.

PAGE 155

1 Marburg—'liebliche deutsche Gotik'—27 July 1905 to Clara Rilke. Cp. also letters of 11 September 1906 to Karl von der Heydt and to the Uexkülls, when the response is somewhat warmer.

2 Naumburg—see Princess Marie Taxis' *Souvenirs*, p. 52.

PAGE 156

1 The present writer's translation of this sonnet, here quoted, was printed in *German Life and Letters*, July 1948.

PAGE 157

1 From *Orpheus*, 18. See Excursus II: 'Problems of the Duinese Credo' (p. 179).

PAGE 158

1 '—das fällt uns leicht und ist nicht erst zu lernen'—*Requiem für Paula Modersohn-Becker* (1908).

2 From the poem 'Baudelaire', written 14 April 1921.

PAGE 159

1 5 June 1896 to Rudolf Christoph Jenny, in *Briefe . . . aus dem Jahre 1896*, p. 25.

PAGE 160

1 2 February 1907, appended to a genuine letter of the same date to Gudrun, Baronin Uexküll.

2 Letter of 13 January 1920 to Frau Gudi Nölke.

3 Letter of 24 April 1924 to Duchess Aurelia Gallarati-Scotti.

4 See Maurice Betz, *Rilke in Frankreich*, p. 173.

PAGE 161

1 Katharina Kippenberg's *Beitrag*, p. 190.

2 Letter of 27 January 1924 to Lisa Heise.

3 *Gesammelte Werke*, vol. v, p. 135.

4 17 December 1912 to Princess Marie Taxis.

5 30 December 1913 to Contessa Pia di Valmarana—original French.

PAGE 162

1 23 February 1914.

2 13 February 1918, to Katharina Kippenberg.

3 J. R. von Salis, *Rilkes Schweizer Jahre*, first edition (1936), p. 136; probably adapted from a letter to Frau Wunderly-Volkart. The word here translated 'familiar landmarks' is in the original 'Vertrautheit'. This passage, like one or two other still more important ones, was, it is interesting to note, suppressed in the extensive revision of the text of von Salis' book for the third edition of 1952.

4 Letter of 26 June 1912 to Princess Marie Taxis—T.T.H., p. 166.

PAGE 163

1 16 November 1920 to Elisabeth von Schmidt-Pauli, printed *in extenso* by Maurice Betz, *Rilke in Frankreich*, pp. 58–60. Elisabeth von Schmidt-Pauli, in publishing this letter in her own *Rainer Maria Rilke—Ein Gedenkbuch* (Basel, 1940, pp. 80–3) suppresses the passage about the 'amerikanisches Vermögen'. [See p. 257] It may be noted that Rilke, with all his proclamation of the ideal of poverty, was by no means immune to hopes of acquiring great wealth. On 26 October 1893 he was counting up all the wonderful things he would do with the vast sum he hoped to gain that day when the Innsbruck lottery was drawn. From his correspondence with Elya Nevar, Katharina Kippenberg and Baladine Klossowska it emerges that he was still buying lottery tickets in 1919 and in 1921. Similarly, as is pointed out by von Salis, when he hoped in his last years

that he might be awarded the Nobel prize, it was not for the sake of the mere glory of it. It was the 'financial independence' that he wanted. (See von Salis, *Rilkes Schweizer Jahre*, p. 150.)

2 It weighs heavily that Rilke will not allow American apples to be real apples in his sense. He was a great apple-eater, apples had for him a symbolical, quasi-sacramental significance. It would be easy to write a study on 'Rilke and the Apple', and to make of it a comprehensive interpretation of his personality, outlook and art.

3 This letter to Witold Hulewicz, bearing the postmark '13 Nov. 1925', has been reprinted innumerable times, and is the chief source of all Rilke interpretations.

PAGE 164

1 A strong case for the view of the older Goethe as a whole-hearted advocate of the American Way of Life is presented with great skill and wit, but also not without some characteristic irony by Thomas Mann in his 'Goethe und die Demokratie' (*Die neue Rundschau*, Summer 1949).

PAGE 165

1 17 January 1926 to Duchess Aurelia Gallarati-Scotti.

PAGE 166

1 See Excursus II: 'Problems of the Duinese Credo'—p. 179.

PAGE 167

1 Gräfin Dobrženský played a decisive part in Rilke's destiny, since it was through her that he received his first invitation to Switzerland in 1918 She also helped him with her hospitality and financially during his first Swiss years, when the German inflation made his situation so precarious. There are references to another long visit paid by the Gräfin to England in Rilke's letters to Baladine Klossowska of 19 March and 19 May 1921—*Lettres françaises à Merline*, pp. 119 and 166. Edith Theresa Hulton, who had only married the 8th Baron Berwick in 1919, came of a family belonging to the British colony in Venice and was therefore known personally to Princess Marie Taxis and perhaps also to Rilke himself.

2 It was, of course, impossible to publish letters in which Rilke fiercely criticized German nationalism so long as the Nazi system prevailed; it is evidently felt that the time for such a publication is still not ripe.

PAGE 168

1 In addition to Gide's translation from *Malte Laurids Brigge* of 1911 there are French versions of passages from the *Stundenbuch* (published in

1910 in *Phalange*) and of ten of his early poems (published in 1913 in an anthology) to be recorded. After this nothing happens till 1923.

2 See letter to Rodin of 27 March 1903, quoted above in n. 4 to p. 82.

3 Jethro Bithell: see above, p. 37.

4 Miss Grantham: see letters from Katharina Kippenberg of 19 August 1913 and to Anton Kippenberg of 5 November 1913; also note in K.K., p. 636.

5 The information given here about translations of Rilke's work into English and about articles on him in English published during his lifetime is based partly on Ritzer's *Bibliographie* (Vienna 1951) and partly on:

(*a*) Hans Galinsky: *Deutsches Schrifttum der Gegenwart in der englischen Kritik der Nachkriegszeit (1919–1935)*, pub. Munich 1938;

(*b*) Richard von Mises: *Rilke in English: A tentative bibliography* (Cambridge, Massachusetts, 1947);

(*c*) Adolf E. Schroeder: *R. M. Rilke in America* (Monatshefte, Wisconsin —1952).

Each of these compilations contains some information which is missing in the other two; one or two items I have myself supplied.

PAGE 169

1 Jessie Lemont: see above, pp. 38 and 124.

2 R. G. L. Barrett: see above, p. 46.

3 Mrs Anne Goodwin-Winslow: see above, p. 46.

PAGE 170

1 The following articles on Rilke in English before December 1926 can be traced:

1915: Reginald H. Wilenski: 'Modern German Poetry', in two issues of *Poetry* (Chicago);

1919: Martin Schuetze: 'R. M. Rilke', in *The Dial* (Camden N.J.);

1920: (anonymous) 'R. M. Rilke, Novelist and Poet', in the *Athenaeum* (an ample article with Faesi's book as point of departure);
(anonymous) review on *The Times Literary Supplement* of the recent re-issue of the *Neue Gedichte*;

1923: (anonymous) review of Heygrodt's *Die Lyrik R. M. Rilkes* in *The Times Literary Supplement* (22 March);
(anonymous) review of the *Sonette an Orpheus* (under the title: 'R. M. Rilke's New Poems') in *The Times Literary Supplement* (6 September);

1924: Pierre Loving: 'R. M. Rilke' in the *Saturday Review of Literature* (New York);

1925: Anne Goodwin-Winslow: 'The Book of Hours', in the *North American Review*;
(anonymous) review of Barrett's translation of the *Life of the Virgin* in *The Times Literary Supplement* (10 November);
1926: 'Austria's greatest poet', anonymous contribution to Littell's *Living Age* (U.S.A.);
Ludwig Lewisohn: 'R. M. Rilke', in the *Saturday Review of Literature*, 4 December.

This list, which could certainly be added to, shows five articles on Rilke traced in two different English periodicals and six articles traced in five different American periodicals or other compilations. There are also references of varying weight to Rilke in general articles on contemporary German literature by Herman George Scheffauer in the *Bookman* in 1923 and 1924 and by Alec W. G. Randall in the *London Mercury* in 1922 and in the *Criterion* in 1926, where interest is shown above all in his translations of Valéry's poems. Further allusions to Rilke are made in the *Criterion* in 1926 by 'F. S. F.', writing on French periodicals, and by Max Rychner, who also in 1927 writes an adequate obituary on Rilke for the *Criterion*. Rilke is on these occasions referred to as a rule as 'the best representative of the German symbolist school' and his name is bracketed with those of Hofmannsthal and George.

2 Cp. also Rilke's letter to Betz of 26 April 1926: 'Ein, wie ich glaube, recht kleiner Teil meiner Arbeiten ist ins Holländische, *Englische,* Italienische und Spanische übersetzt worden.... "Rodin", eine Auswahl Gedichte und ein dritter Band sind schon vor sehr langer Zeit *in Amerika* veröffentlicht worden; aber auch darüber weiß ich nichts Näheres' ('Part of my work, but, I think, only a very small part, has been translated into Dutch, English, Italian and Spanish.... "Rodin", a selection of poems and a third volume were published a very long time ago in America; but that too is something about which I do not know any details') Betz, *Rilke in Frankreich,* pp. 236–7).

PAGE 171

1 This letter is found only in the later, two-volume edition of the *Briefe an seinen Verleger,* p. 428. The payment in question was presumably in respect of the thirteen poems of Rilke's published in translation in 1923 by Babette Deutsch and Avrahm Yarmolinsky in their *Contemporary German Poetry*—see text, p. 169.

2 See the *Correspondance* of Rilke and Gide, pp. 187, 188, 191 and 192. Paul Desjardins had in 1910 inaugurated annual, unofficial, international con-

ferences of authors and *savants* at the Abbaye de Pontigny. It was a high honour to be invited to these gatherings.

PAGE 172

1 See *Sämtliche Werke*, vol. II, pp. 346–7.

2 'Aufgefallen ist mir, mit zahlreichen Unterschriften ausgestattet, ein grosses Schreiben des "German Department" der Universität Edinburg.' ('I was struck by a large document furnished with numerous signatures from the German Department of the University of Edinburgh') (7 December 1925 to Anton Kippenberg). As everything about Rilke is conducive to hyperbole and to the evolution of legends, it need not surprise us to find von Salis (*Rilkes Schweizer Jahre,* first edition, p. 150) declaring, with reference to this incident, 'dass im Jahre 1925 die Universität Edinburg ihm feierlich ihre Bewunderung ausdrückte' ('that in 1925 the University of Edinburgh solemnly expressed its admiration to him').

3 Translated from a copy of Professor Schlapp's letter, kindly lent to me by Dr Robert Schlapp. The whole text of the letter, together with that of Rilke's reply, is given in the original German in the Appendix on pp. 187–93.

PAGE 174

1 Hans-Egon Holthusen: 'Rilke nach dreißig Jahren', in *Neue Zürcher Zeitung,* 25 August 1957. I have Dr Holthusen's authorization for translating his words 'in allen Ländern der freien Welt' as 'in all *the other* countries of the free world'.

PAGE 175

1 Curtius, in *T. S. Eliot—A Symposium,* compiled by Richard Marsh and Tambimuttu (P.L., London 1948), p. 121.

PAGE 176

1 4 November 1909 to Elisabeth Freiin Schenk zu Schweinsberg.

2 See Rilke's letter to Fürstin Marie Taxis of 31 October 1913 and her reply of 17 November 1913—here Rilke is contemplating obtaining a divorce for himself; see also Lou Albert-Lasard, *Wege mit Rilke,* pp. 55, 82 and 89—in this case, if it had gone through, Rilke would have figured as co-respondent.

3 Some of Rilke's letters to Paula Modersohn-Becker of February–April 1906 appear in the *Collected Letters*.

4 26 December 1921 to R. H. Junghanns—publication of Vereinigung Oltner Bücherfreunde, 1945.

5 S. Trebitsch, 'Meine erste Begegnung mit R. M. Rilke', *Neue Zürcher Zeitung,* 27 April 1951.

PAGE 177

1 *Toskanisches Tagebuch,* pp. 115–16.

2 *Aufzeichnungen des Malte Laurids Brigge,* pp. 291–300.

3 Herbert Steiner: 'Ueber Rilke', *Neue Zürcher Zeitung,* 18 October 1952.

4 Magda von Hattingberg, *Rilke und Benvenuta,* p. 236.

5 23 September 1911 to Princess Marie Taxis, T.T.H., p. 64.

PAGE 178

1 9 October 1915 to Ilse Erdmann—only in Collected Edition C.

PAGE 180

1 13 March 1922 to Rudolf Bodländer.

PAGE 181

1 2 December 1921 to Countess Mariette Mirbach.

PAGE 190

1 From 'The Panther' (*New Poems,* vol. 1)—quoted here with a remarkable alteration in the text, the substitution of 'bewußt' ('conscious') for 'betäubt' ('benumbed'). By this change Schlapp adapts the verses to Rilke's own artistry as he sees it, that is to say as an emphatically *deliberate* artistry. The translation here given is adapted from one of E. C. Mason's which was published in *Windfall* (Edinburgh, 1954), p. 21.

PAGE 191

1 *Sonnets to Orpheus* I, 1.

2 *Sonnets to Orpheus* I, 3.

3 *Duinese Elegies* VII.

4 *Sonnets to Orpheus* I, 7. (Translation by E. C. Mason, published in *German Life and Letters* July 1948.)

5 Freely adapted from 'Self-portrait from the year 1906' (*New Poems* I). The original runs: 'noch nie im Leiden oder im Gelingen / zusammgefaßt zu dauerndem Durchdringen.'

6 From the *Note-books of Malte Laurids Brigge,* the passage on Sappho—p. 278, in vol. v of the *Gesammelte Werke.* The interpretation of the word 'Bruch' (translated 'flexure') presents problems here.

7 From the first of the little cycle of poems 'The Parks' ('Die Parke') in *New Poems II.*

8 *Sonnets to Orpheus* I, 7.

9 From the *Book of Hours,* Part I—the poem beginning: 'Wenn es nur einmal so ganz stille wäre . . . .'

10 Isaiah 63, 3.

11 This poem 'Magnificat' occurs in *New Poems II.*

GENERAL INDEX

Craven

INDEX OF RILKE'S WRITINGS

The works and poems are indexed according to their German titles or first lines.

I. WORKS

2. SINGLE POEMS

Those to which only the year of composition is attached were not included in any of the great cycles; first lines are given for poems without distinctive titles.

ADDENDA

p. 206 (Addition to note 2 to p. 18.) A further favourable comment on Austria which should have been recorded here occurs in a review in letter-form of Richard Schaukal's poems, written in autumn 1904, where Rilke confesses to 'a certain sympathy with the Austrian character of your culture, with what is soft, supple and finely-wrought in it.' (*Bücher—Theater—Kunst*, p. 136.)

p. 241 (Addition to the opening of note 1 on p. 163.) On 10 June 1921, at the time when the new de luxe edition of the *Book of Hours* was on the point of being published by the Insel-Verlag, Rilke wrote to Kippenberg: 'I shall have to ask for a copy of this precious edition to be sent to a certain person in America who has quite unexpectedly rendered me a very important service, and to whom I should like—how lucky I am to be able to do it!—to express my gratitude in a monumental form.' This is evidently a confidential matter about which Rilke prefers to give Kippenberg no definite details. Possibly it has something to do with the 'American capital' referred to in the letter written to Elisabeth von Schmidt-Pauli seven months earlier. Elisabeth von Schmidt-Pauli seems herself to have been back in Germany at this time, but preparing for a journey to South America. It is impossible to tell who the 'certain person in America' here referred to was, or what 'very important services' she or he had unexpectedly rendered to Rilke.